the Ethical Canary

Science, Society and the Human Spirit

Margaret Somerville

VIKING

VIKING

Published by the Penguin Group

Penguin Books Canada Ltd, 10 Alcorn Avenue, Toronto, Ontario, Canada M4V 3B2

Penguin Books Ltd, 27 Wrights Lane, London W8 5TZ, England

Penguin Putnam Inc., 375 Hudson Street, New York, New York 10014, U.S.A.

Penguin Books Australia Ltd, Ringwood, Victoria, Australia

Penguin Books (NZ) Ltd, cnr Rosedale and Airborne Roads, Albany, Auckland 1310, New Zealand

Penguin Books Ltd, Registered Offices: Harmondsworth, Middlesex, England

First published 2000

1 3 5 7 9 10 8 6 4 2

Printed and bound in Canada on acid free paper ⊗

Text design and typesetting by Laura Brady

CANADIAN CATALOGUING IN PUBLICATION DATA

Somerville, Margaret A., 1942–

The ethical canary : science, society and the human spirit

ISBN 0-670-89302-1

1. Medical ethics. 2. Bioethics. I. Title.

R724.S65 2000   174'.2   C00-931620-5

Visit Penguin Canada's website at **www.penguin.ca**

for Veronica, Bob and Anne

Contents

Prologue

The scene was a magnificent guildhall in Lübeck, one of the powerful Hanseatic League cities in northern Germany. In the past, this hall had been the meeting place of the ships' captains and seamen who brought great wealth to the region through their trade. I was there to give the opening speech for a conference called "Health Care Systems at the Crossroads: Balancing Individual Needs with Financial Limitations" and organized by the Dräger Foundation, a German charitable foundation. There were around 250 people present, and we had already begun the evening with cocktails.

After my hosts introduced me in the full German tradition, as "Professor, Professor, Doctor," I suddenly wondered how I was going to be able to capture the attention of these people, all of whom were obviously having a good time. The subject of my address was unlikely to x do the trick. It was on the serious and distinctly non-humorous topic of the ethical allocation of healthcare resources.

Completely by chance, I was wearing a very bright yellow jacket over black pants—authentic canary colours. I stood up, tucked my hands under my armpits and flapped my folded arms as though they were wings. The audience stopped talking instantly and looked somewhat astonished. "I am an ethical canary," I announced, "or rather the allocation of resources to health care is such a canary: How we deal with this issue will test the ethical air in our societal mineshaft. And if the ethical healthcare canary is sick, we will need to worry about the ethical tone of our society as a whole."

I went on to explain that there are many of these ethical canaries and that they send us early-warning signals about the ethical climate in our society. Some of them are everyday but nonetheless immensely important issues, like the range of treatment we make available to terminally ill people to relieve their pain and suffering. Others are among the most avant-garde issues we face, like human cloning and xenotransplantation (the transfer of human genes to pigs and the transplanting of the resulting transgenic pig organs to humans).

At the end of my speech, my hosts from the Dräger Foundation expressed their delight at the image I had used. I was pleased but puzzled until they explained what they assumed I already knew: Their corporation, Drägerwerk AG, had invented the equipment that replaced the canaries used to detect toxic gases in the real mineshafts. Even today, the men who operate this equipment, which led to much safer working conditions for miners, are called Draegermen.

THIS BOOK EXPLORES A selection of issues that I believe are among the most important ethical canaries in our contemporary societal mineshafts. In many ways, indeed, they are all feathers of the same bird. But it is only when we look at them as a collective, as we do in this book, rather than as isolated individual issues, that we can see the commonalities among them. These issues range from the ancient, such as infant male circumcision, to the everyday, such as a family's conflict with physicians over whether their father should be taken off a respirator that is providing life support, to the avant-garde, such as new reproductive technologies. Inevitably, we will ruffle one another's feathers in discussing these matters, because they involve our most important personal and societal values and intimate and community relationships.

The larger themes and concepts that underlie and link these issues can be summarized fairly briefly: First, just because we are able to do something does not mean that it is right to do it. Moreover, what is possible and even legal might not be ethical. Therefore, we must ask, especially regarding the new science: Is it right? Is it ethical?

To answer, we must first ask whether what we plan to do is inherently wrong. Although as societies we once commonly addressed this question—probably because our societies based their collective morality on religion—in the recent past we have abandoned it. As I discuss in Chapter 1, a wide variety of societal factors have led us as societies to rely instead on a situational ethics approach that says that nothing is inherently wrong, rather it all depends on the situation. The primary question in this approach is: "Does it do any good?" But in developing and using our new science and technology, we fail to ask "Is it inherently wrong?" at our ethical peril. If it is, then we must not do it, no matter how much good could come from it: "Doing good" is not a justification for doing that which is inherently wrong.

How can we have an approach that hinges on inherent wrongness in a secular society? In such a society, by definition, we do not all belong to the same—or any—religion, and we have no external, absolute moral authority. I propose, however, that we can view as inherently wrong that which breaches either of two values. These values are that we must have profound respect for life, in particular human life, and we must act to protect the human spirit—the intangible, invisible, immeasurable reality that we need to find meaning in life and to make life worth living—that deeply intuitive sense of relatedness or connectedness to the world and the universe in which we live. That which fails to show respect for life, in particular human life, or puts at serious risk or harms the human spirit is inherently wrong. Throughout this book I explore how some uses of our new science and technology or approaches to health care or medical treatment might breach one or other or both of these values.

Accepting that some things are inherently wrong, and that this can be established without necessarily having recourse to the supernatural, can lead us to a concept of the "secular sacred"—the idea that there are some things that deserve the utmost respect. We seem to be coming close to recognizing that our relationship with the Earth must be of this nature. But we can go further. I believe that our relationship with life itself must also be of this kind. Indeed, if it were, it would encompass a secular-sacred relationship with the Earth.

If something is not inherently wrong, we must then decide whether in all the circumstances it is ethical to proceed and, if so, under what conditions. To decide, we must weigh the benefits and potential benefits against the risks and harms—not only to our physical realities but also to our metaphysical ones, our values, attitudes and beliefs. Many of the discussions about issues addressed in this book are aimed at identifying and articulating what these conditions might be in various circumstances. For instance, when is it ethical to override parents' refusal of medical treatment for their child; or to take a critically ill old man off life support when his sons strongly object to this; or not to tell a cancer patient that there is a better treatment because the hospital budget has been exhausted and this means that the treatment is not available; or to place the public at risk through medical research?

Doing ethics, especially when this includes an approach based on an enquiry as to inherent wrongness, can, alas, be perceived as authoritarian, paternalistic and, often, outmoded—as belonging to the Dark Ages. Thus, too often, doing ethics is characterized as an exercise in moral policing with the primary function of restricting and inhibiting people—a litany of "do's and don'ts." But this is not the only way to view doing ethics. We can, alternatively, see it, as I believe we should, as the great contemporary exploration of our moral universe, an exploration that parallels that of our physical universe throughout the new science. We could even regard the current search for ethics as a further development in the formation of values. Rather than seeing our values as just being handed down to us and our passively adopting them, we can view our values as coming out of our search and that, in turn, can result in our shared commitment to them. Such a view could mean that we will care more, as both individuals and a society, about upholding and protecting our values.

But there are also serious dangers to which we must pay heed in choosing our values and there is a huge responsibility in doing so. For instance, just because a majority of people believes that certain conduct is ethical does not necessarily make it so. And seeing ourselves as having the opportunity to choose the values to which we will commit could be interpreted as meaning that our values will necessarily change. This is not correct. Many, or even all, of the values we choose might not be different from the ones that we respected in the past. Moreover, such an approach might be interpreted as an abnegation of the belief that some things are inherently wrong and as the adoption of a pure situational ethics approach. It is not: Indeed, it allows us to decide for ourselves that some things are inherently wrong.

We must remember also that in choosing our values, attitudes and beliefs, we are choosing not only for ourselves as individuals, but also for our world. If, therefore, the contemporary search for ethics is the search for the values on which we will base our societies, we must all, especially as citizens of the global commons, be engaged in it. This is especially true in relation to the values that should guide scientific progress, because of the enormous—indeed unprecedented—power for good and harm that this has given us. Scientific progress alone would be a hollow victory without the moral and ethical progress that must accompany it and ensure the humanization and humanity of our development and use of science.

AS I AIM TO SHOW throughout this book, it is not enough just to identify and articulate problems, especially ethical ones. We have to seek constructive ways to remedy them and we must create a climate that supports and encourages us to do so. I believe that a commitment to generating hope on the part of each of us, both as individuals and as a society, is the most important single step we can take towards creating such a climate and a more ethical world. It will require difficult, detailed work, hard decisions and often grief. But we have no choice. A loss of hope is an immense danger in our world because it generates cynicism and nihilism, which in turn corrode and destroy the human spirit, especially in young people.

Hope is our connection, as both individuals and societies, to the future. Hope is also the element common to science, society and the human spirit. If we had no hope, seeking to understand ourselves, our world and our universe through science would be pointless. Without hope for the common good, we are not able to form community. And hope is the oxygen of the human spirit; without it our spirit dies, whereas with it, it can survive even appalling suffering.

THIS LEADS ME TO THE cover of this book, the raised open hand with the delicate feather. As was true with my "canary act" as the prelude to my speech in Germany, this image involved no planning on my part. It was produced by my publishers. And yet it captures so much of the message that I would like to convey. My friend and colleague Katherine Young, who is a specialist in Hinduism, tells me that in that tradition a hand in this position means "have no fear." I thought that was wonderful, because a major message of this book is that we must have the courage both to act and to refuse to act on the basis of ethics in developing and using the new science. This sign is also that of a peaceful encounter: "Have no fear, I come in peace and will not hurt you." This maxim resonates with the one that has guided physicians through the centuries and that, I believe, must now be fully adopted by scientists: "*Primum non nocere*, first do no harm." The hand is also in the position in which we take an oath: For me that would be a commitment to respect for all life, the human spirit and our world both present and future. The hand also carries a message of honesty, trust, openness and transparency, important elements in doing ethics. And, finally, and possibly most importantly, it is a sign to stop—whether temporarily or permanently—a warning to be cautious, to take care and pay heed, to both think and feel, and to integrate our thinking and feeling.

And what about the fragile yellow feather? Has the ethical canary lost the feather and just escaped with its life? Or is it a gift left behind as a reminder that in dealing with scientific advances, we must protect the human spirit? Are the ethical canaries in our present society endangered—out on a limb? If so, which decisions about science, society and the human spirit will kill them (cause them, as we say in Australia, to drop off the perch) and which will help them to flourish? The feather also shares a symbolic message with the hand raised to take an oath: In Egyptian mythology the single feather represents truth, in particular, the truth of the soul. And the single feather, the traditional quill pen—the image and the word. We need both images and words in doing ethics—perhaps most of all we need poetry.

Together the hand and feather bring yet another message. Through the new science, life has placed itself in the palm of our hand. Can it trust us to hold it gently and safely, to respect its fragility and mystery?

The Australian aborigines believe that all people can be divided into two groups: those who dance and those who do not. Our human spirit can be fully expressed only when we are among the dancers. But in order to dance with the joy, hope and wonder of which we are capable—to come to a deep knowledge and perhaps wisdom about the dance of life—we must pay more attention than we might have been doing to the songs of the ethical canaries.

1. Searching for Ethics in a Secular Society

Recently, the search for ethics seems to have been everywhere. One has only to pick up the daily newspapers to see the perceived relevance of "ethics talk" to much of what goes on in our lives as individuals and communities. We are now exploring the ethics of politics and politicians; the ethics of public policy, governmental bureaucracy and public accountability; ethics in academia, business, industry and health care; the ethics of our treatment of animals; environmental ethics; ethics in the media; ethics in sport; the ethics of armed conflict; and the ethics of scientific and medical research and the new technologies resulting from it. This widespread search for ethics can be seen as a turn-of-the-millennium revolution in conscience and consciousness, in the sense of awareness of the need to ask the question "Is it right?" in a wide variety of contexts.

Science and technology is only one of these contexts, but, as I hope to convince you in this book, it is an especially important one.

Why has this search for ethics emerged now? Our postmodern, industrialized Western democracies are characterized by being pluralistic, secular and multicultural. These same features also mean that these societies lack a "shared story"—the collection of fundamental values, principles, attitudes, beliefs, myths and commitments that we need to buy into in order to function as a society, and that we use to give meaning to our communal and individual lives. This story, or societal-cultural paradigm, is the glue that holds us together.

However, at present, in secular societies we are in search of a new story. Some of the factors that have caused the collapse of our old story result from the extraordinary advances in science and technology, whether information technology, the neurosciences, nanotechnology, artificial intelligence or molecular biology and genetics. The possibilities these advances open up are mind-altering, society-altering and world-altering and, depending on how we use them, could radically alter our human nature or even annihilate us. We have become very sensitive to the threats that these new technologies present to our physical existence and our planet. Our contemporary search for ethics shows, I believe, that we are becoming much more sensitive than we have been to their threats to our human spirit—the deeply intuitive sense of connectedness to the world and the universe in which we live, the metaphysical reality (that which is beyond the physical) that we need to live fully human lives and to find meaning in life.

Our shared story has always focused on the major life events of birth and death. Indeed, the general level of respect for human life that permeates a given society is largely determined in these contexts. We also structure both our rational and non-rational knowing in a coherent framework through focusing on human beginnings and endings. Many rituals of celebration and mourning have human beginnings and endings as pivotal motifs. We use these rituals to create the sense of community that we need to enrich our experience or to sustain us, both at the time of these events and more generally.

Contemporary ethics talk often focuses on the possibilities that new scientific developments have opened up in relation to birth and death. At one end of the life span, we are faced with a stunning power that no humans in previous ages ever possessed: the potential to alter, through the use of a combination of genetic and new reproductive technologies, the very basis of human life and its mode of transmission. The possibilities presented by these technologies include *in vitro* fertilization; cloning human embryos; cloning our adult selves; using ova from aborted fetuses to produce children whose "mother" was never born; and designing our progeny through genetic manipulation in ways that range from choosing certain physical characteristics— such as height or eye or hair colour—to dramatically augmenting their intelligence through a so-called smart gene and even creating disease-proofed children. At the other end of the life span, we face issues of the allocation of very expensive life-prolonging treatments; xenotransplantation; withdrawal of life-support treatments from ter- minally ill people; and euthanasia.

In the past, we wove the metaphysical fabric in which we wrapped the events of birth and death mainly using the resources that we found in religion. And we bonded together through a shared reli- gion—both in the present and with past and future generations. After all, the word *religion* comes from *re-ligare*—to bind together. The great religions have traditionally given us a compelling shared story, allowed us to pass on our most important values to future genera- tions, enabled us to form and live in families and communities, and stimulated and extended our human imagination. But in the mid- 1970s we began to transfer our "collective faith" from religion to the extraordinary new science that was emerging. In particular, modern medical "miracles" held out hope, if not of immortality as most reli- gions do, at least of delayed mortality. This new science radically altered our perceptions of the nature of human life, its transmission and its passing. Consequently it forced us to re-evaluate the meaning we give to the major life events of birth and death, and, therefore, the nature of the society we will create. Moreover, in postmodern, secular, pluralist societies such as Canada, by definition, religion—or at least traditional, institutional religion—can no longer be used to create our shared story, at least not as a sole mechanism. Quite apart from the fact that today many people do not adhere to an institutionalized religion, even those who do are likely to practise one that is different from that of their neighbours. And yet for many people, religion remains an important lens through which to see life and the values and meaning that we attribute to and find in it. The secular-societal paradigm we create must, therefore, as we see articulated in all declarations of fundamental human rights, accommodate and respect people's freedom of conscience and religion.

One of the substitute forums for religion that has emerged in secular societies in the last fifty years is medicine and health care. Because we all personally relate to and identify with health care, it is a very important forum for creating values, implementing those values and carrying them forward. Health care is also the forum in which new scientific developments and the ethical issues they raise are encountered by people most directly and personally—and often most dramatically. Within this primary forum of health care, we will work out the ethics that should govern these new technologies and decide what we may, must and must not do with them. Thus health care is an ethics laboratory for societies like Canada. Our decisions about health care, especially when those decisions concern new scientific and technological developments, are never just about health care. They have a much wider impact on society as a whole.

For example, extraordinary new advances in medical science have shocked us into recognizing that we do not have consensus about the values that we need in order to address the immense ethical issues these new technologies raise. We have also recognized that these issues must be accommodated within our general societal paradigm; we would deal with them in isolation at our peril. The search for ethics is part of this accommodation process.

Our search for ethics is also related to a change in the basis of trust in our societies. Jay Katz, a psychiatrist and law professor at Yale

University, has described this as a shift from "blind trust" ("Trust me, because I know what is best for you") to "earned trust" ("Trust me because I will show that I can be trusted"). Just as we can no longer assume that there is consensus on the values we will uphold, likewise, we can no longer assume the presence of trust in our society and its institutions. Rather we must take steps to ensure that it is present.

One way to view the search for ethics, then, is as the search for societal values in a secular democracy. In this type of society, we no longer automatically have access to a received set of values through a shared religion, and we can no longer impose values or assume there is consensus on them. We must, rather, find and agree on these values and a very important context in which we are seeking to do this is in relation to how we should and should not use the new science.

I WANT TO IDENTIFY SOME particular changes that have resulted from the overall shift in the general societal context I have just described, changes that are powerful forces in precipitating the search for ethics. These include a move to intense individualism; the adoption of a situational ethics approach in searching for shared values; the impact of the media; the increased use of law in resolving disputes about values; the effects of the unprecedented powers provided by new science and technology; the emergence of new fears; the impact of a "gene machine" mind-set on our societal-cultural paradigm; an intolerance of mystery; a loss of our sense of the sacred, and of wonder, awe, play and humour; the emergence of a market-place approach to values and, subsequently, post-materialism. Let us examine some of these in more detail.

Secular Western societies are based on *intense individualism*—possibly individualism to the exclusion of any real sense of community. In fact, one way to view intense individualism is as the institutionalization of a sense of disconnection from each other. And yet we humans cannot live fully human lives without having a sense of belonging to a community—whether the smallest community of family, the larger one of our immediate friends, peers, neighbours, village or city, or the even larger one of society, as a whole. Many of us have difficulty eliciting this sense that we are part of something larger than ourselves. Indeed, Daniel Yankelovich, a leading survey researcher in the United States whose work focuses on changes in the values of the American population, found that the fastest growing trend was people's longing to belong to something larger than themselves, a yearning for some form of transcendence.

Did the adoption of intense individualism mean that we lost a sense of community or did we reject a sense of community and adopt intense individualism to fill the void? If the latter is correct, why would we reject community? Might we have confused community with "the system" that we use to run our society—especially the bureaucracy that makes up this system—and rightly rejected the notion that a system would ever be considered more important than individuals or take priority over them? But there is a difference between a system that runs a community—including when that community is a society—and a community, itself. The latter is a living entity; it has, for want of a better word, a soul. The former does not. Sometimes a community might take precedence over individuals; a system should not.

John Ralston Saul in his book *The Unconscious Civilization* describes a phenomenon he calls "corporatism." He points out that although the foundation of democracy is that each person's voice should be heard and each person's vote should count, modern democracy functions in response to interest groups—corporate entities ranging from grassroots groups to trans-national industries—who advocate approaches that favour them but not necessarily the society as a whole or the common good. The individual is powerless—his or her voice is not heard and a vote does not count. Is there a relationship between this development and intense individualism? Could intense individualism have given rise to corporatism—individuals coalesce as individuals in order to exercise power to their own advantage? Is corporatism an example of collective intense individualism?

We can see the impact of intense individualism in relation to science and medicine in some of the approaches taken, for example, to the new reproductive technologies and euthanasia. If we give preeminence to the values of personal autonomy and self-determination, and competent adults' rights to decide for themselves, the result is highly likely to be a judgment that most applications of reproductive technology and euthanasia are acceptable. But respecting the rights of the individuals who make up a society, important as this is, is not always sufficient to protect the society itself. Sometimes, in carefully justified instances, to do so we must give priority to the needs of the community over the claims of individuals.

Intense individualism can also be connected with a loss of respect for ourselves, others and our environment. *Re-spect* comes from the Latin word meaning to look back on. If we cannot see ourselves in context, if we lose our ties with the past—if we fail to look back—progress becomes synonymous with amnesia. The philosopher Mark Kingwell calls this the great fiction of the "eternal now." We fail to remember at our ethical peril. Respect is the mechanism through which we remember, and it requires us to see ourselves in a larger context than just ourselves. Intense individualism functions from the opposite basis and is, therefore, incompatible with this type of respect. (One area where exploration of the conflict between respect and intense individualism could provide insights is that of the allocation of and access to healthcare resources.)

Intense individualism is probably, in part, a response to globalization. Because the vastness of the connection that globalization represents can make us feel so small, insignificant and anonymous, we seek refuge for our ego—reassurance that we exist and, perhaps, matter—in intense individualism, tribalism or both. The danger of tribalism, which in some ways is also a collective form of intense individualism, can be seen in many of the horrific armed conflicts and massacres in various parts of the world in the last decade. Such examples make us realize that intense individualism can be an attempt to fulfil a need to take control in a situation in which we feel abandoned and afraid because we have an overwhelming sense that indeed we are only an individual—we are alone.

There is, however, a paradoxical side to intense individualism. People who espouse it (strong civil libertarians, for instance) can bond through their belief—it can function as an ideology binding them together, as a substitute for the bonding that religion used to provide. Moreover, the experience of going through a stage of intense individualism might be the template for a new—or a return to a very old—form of community. This change would occur if we moved beyond the focus of intense individualism just on individual rights to an equal and balancing focus on individual responsibilities, especially for those people who are vulnerable, for community and for the common good. A concern raised by the predominance of intense individualism is that it has caused us to lose a sense of the common good and of what is required of us if we are to protect and promote the common good. The current search for ethics could indicate the emergence of a focus on individual responsibilities as well as rights and a renewed willingness to act in the interests of furthering the common good.

In contrast, if we apply intense individualism to our search for values, they can be reduced to simply what I as an individual prefer, which means that it is very difficult to find consensus and, as a result, to form community and protect the common good. The political scientist Francis Fukuyama, in his controversial book *The Great Disruption: Human Nature and the Reconstitution of Social Order* (with at least some of whose arguments and beliefs we might take issue), sums up this phenomenon as "moral individualism" resulting in "miniaturization of the community." But for the purposes of the line of argument I want to develop in this book, the most important effect of the loss of consensus on values is the adoption of a situational ethics approach. In taking a situational ethics approach to the formation of values—adopting moral relativism—so that we can keep all our values' options open, we seem to have lost the ability to agree that anything is *inherently wrong*—that is, wrong no matter how much good could come from doing it.

But can we in practice implement a view that something—for instance, human cloning—is inherently wrong in a society that has no absolute moral rules or no external source of authority for those moral rules that it does have? Can we believe in a moral absolute, even if we are not religious and even if we do not believe in a supernatural being as the ultimate authority? As I propose in the introduction, we can do this by accepting two values, which are probably two sides of the same coin, as absolutes. First, we must always act to ensure profound respect for life, in particular, human life; second, we must protect and promote the human spirit. If our development or use of any given scientific technology, for example, would seriously harm the fulfilment of either of these two values, it is inherently wrong. I return to this theme in the chapter on human cloning.

Another change from the past is that we are *media societies*. This, in turn, has changed the nature of the public discourse through which we create the shared concepts, ranging from values to laws, that govern our collective life. We are the first age in which our collective story-telling takes place through television—and now, increasingly, the Internet—and, consequently, at a physical distance from each other. We do not know how, in the long run, this change will affect the stories we tell each other in order to create our societal-cultural paradigm. Creating our "shared story" through the media may, moreover, alter the balance between the various components that go to make it up. For example, with our current fear-attraction-obsession reaction to death, we may engage in too much "death talk" and too little "life talk," or too much despair and horror and too little hope and joy. Moreover, the unprecedented, almost daily exposure of virtually everyone in the society to violence, cruelty and death—seeing the horrors of war, for example, each night in our living rooms—may overwhelm and dull our sensitivity to these atrocities and to the awesomeness of death and, similarly, of inflicting death, whether in war or by euthanasia. The adverse effects of this phenomenon are often discussed, but we need to be especially aware of its impact in the context of doing ethics.

Our frequent failure to take into account social issues in doing ethics is also connected with the increasing use of the media as the means through which we engage in our societal dialogues. The media encourage us to focus on the individuals whom we can see and listen to. For instance, it is difficult to present the argument on television that in governing the new reproductive technologies we must put future children at the centre of the infertility business and consider what is best for them, rather than simply what the person seeking to use this technology wants, or what investors in fertility clinics promote as "good for business." It is much easier to show a happy mother and a beautiful child who resulted from using this technology, thus making the case for such use.

We face the same dilemma in arguing against euthanasia. It makes dramatic, emotionally gripping television to feature an articulate, courageous, forty-two-year-old divorced woman who is dying of amyotrophic lateral sclerosis, begging to be allowed to have euthanasia made available, and threatening to commit suicide while she is still able if she is refused such access.

In short, the arguments against reproductive technology or euthanasia that are based on the harm they would do to society are especially difficult to present in the media. They do not make dramatic and compelling television. Visual images are difficult to find; we do not personally identify with either the arguments or the people presenting them in the same way we do with those of happy parents playing with children produced through reproductive technology or dying people who seek euthanasia; and society cannot be interviewed on television and become a familiar, empathy-evoking figure to the viewing public.

In order to identify and articulate the values that we need and can share, we must engage in "values talk." Our places of religious worship used to be our main forums for engaging in these discussions. But values talk has been transferred to the media as "ethics talk." This ethics talk is frequently interwoven with "law talk" concerning the same issues.

The role of the legal process (and, probably, of law) in forming our societal values has also changed. Matters such as reproductive rights or rights to refuse medical treatment that would have been largely the subject of moral or religious discourse are now explored in our courts and legislatures, in particular through concepts of individual human rights, civil rights and constitutional rights. When this happens, the cathedrals of a secular society—its highest courts and parliaments—become the forums in which the talk that forms societal values takes place. Consequently, it is not surprising that many of the issues surrounding new scientific developments that evoke widespread public discussion, hope and concern are also, in one form or another, ending up in the courts. For instance, in some countries, people are currently arguing in court about the patenting of human DNA and other life forms, including genetically altered animals; others are seeking injunctions against the release of genetically engineered micro-organisms into the environment; and products liability law is being used to require the labelling of genetically altered food.

We have become legalistic societies, and this change is connected with a loss of consensus on values, probably intense individualism and the impact of media. Law provides a bottom line, working consensus on values, even if in substance we still disagree. Law is also the most powerful way for individuals to challenge the state and has a very prominent role in establishing the values and symbolism of a secular society. People who are seeking to change these values and symbols use debates such as those on reproductive technologies, abortion and euthanasia as opportunities to further their aims. They do this through taking test cases to the courts and by advocating for changes in legislation. The response of those who oppose these changes can often be to propose harsh measures—for instance, framing them in criminal law—to reject the new values and affirm the old. (For example, recent legislation specifically criminalizing the transmission of HIV in some American states indicates a backlash by those with conservative values against society's tolerance of homosexuality and drug use. But these people might also see enacting such laws as a way to affirm values that are threatened by this tolerance.)

It might also be that taking test cases to the courts is some people's way of forming community, somewhat paradoxically, out of intense individualism. Being committed to individual rights—especially those that confront traditional conservative values, such as women's rights to equal pay for work of equal value or the right to marry for same-sex couples—can form the basis for a collective identity, usually one based on "minority status." This identity and the shared values that underlie it can be affirmed through successful litigation. These cases might also be showing a further shift in the locus of our decision-making about societal values. The locus of such decision-making has moved from religion and the clergy to the legislatures and politicians and now to the courts and judges. It is interesting to speculate whether there could be another shift and, if so, where this would be.

Yet another reason why the search for ethics has emerged now is that the new science has moved us *from chance to choice* in many matters—for instance, reproduction. With choice comes the responsibility to use that choice ethically. Doing so requires two kinds of courage: the courage to go forward with the new science and technology when it is morally and ethically acceptable to do so, and the courage to exercise restraint when it is morally and ethically required.

Fear also plays an important and complex role in our responses, both as individuals and as a society, to new scientific developments. Sometimes the fear we experience is unjustified. But sometimes a moral anxiety or an ethical intuition is at the base of our fear and should be heeded. Often we deal with fear by seeking to take control over the situation that elicits it. Consequently, we are likely to adopt new scientific developments that we see as giving us control and to reject those that we see as the source of our fear. We need to carefully research how fear affects our individual and societal psyches and, as a result, our assessment of what is ethical in relation to new scientific developments.

The fact that we are very *intolerant of mystery* can also cause ethical difficulties. Sometimes, we eliminate mysteries by converting them into problems. For example, if we convert the mystery of death into the problem of death, euthanasia can be seen as a solution. An inability to live comfortably with uncertainty—which is a variation on discomfort with mystery—can also cause us to adopt simplistic, reductionist approaches to very complex realities. Genetic reductionism—the view that we are nothing more than the expression of our genes—is a good example in this regard. Often these approaches lead us astray ethically.

Similarly, many of us have *lost access to a sense of the sacred*, including the notion that we, as human beings, are sacred in any meaning of this term. There are multiple causes of this loss over the last half-century, including our extraordinary scientific advances. By a sense of the sacred, I mean the recognition and protection of the human spirit—a sense of what I call the secular sacred. This might be more a new label or awareness than a new reality. For instance, we are using this concept often without recognizing that we are doing so to come to a new realization about what is required for respectful human-Earth relationships.

New genetic discoveries and technologies have, along with new reproductive technologies, had a major impact on our sense of the sacred. They can lead us to believe that we understand the origin and nature of human life and that, because we can, we may manipulate—or even "create"—such life. If we transfer these same sentiments to the other end of life, they would support a view that euthanasia is acceptable, that is, if we can create life we may dispose of it. In other words, we can regard the current movement for the legalization of euthanasia as a correlative development with the new genetics, and its emergence, therefore, as expected. According to this view, it is not an accident that we are currently concerned with both eu-genics ("good" genetics—good at birth) and eu-thanasia ("good" death—or, perhaps, good at death, that is, of no trouble to anyone else). We could even expand this connection between genetics and euthanasia.

14   This expansion could stem from a new perception that we have the ability to ensure our genetic immortality—seeing ourselves as an immortal gene collection—and, as a result, we could reduce somewhat our deep anxiety about the annihilation presented by death.

Our new genetics has also informed us of the connectedness of all life and of the vast amount of genetic heritage that we share with other animal species. This knowledge has led some to ask why we should regard ourselves as sacred if we do not regard these other species as sacred. In fact, Princeton bioethicist Peter Singer has given a label to the practice of distinguishing between humans and other animals. He calls it "speciesism"—a form of wrongful discrimination. Some people, especially those with traditional religious beliefs, are outraged by equating humans with other animals. I suggest that we should see all life as sacred—that is, as requiring profound respect—but human life as demanding a special degree of respect.

The frameworks that we use to structure our knowledge, in general, have always been influenced by scientific advances. For instance, Darwin's theory of evolution and the survival of the fittest has affected fields as diverse as sociology, psychology, political science and economics. Advances in genetics and molecular biology are likewise influencing fields well beyond the borders of the science of genetics. New schools of thought that are influenced by genetics are emerging. These new ideas can challenge our traditional concepts of what it means to be human and what is required to respect human life. For instance, sociobiology asks us to see the characteristics that we have usually identified as the unique markers of being human and as differentiating us from the other animals—namely, our most intimate, humane, altruistic and moral impulses—as also being the products of the evolution of our genes. At a macro-genetic level, deep concern about overpopulation of the earth, unlike the fears of extinction of the human species through underpopulation in earlier ages, might have thrust us towards losing a sense of sacredness in relation to human life.

The new science can, however, be linked with eliciting a sense of the sacred; it just depends on how we view it. For example, rather than viewing the new genetics as a totally comprehensive explanation of life, we can experience it as deepening our sense of wonder and awe not only at that which we now know, but even more powerfully at that which we now know that we do not know. We can thus see the new genetics and the rest of our science as only one of the lenses through which we are able to search for "the truth." In short, we must place science in a broad human perspective and view it within this context and not, as we have been doing, place human life in a narrow scientific perspective.

Instead, we should take an approach that is captured in a Japanese saying: As the radius of knowledge increases, the circumference of ignorance expands. The more we know, the more we know the extent of that which we do not know. I often think of new knowledge as a laser beam going out into the dark unknown, opening up a path that we can see and follow but, in doing so, increasing the area of darkness of which we then become aware. Recognition of this darkness, this unknowingness, can connect us with a sense of mystery. Ironically, this means that our scientific discoveries could increase our awareness of mystery, not destroy it. It all depends upon how we view what we learn.

Some people may have a "so what?" reaction to another change in our societies, yet another group of losses, those of a sense of *wonder* and of *awe,* of *play* and of *humour.* They may even welcome the loss of some of them. But these losses could impoverish our ethical sense. By a sense of play, I mean the childlike, but not childish, feeling that all is right with the world, even though we do not feel we are in control of it. We often make ethical mistakes when we seek certainty—a sense of control—in situations that are necessarily uncertain. Could our intense need for control be connected with a loss of a sense of play? And could this loss result from an undue emphasis on reason to the exclusion of imagination and intuition as ways of knowing? Does this mean that we should be concerned about a loss of the moral imagination and intuition that is essential in doing ethics?

Similarly, should we be concerned about a loss of a sense of humour in its deep meaning of a sense of balance and wise perspective in relation to any particular issue? This sense gives us access to common sense and good judgment, which are crucial faculties in doing ethics, especially in relation to the new science.

We are also highly *materialist, consumeristic societies,* and our search for ethics could help to avert the threats this behaviour presents. Intense materialism creates a danger that people can be equated to products and treated accordingly. For instance, if worn-out people are equated with worn-out products, the people can then be seen simply as a "disposal" problem. This view would favour euthanasia. Intense materialism would likewise favour the use of human embryos as therapeutic products for the benefit of others. And, if we see our children as products, especially products that reflect on our worth—as designer logos are seen to do—we are likely to want to design them to fulfil high standards of physical attractiveness and intelligence through genetic manipulation. This, of course, raises major ethical issues.

Yet another change relevant to the emergence of the search for ethics is the use, in some instances, of capitalism (perhaps as a substitute for religion or even a substitute religion itself) in the formation of societal values in secular Western democracies. For instance, some people, including some prominent scientists who do not want to have any explicit ethical restrictions placed on their pursuit of knowledge, argue that the "morality of the market place" will—and should be allowed to—regulate their science. According to this view, members of the public must be assumed to be moral, and, therefore, it is argued, they will not purchase or use technologies that they consider to be ethically unacceptable. The adherents of this belief propose that the market place can function to ensure ethics: Immoral or unethical uses of new technologies will not be commercially viable. But this approach requires the market to bear a moral weight it is not designed or employed to support. Moreover, even if the market place could act as a moral arbiter, what effect would advertising have on its ability to function in this way?

That said, and without detracting from a belief that market-place morality is an inadequate ethical regulator, the philosophical underpinnings of the market may be changing in a way that could be ethically relevant. If, as some commentators believe, we are moving from an age of materialism to one of post-materialism with regard to our pre-eminent values, business, especially the scientific-industrial complex, needs a new bottom line, whether we describe this as "new capitalism," "the third way," or "post-capitalism." This new bottom line will not abandon the component of the old single bottom line, that of profit, but it will integrate it with protection of the environment, concern for maintaining a sense of community and social cohesion, and ethics. The idea that bad ethics is bad business is, it appears, becoming more broadly accepted, not only in theory, but also in practice. It might even be that this fourfold combination will prove to be a "fourth way," one that takes account of the need to protect and foster the human spirit.

THE ABOVE DISCUSSION leads to an important insight: We are searching for a new world-view as a basis for a new societal-cultural paradigm. There are, I propose, three competing possibilities, each of which has a very different relationship to the new science.

The first is the "pure science" view, which takes a position that science does, or will be able to, explain everything, including those characteristics such as altruism and morality that we regard as distinguishing us from other animals and most clearly identifying us as human. This profoundly biological view of human life is a gene-machine approach. It seeks meaning in human life mainly or only through science and similarly seeks to exercise control through science. Such control can be implemented through the development and use of technologies that scientific discoveries make possible—the tangible reality of science—and at a more inchoate level through the use of the language and concepts of science. What it means to be human and the meaning of human life are seen and explained only in terms of scientific constructs. Genetic reductionism and an exclusive focus on sociobiology (our biology explains all that we are and can become with regard to our behaviour) to explain human aspirations and behaviour are two examples of such an approach. The pure science view is intolerant of the belief that there is a mystery in human existence—which often results in the negation of a sense of wonder—and within its parameters there is no recognized space for spirit.

The proponents of this view are comfortable with the use of reproductive technologies and with euthanasia, seeing most decisions concerning reproduction or one's own death as personal matters involving only individual values and preferences. The gene-machine approach to reproduction is epitomized by a current development in Britain. It has been reported that a private clinic is offering women having abortions the option of storing their fetuses in liquid nitrogen so that they may later use a cell from the fetus and the cloning technique that produced the sheep Dolly to create an embryo genetically identical to the aborted fetus. The fetus is not a unique human being but becomes a replaceable object—one that will be reconstructed when it is convenient to do so. The gene-machine approach is also operative, although in a less obvious and dramatic way, in practices that commercialize the human body or human reproduction, such as the buying and selling of human gametes or embryos, or for-profit surrogate motherhood.

The gene-machine approach to euthanasia can be summed up in the words of one Australian politician who, speaking in favour of it, said, "When we are past our best-before date, we should be disposed of as quickly, cheaply, efficiently and painlessly as possible." The tone of such extreme versions of the gene-machine view can also be captured in the image of human embryos as products in a supermarket.

In contrast, the second view, the "pure mystery" view, often decries science or is expressly anti-scientific (as can be seen, for example, in the creationists' legal suits against teaching evolutionary biology in schools). This view adopts an intense sanctity-of-life stance, which can be compared to respect or reverence for life, and to respect or reverence for death. For instance, many people who hold a pure mystery view believe that all medical treatment must be continued until no vestige of life remains. These same people could also have moral difficulties with providing necessary pain-relief treatment that could or would shorten life. Often, this view is derived from fundamentalist religious beliefs. It seeks meaning, and likewise control, through religion. This view does encompass a sense of wonder, but the wonder is not elicited by the new science, which is seen as frightening, at best, and possibly evil.

In her book *The Battle for God*, Karen Armstrong, a leading commentator and teacher on religious affairs, says that the fundamentalist movement is, at least on the surface, an anti-modernist movement; it is based on an intense fear of modernism and is a rejection of it. Because science is associated with modernism, especially in its emphasis on reason to the exclusion of other ways of knowing, we can expect that science would be feared and rejected. Fundamentalists fear modernism because they see it as annihilating them. Armstrong compares and contrasts access to knowledge through logos (science) and mythos (myths). The fundamentalists are returning to mythos, that is, earlier beliefs, but to a very literal interpretation of the myths on which these beliefs were based. People in previous ages realized that these myths were meant to function as ways of access to the psyche, but now these myths and the beliefs to which they give rise are being treated literally. It is not surprising, therefore, that the views of these fundamentalists are incompatible with those based on contemporary science. Armstrong goes on to explain, however, that at a deeper level the fundamentalist movement is essentially a modernizing movement: It is a way in which people who find the modern frightening and threatening can make a transition to the modern.

The "science-spirit" view, the third view, seeks a structure to hold both science and the human spirit. For some people, this view is expressed through religion, but it can be, and possibly for most people is, held independently of being religious, at least in a traditional sense. It recognizes that human life consists of more than its biological component, wondrous as this is. It also involves a sense of mystery—made up of at least the mystery of the unknown or the mystery of the nameless, or both—of which we have a sense through our intuitions, especially our moral intuitions, and accepts that we should respect this mystery. This world-view includes a sense of a space for the (human) spirit and of the secular-sacred. This view experiences our new science as eliciting wonder at both what we know and, as a result, what we now know that we do not know. It seeks meaning through a combination of science and spirit, which could create a different reality from the other two views.

We can compare and contrast these views. The pure science and pure mystery views represent opposite poles on a spectrum and as a result tend to be two-dimensional or linear. In contrast, the tension created through seeking a combination of science and spirit might create a third dimension—a space for human spirit, one that also fosters our imagination and creativity.

The pure science view operates from a basic presumption of doubt (although an alternative view is that it operates from a presumption of faith in science and that which science reveals, which brings it very close to a religion—or substitute for one—or an ideology). The pure mystery view operates from a basic presumption of faith in revealed doctrine (revelation). Paradoxically, to the extent that revelation offers an explanation, for instance, of the origin of the universe or the purpose of human life, it could be seen as reducing a sense of mystery. Adherents of both the pure science and the pure mystery views believe that their basic presumption is the only correct one and that the other's view is wrong. It can be argued, however, that the approach taken to forming a world-view by the proponents of each of these views is identical, and it is just the content of each view that differs radically from the other. In contrast, the basic presumption of the science-spirit view is more difficult to identify and the approach taken to forming it differs from that of the other two views. Perhaps it is best described as an openness to all ways of knowing, a comfort with uncertainty, ambiguity and paradox, and the courage to admit that one does not know and to change one's mind. It is a complex, active, constantly changing interweaving of certainty and uncertainty—with the certain open to becoming uncertain, and vice versa. I hasten to add that this is not equivalent to adopting a situational ethics approach. Recognition of unavoidable uncertainty is not incompatible with regarding some things as inherently wrong.

Those who subscribe to the science-spirit view may also be less likely to seek control than adherents of the other two views, probably because this view recognizes that it is less certain; indeed, it has respect for uncertainty and requires us to act in situations that involve uncertainty, under a precautionary ethical principle.

Most importantly, the science-spirit view recognizes that there is more that we *can* do with our new science than what we *ought* to do, so it opens up the debate on what we should and should not do. For instance, under this view, we could regard certain genetic interventions on a human embryo as acceptable (for example, those aimed at therapy for that embryo). But others—for example, those involving alteration of the human germ-cell line (the fundamental genetic inheritance that is passed from generation to generation) or human cloning —as inherently wrong. This view would also accept both refusals of treatment and the provision of necessary pain-relief treatment that would shorten life, but reject physician-assisted suicide and euthanasia. This view requires the courage to live with the uncertainty that making such distinctions involves.

The science-spirit view recognizes there are many questions we must ask about any given issue, but that there may be no one right answer. Its fundamental premise is that it is only through an undivided science-spirit approach that it will be possible to tell a collective story—to create a societal-cultural paradigm—of sufficient depth, breadth and width to capture our collective mind, heart and imagination. It will be the greatest challenge of the twenty-first century to realize the potential of this view. That is why we are now searching for ethics, especially in relation to the new science.

2. Making and Un-Making Babies

The Ethics of Human Reproduction

A young professional couple had telephoned to make an appointment. When they arrived in my office, they looked tense and distressed. The woman had had five pregnancies in a short time. Four had resulted in very late-term stillbirths. A baby was born at the end of the fifth pregnancy. At first all had seemed well, and the parents were overjoyed. After about eight weeks, however, the baby's health began to deteriorate and, six months later, he died of a serious genetic disease.

The couple then underwent extensive genetic testing and were told that they were genetically incompatible (this is called dysgenesis). The choices, if they were to have a child genetically related to one of them—which they wanted desperately—were artificial insemination of the woman by a sperm donor or using the husband's sperm to artificially inseminate a surrogate mother. The woman's physicians strongly recommended that she not become pregnant again; to do so, they said, would seriously endanger her health. The couple wanted to "hire" a surrogate mother but were concerned about the legality of doing so. They had read some of my remarks reported in the press, in which I had spoken out against commercial surrogate motherhood and pointed out its doubtful legal status. The woman looked at me with tears rolling down her cheeks. She said, "I can't believe that you would want to prohibit us from doing the only thing we can to have our own child. How can you be so cruel?" Her challenge was, indeed, food for thought.

Surrogate motherhood is not a new option, as the often-cited biblical example of Abraham fathering a child with Sarah's maid servant Hagar shows. But it is usually included among the new reproductive technologies. The advent of reproductive and genetic technologies, and changes in social mores and values regarding sexual relationships and reproduction, have recently led to a wide variety of situations in which we have been confronted with two related questions: What are our ethical responsibilities as individuals and a society with respect to the transmission of human life from one generation to the next, especially when technology is involved in this transmission? And what are our ethical responsibilities to early human life? (I use this term to describe human life at all stages from fertilization—the union of a sperm and ovum—to the moment of birth.) These questions link the different topics discussed in this chapter. They also link this chapter with the next one on human cloning.

Advances in science can cause us to revisit situations that we have accepted as ethical and to view them and similar situations in a new light. For instance, advances in reproductive technology that have made the donation of ova by women possible have caused us to look again at the ethics of sperm donation, which in recent times has not been seen as raising any great ethical difficulties. Likewise, people's concern over the creation of human embryos as a source of therapeutic products can cause us, if not to review the ethics of abortion, at least to review those of the use of aborted fetuses.

　　　And sometimes, new facts can send us back to reconsider the ethics of that which we have accepted. For instance, the abortion figures for 1998 show that a record 31,329 pregnancies were terminated in Quebec's hospitals and clinics, and 75,757 babies were born that year. This means there were forty-one abortions for every hundred live births, twice the rate of abortion twenty years ago. What does this tell us about our society's views of the ethics of the transmission of human life? Have these views been affected by new scientific developments, particularly in reproductive technologies and genetics? What does respect for human embryos or fetuses require that we not do? What harm will we do to ethical principles and values if we fail to respect early human life? These questions are explored in this chapter.

　　　The nature of our responsibility towards early human life has recently been prominent in the media. For example, in Canada, we saw the introduction of the Human Reproductive and Genetic Technologies Act in Parliament, which would, had it become law, have banned certain uses of these technologies and regulated others (the bill lapsed when Parliament was dissolved for an election). In a Winnipeg case, which is discussed in Chapter 7, the court ordered a young pregnant woman, Ms. G., into custody under its *parens patriae* power, because her glue-sniffing addiction was placing at risk the fetus she intended to carry to term. (Subsequently, the Supreme Court of Canada upheld the ruling of the Court of Appeal of Manitoba, reversing this order.) And there was the case of the Ottawa woman who discharged a BB gun in her vagina with the result that a pellet lodged in the brain of her fetus *in utero*. She was charged with attempted murder after its live birth, a charge that was later dismissed on the grounds that a fetus *in utero* was not a person and, therefore, could not be the subject of an attempted murder charge.

　　　Other countries have also faced the question of the ethics of how we treat early human life. In the United Kingdom, the proposed destruction of large numbers of stored, "abandoned" frozen embryos under their Human Fertilisation and Embryology Act caused a public outcry. The decision of an English woman and her obstetrician to "abort" one of the twins she was carrying because the woman said she was "too poor to raise twins" but wanted to have one baby was the focus of heated public debate. This procedure is not an abortion, properly so-called, but rather involves an intervention called selective reduction of multiple pregnancy in which one or more fetuses are killed *in utero* by exsanguination or a lethal injection and delivered dead at the same time as the wanted fetus(es) are born alive.

The cases described above raise deep concerns for those opposed to abortion who see all forms of early human life as having the same rights to protection as the rest of us. But why, apart from their potential, depending on how they are dealt with, to limit rights to abortion or set precedents for the coercion of women, have these cases also raised other deep concerns among people not opposed to abortion?

The usual justification of abortion is that a woman has the right to determine what should happen to her own body, in particular whether to continue or to terminate a pregnancy. The focus is on the woman's right to self-determination; the destruction of the fetus is regarded as a secondary, or perhaps an indirect, consequence of the exercise of this right. In contrast, the focus is on the embryo or fetus when someone destroys frozen embryos or one fetus while allowing the pregnancy to continue, because the destruction is the sole purpose of the intervention.

The same is true of *in utero* sex selection, and many people not opposed to abortion oppose sex selection. Even countries with liberal abortion laws have legally prohibited sex selection. In short, it can make a difference—at least to people's perception of the situation and the ethical acceptability of abortion in that situation—whether the primary reason for carrying out an abortion is focused on the fetus and a desire to eliminate it, or focused on the pregnant woman and a desire to respect her right to self-determination. When the primary reason for the abortion is related directly to eliminating the fetus and not to respecting the woman's right to self-determination, even those who view abortion on demand as acceptable can characterize such an abortion as ethically unacceptable.

We might also see the destruction of early human life or the failure to protect it as more tolerable in some cases than others depending on the nature of our personal identification—whether with the
woman or the fetus—or the degrees to which different interventions
overtly challenge the value of respect for human life. When people
primarily identify with a woman faced with a decision about abortion, those not opposed to abortion on moral grounds see the
woman as having a right to an abortion. On the other hand, when
people primarily identify with the embryo or fetus—and, let's face it,
we are all ex-embryos and ex-fetuses—we are concerned with protecting the embryo or fetus. Behind this concern lies a deeper concern: to maintain respect for human life itself. Such respect is
challenged much more overtly by the direct destruction of *ex utero*
human embryos and, even more so, by the selective reduction of
multiple pregnancy than it is when we justify abortion on the
grounds of respecting a woman's right to self-determination. In the
former situations, there are no competing claims to balance against
and override the harms involved in the destruction of the early
human life. If we apply this analysis to the glue-sniffing pregnant
woman in Winnipeg who intended to give birth to the baby she was
carrying, the cause of our dilemma becomes clear. It arises in part
because we have a dual focus—on the woman and her rights, and on
the child that will be born and its need for protection—and we do
not agree which should predominate because, as we see it (although
some would disagree), there is conflict between our ethical obligations to the woman (to respect her liberty and autonomy) and our
ethical obligations to the fetus (to protect it).

Some people object to any intervention that is aimed at protecting a fetus to which a woman intends to give birth and that also
would infringe on a woman's liberty. They regard such interventions
as inherently wrong and demeaning to women; moreover, they
believe the interventions would set a precedent that could be open
to abuse. These are valid concerns. However, many of us have
strong moral intuitions that doing nothing, that standing by and

simply "watching" serious harm being caused to a fetus that we know will be born, is ethically unacceptable. If we do intervene, we have the burden of proving the intervention is justified. There must be a threat of serious harm to the fetus that cannot be avoided in any other way, and the intervention must be highly likely to avoid or substantially reduce this harm. Moreover, ethically the intervention must be the least restrictive and invasive way that is reasonably available to avoid the harm or risk.

As is true in so many areas of applied ethics, in considering our objections to either intervening or not intervening to protect a fetus *in utero,* we must be honest about the true bases of these objections. In the *Ms. G.* case, for instance, as some opponents of allowing any intervention admitted, one of their main concerns was that to permit this intervention could be the thin edge of the wedge for placing restrictions on abortion: Intervening to protect the health of the fetus could be used as a precedent for intervening to protect its life. Justifying such an intervention would also be to acknowledge that the fetus, although not recognized as a person by the law, is still protected by the law—although in a lesser way than if it were a person—as indeed are baby seals and puppies. I would suggest that we can, however, separate abortion from interventions to protect fetuses from the risk of serious harm, by recognizing that a woman's decision to have an abortion on demand takes priority—although I believe that such a decision should be limited to the first trimester of pregnancy, unless it is for genuine health protection reasons. Those people who are anti-abortion could, I suggest, adopt such an approach without compromising their opposition to abortion if they did so on the basis that the use of law to prohibit early abortion is ineffective—especially in view of new methods of abortion such as the "morning-after pill"—and does more harm than good. They are not approving of abortion but, rather, recognizing that it is not feasible to use the law to prohibit it in the early stages of pregnancy. The danger in allowing coercive interventions to protect the fetus is that women might choose to have an abortion when they would not otherwise have done so, in order to avoid an intervention aimed at protecting the fetus. This area of decision-making is indeed a world of competing sorrows.

THE SELECTIVE REDUCTION of multiple pregnancies raises some of the same issues as abortion but presents us with an outcome different from that of abortion. In an article in the *New England Journal of Medicine* in 1981, an obstetrician described how he had exsanguinated an unwanted fetal twin by placing a needle in its heart. A dramatic graph illustrated the continued growth of the "wanted" fetus and shrinkage of the "unwanted" fetus. One live baby and one "mummified" fetus were delivered at term. In seeing the live baby, we see exactly what the dead fetus could have been. This image can change our perception of the ethical acceptability of the interventions that gave rise to this outcome—it may, for instance, affect our moral intuitions about such interventions.

Some methods of disposing of or destroying human embryos left over from *in vitro* fertilization could also be more problematic than others. (We must also ask whether it is ethical to create situations in which we have such embryos, but the present reality is that we do and they must be dealt with.) Human embryos are preserved by freezing them in liquid nitrogen below minus 196° Celsius. In at least one case in England, unclaimed embryos were destroyed by removing them from the liquid nitrogen and placing them in a solution of alcohol and vinegar. As the euthanasia debate shows, how we die can make a difference ethically, legally and emotionally to those who either are involved in causing the death or identify with the human who dies. Simply removing the embryos from the liquid nitrogen and allowing them to die naturally may have been marginally less ethically troublesome and less emotionally traumatic than actively killing them. Removing them from the liquid nitrogen and doing no more can be compared with the withdrawal of life support. In contrast, killing the embryos resonates more with euthanasia, which raises greater ethical difficulties. The result, of course, is the same.

The fact that the mass killing of the human embryos in Britain was legally required under the terms of the Human Fertilisation and Embryology Act, which placed a limit on the time for which embryos could be stored, also raises ethical concerns that might be lessened if the decision concerning each embryo were made on a case-by-case basis. An individualized approach would avoid having an intervention—moreover, one that there is a legal requirement to undertake—that can be described, as it was in the press, as a "human embryo holocaust." There is something grossly wrong with our moral intuition if a law that mandates mass extermination of any form of human life does not raise the most profound ethical concerns.

We often regard further advances in science and technology as a one-way street creating only new ethical dilemmas. But some advances may solve existing dilemmas. When we are able to store human ova as successfully as we are currently able to store human sperm, it will be unnecessary to create embryos prior to their being needed for implantation. But this technology could also raise ethical concerns in a different area, that of research on human embryos. In general, the creation of human embryos for research purposes is regarded as unethical and is legally prohibited in some countries. Such research is allowed only on so-called spare embryos—embryos left over from *in vitro* fertilization programs whose "parents" have consented to their use in research. Does this restriction result in pressure to create as many embryos as possible for *in vitro* fertilization in order to have some remaining for research? To do so would not be ethically acceptable. And what about cloning "spare embryos" to create large numbers of embryos to use in research. Is this ethical? This issue is discussed in the next chapter, but the point to note here is that advances in science can have a paradoxical effect: They may solve some existing ethical problems, but in doing so, open up different or new ones.

Preimplantation genetic diagnosis (PGD) is another ethically controversial new technology. It involves taking one cell from an early *ex utero* embryo and genetically analyzing that cell. If the embryo has

30   genetic abnormalities, it will be discarded. People with the same disabilities as those that are the basis for discarding embryos argue, with good reason, that this practice devalues them and their lives and sends a message that they are disposable people. This practice is also criticized as being a eugenics program. As such, it is ethically objectionable in itself. But it also raises further concerns. There is concern, for instance, especially as we develop tests for a wide range of genetic disorders, that we will "lose" the most brilliant and creative people from the next generation. Many geniuses in the past have suffered from bipolar manic-depressive illness, unipolar depression or other psychiatric disorders. Some others had physical disabilities that can now be traced to "defective" genes. Would we discard embryos who were at risk for these disorders? And what does it say about us, our values and our society, if we want to eliminate all people with Down's syndrome, which results from a defect in the twenty-first chromosome (Trisomy 21)? Moreover, even speaking just from a selfish point of view, what would we lose and what harm would it do to our society to systematically eliminate people with Down's syndrome? Recently, Bill Joy, the chief scientist and co-founder of Sun Micro Systems and a highly respected architect of the Information Age, warned in an article in *Wired*, "Why the Future Doesn't Need Us," that we need to take great care and exercise restraint in developing artificial intelligence, because at a certain point spontaneous consciousness might emerge and the "beings" with this intelligence might see us as inferior and disposable. Even if we do not believe this prospect is likely, contemplating it could provide important insights into the ethics of our acting likewise with regard to those we see as less worthy of life than ourselves.

WE CANNOT AVOID ENTERING a minefield of ethical and legal issues in deciding what is required of us in dealing with early human life. We will be forced to take into account in new ways some of our deepest human emotions and to re-evaluate the nature of our bonding—or lack of it—to living beings at these youngest stages of life. We need profoundly thoughtful discussion of what is required to maintain our overall respect, as both individuals and a society, for both individuals and human life itself.

Nowhere is this likely to be more true than in relation to abortion. Many of the ethical issues surrounding abortion are far from new. But recent technologies mean that we will also face different issues. For instance, as the age at which the fetus becomes viable (that is, can live outside the mother's body with or without assistance—at present this is placed at twenty to twenty-two weeks' gestation) decreases and ectogenesis (gestation outside a woman's body in an artificial uterus) becomes more likely, we could be faced with the issue of whether we are justified in destroying a fetus that could survive outside its mother's body, but only with very expensive medical care, when its mother decides not to continue her pregnancy. Or what are the ethical limits on using aborted fetuses as they become an increasingly valuable source of therapeutic products? I want to turn, here, however, to the primary and oldest ethical question, that of the ethics of abortion itself, and to discuss how—if we are to judge from the abortion statistics for Quebec, for instance—many people's view of abortion might have changed.

In response to these abortion statistics, The [Montreal] Gazette published an editorial in which the writers expressed grave concern about the large number of abortions. They said that the only question was "what practical steps might help to make . . . [abortions] less necessary. . . . Like it or not, society's moral debate on abortion is over: the courts have said abortion on demand is here to stay." The last part of this statement is correct in practice (though not in legal theory), but the first part is wrong.

Because abortion is legal does not mean that it is right, in the sense of ethically and morally right, in all circumstances. And society's moral debate on the ethics of abortion is *not* over. To regard, as *The Gazette* notes, the growing frequency of abortion as "one of society's great tragedies" and as "inflict[ing] a difficult emotional legacy" shows this continued concern. Indeed, one reason for the increase in abortion might be that many women (and men, to the extent that they participate in women's decisions to have an abortion) have made the same error as *The Gazette*, namely, they have assumed that because abortion is not illegal, it is ethically and morally acceptable in all circumstances. We need, however, a more careful and precise analysis than this.

Some people do not believe that abortion raises ethical or moral concerns. They support abortion on demand and would regard the idea that there should be ethical justification of abortion as reflecting a mind-set or ideology that they do not share. And some other people are against abortion no matter what the woman's reason for seeking it. Many people believe, however, that there can be an ethical justification for abortion in some circumstances, even if they, personally, would never have an abortion. Where they disagree is what these circumstances are.

The differing beliefs of this last group can be placed on a continuum: At one end, there is strong consensus that when a woman's life is in danger or her health is seriously threatened by continuance of the pregnancy, she must have the choice of whether or not to continue the pregnancy. Farther along this continuum, many people accept a wider range of ethical and moral justifications for abortion than just a serious threat to the woman's life or health. And, at its other end, there are some, but many fewer, people who regard abortion as a form of contraception, an insignificant event—more or less ethically and morally equivalent to having one's teeth cleaned. Consequently, where most of us differ is not on whether abortion needs to be ethically justified (many and probably most people, including those who are pro-choice, believe that it does), but on what constitutes a sufficient justification for it.

We might, however, have lost the capacity to convey the message, especially to young women—in Canada the major increase in abortion has occurred in the twenty- to twenty-five-year-old age group— that all abortions require ethical justification. This situation is probably a result of the polarization of the abortion debate into the two extreme views, on the one hand, that abortion is never ethically justified and should always be illegal, and, on the other hand, that abortion requires no ethical justification and there should be no legal restrictions on it. Women who believe that their only option is to choose between these two alternatives are likely to choose the latter.

Requiring ethical justification for abortion is necessary if we are to pass on to future generations a value of profound respect for the transmission of human life from one generation to the next. This respect could be based on a sense of the secular sacred, which I discussed earlier. Such a sense of the secular sacred would require that we treat the passing on of human life with the utmost respect and that we act with great responsibility in doing so. Thus, while we might engage in casual sex (and, even here, we should consider our personal ethics), we should never engage in the casual transmission of human life. Probably this distinction is yet another that we have not communicated to young people. Women or men who knowingly and deliberately take the risk of conceiving a child they would abort if pregnancy resulted are not, in my view, acting ethically with respect to the transmission of life.

There are other reasons that abortion might not be treated by young women with the ethical seriousness that it deserves. To be pro-choice has been characterized as being pro-women and their rights, and as feminist. Having ethical reservations about abortion has been characterized in the opposite way. It is not surprising, therefore, that young women ally themselves with the former perspective. But a woman can have deep ethical concerns about abortion and still be a feminist. The belief that she cannot both have these concerns and be a feminist—and, moreover, that it is politically incorrect to reject abortion—is an example of an increasingly common and worrying way in which political correctness can border on totalitarianism. Historically, it is understandable why access to safe abortion was linked to recognition of women's rights. Women placed their lives and health in danger by seeking unsafe, illegal abortions. Legal prohibitions on early abortion were ineffective and the harm they caused was very serious. As noted previously, such prohibitions would be almost entirely ineffective today when the "abortion pill" is available. But just because abortion is easily accessible should not be interpreted to mean that it is ethically acceptable—at least in all circumstances. If we believe that it is not acceptable, we must try to persuade others to regard it as unethical. We should be seriously concerned if, as we seem to have done, we lose the sense that abortion raises serious ethical questions. This loss of sensibility to the ethical issues raised by abortion places women at risk to their emotional, psychological and, for some, spiritual well-being, just as the total legal ban on abortions placed them at serious physical risk. Not to see abortion as raising serious ethical issues is also, I believe, very damaging to the human spirit and, therefore, to society.

The change in attitudes to abortion may also have come about because of a change in the basic presumption governing access to it. In Canada, this change resulted from the *Morgentaler* cases, which struck down the Criminal Code provision that limited, but did not preclude, access to abortion. Abortion was allowed when continuation of the pregnancy could put at risk a woman's life or health and a therapeutic abortion committee certified the danger. The Supreme Court of Canada held that this provision was unconstitutional because it infringed on a woman's right under the Canadian Charter of Rights and Freedoms to security of her person. The process prescribed in the Criminal Code for obtaining the committee's authorization was too uncertain: A woman who needed an abortion to protect her life or health might not be able to obtain it. Prior to the *Morgentaler* cases the basic presumption, which was reflected in the law, was that carrying out an abortion was an exception to the general principle that abortion was not ethically and morally acceptable. The basic presumption, now, especially in view of the fact that there is no law in Canada limiting abortion, is that abortion is acceptable and only in exceptional cases (for instance, when a fetus is clearly viable and the woman seeks an abortion for no medical reason) would it be seen as ethically unacceptable. Keep in mind that even in these very late-term abortion-on-demand cases, because there is no abortion law in Canada, such an abortion would be legal.

The messages given by these two different presumptions can each be described in another way: The first is "No, abortion is not ethically acceptable, but in some circumstances it can be justified." The second is "Yes, abortion is ethically acceptable, but in exceptional circumstances it would not be ethical (even though it is legal)." The choice between these two basic presumptions will affect the societal values about abortion that are handed on to the next generation. And if abortion is seen by society as *prima facie* ethically acceptable—or, even more so, if it is not seen as raising any ethical issues at all, and in no circumstances is it restricted by law—it should not be surprising that women, especially young women who have never seen it regarded in any other way, would increasingly use it.

Recognizing that the transmission of human life is a matter of the secular sacred could help to prevent this trend. Applying a concept of the secular sacred would mean that, whether we are religious or not, our moral and ethical views would include a recognition that the passing on of human life to the next generation deserves the deepest respect. Both personally and as a society, we must then consider what is required of us in acting out this respect. Using abortion as a form of contraception, regarding it as a trivial event or mere inconvenience, would not fulfil these requirements.

The Gazette editorial focuses on sex education as the solution to their concerns about the rise in abortion rates. While education might help, I very much doubt that it will be anywhere near sufficient. It is reminiscent of many scientists' response to the public's concern about some of the uses of the new genetics, which I discuss in relation to human cloning in the next chapter. These scientists assume that the public is scientifically ignorant, that their concerns arise from this ignorance, and that education will remedy their mistaken views. In fact, much of the public's concern arises from a deep moral anxiety about these technologies, not a failure of understanding. The same might be true, but in the opposite direction, concerning abortion. We may have a generation of women (and, it seems reasonable to assume, men) who have no moral anxiety about abortion and simply educating them, which often results in rational but not emotional or moral understanding, is unlikely to change this situation.

The values that govern the transmission of human life are not just a matter of information or something that can be brought up, on the side, by teachers "when discussing literature or biology" as the editorial suggests should be done. In order to "talk about sex" in its fullest context, in the richness it deserves, we must communicate a sense of the human spirit as well as factual information. This form of education requires a larger sphere than just the classroom. The values communicated to future generations about matters such as abortion—which are really values about respect for life itself, its transmission and, in the context of the new genetics, its inherent integrity—must also come from families, communities and society.

In our secular, pluralistic, multicultural societies, where we cannot find a ready consensus on important values, it is very difficult to communicate the values that should govern an issue such as abortion. But this difficulty makes it more, not less, important to try to do so. We cannot afford a values vacuum regarding abortion, no matter what our views about it.

LET'S TURN NOW FROM the ethics of interrupting pregnancy through abortion, to the opposite situation, the ethics of making pregnancy possible outside a woman's natural reproductive life span. A combination of new technologies and entrepreneurship is emerging in response to this new possibility. For instance, ovarian tissue transplants (taking ovarian tissue from the woman herself and storing it to use at a later time, or taking it from a donor—the possibilities are from another woman or a fetus) mean that women can avoid or reverse menopause. This tissue will function as substitute ovaries in the woman who receives the transplant. An example of entrepreneurship is the Web site "ronsangels," run by a fashion photographer who is auctioning off the ova of fashion models to the highest bidder. The site explicitly encourages rich men who want to have beautiful children to use its services. And advertisements are appearing in university newspapers offering young women $50,000 (U.S.) and more to donate their ova. Some of these ads are very precise, specifying that the donor must have high grades and blond hair and be tall, athletic and a graduate of a specific Ivy League university. What are the ethics of these dealings with and in human ova?

One use of ovarian tissue transplants would be by women with a disease such as cancer, the treatment for which might make it impossible for them to have their own children later. They could store their ovarian tissue prior to chemotherapy or radiation treatment. Later, they could have this healthy tissue put back in place, either to become pregnant or just to reverse an early menopause caused by the treatment. Such a use raises no ethical difficulties. Facing cancer is traumatic, and even more so when the treatment could result in sterility. We have ethical obligations to relieve any of these traumas that we can.

Another group of ethical issues raised by ovarian tissue transplants relates to the use of aborted fetuses as the source of the transplanted ovarian tissue. Should a woman with such a transplant conceive a child, this child would genetically be that of the fetus, not of the woman who received the transplant. Women have the maximum number of potential ova (eggs) that they will ever have in their lives when they are approximately five-month-old fetuses—from then on it is all downhill to menopause, which is the cessation of ovarian function. Ovarian tissue taken from a donor will generate ova that carry the donor's genes. Consequently, the child conceived by a recipient of an ovarian tissue transplant will be the genetic child of the donor of the ovarian tissue, not of the transplant recipient who gives birth to the child (unless the transplant involves replacing the donor's own stored ovarian tissue). There is something profoundly cynical and dehumanizing about using a fetus, who itself never came to live its life, as the source of a child. It raises ethical issues about treating the fetus as a commodity, an object or a thing. The Canadian Royal Commission on New Reproductive Technologies describes the "fertilisation of eggs obtained from female fetuses . . . [as] deeply offensive to all notions of human dignity." The ethical issues raised by using ova from aborted fetuses is but one example of a larger group of such issues. In using new reproductive technologies, ethical issues are raised about what is required of us if we are to ensure that we maintain great respect for the way in which human life is transmitted, as well as for each individual human life, and human life itself. (What is required in these respects is discussed more fully in the next chapter, in the context of human cloning.)

The use of ova from aborted fetuses also raises consequential ethical concerns, such as the possibility of encouraging a market in aborted fetuses or of women becoming pregnant in order to benefit financially from the use of the subsequently aborted fetus. It is possible that ovarian tissue or ova from aborted fetuses would be offered for sale on a Web site—as mentioned previously, there already are "ova for sale" sites; there is also a site with the price list for dead human fetuses or their parts for use in medical research.

To examine the ethics of ova donation, let's compare ova donation to sperm donation. Do we have greater hesitancy, ethically, about one than the other? Are there reasons for this, other than the fact that ova donation involves greater risks and a greater need for medical intervention? One reason might be that we treat regenerative tissue differently from non-regenerative in the larger context of the donation of tissues and organs for transplantation. Sperm are regenerative, ova are not—although the potential supply is large during a woman's reproductive years. Or might this hesitancy be connected with social, cultural or religious factors?

Until *in vitro* fertilization and embryo transfer became possible and, with them, the possibilities of donating ova and, just recently, ovarian tissue, we always knew that a child was the genetic child of the woman who gave birth to it. This knowledge is probably one reason that some cultures trace their ancestry through the maternal rather than the paternal line. But we can no longer be certain that a woman who gives birth to a child has not used reproductive technology and is its genetic mother, just as we cannot be certain of its paternity, unless we use genetic testing—which can allow us to be almost certain about this. Are we concerned about the genetic uncertainty that ova donation opens up? If so, do we fear it as individuals or a society? Is there, in some larger sense, a feeling that a woman bearing a child conceived from a donated ovum is acting as an incubator—Margaret Atwood's chilling portrayal in *The Handmaid's Tale* of a society in which women were seen in this way comes to mind—which would be to demean women? Or should we see the donation of ova as the most precious gift one woman could make to another and as affirming that fundamentally we all share the same human genome and human life? The questions we ask, the language we use, the analogies and metaphors we employ in searching for ethics in relation to these new reproductive technologies, are definitely not neutral in relation to the ethics we will adopt.

Or might there be even less obvious factors at play in our ethical hesitation about ova donation as compared with that of sperm? Our society's general reaction to surrogate motherhood was one of shock and concern, even if some people would accept it in some exceptional cases. We were appalled by the fact that a woman would plan to become pregnant in order to give away her child. "What type of women would do this?" we enquired, implying that she must be morally degenerate or psychologically abnormal in failing to bond with her child. Yet we experience nothing like the same reaction to men who father children and fail to bond with them.

We see this same contrast in societal attitudes towards women as compared with men who fail to bond to their children, in an historical example: Young Victorian women who left their babies on church steps were pursued and legally prosecuted. Young men, who "sowed some wild oats" and went to the colonies for an extended vacation, leaving a young pregnant woman behind, were more often considered cunning and clever. Even today a system being tried in Hamburg, Germany, and possibly elsewhere, which attempts to save unwanted babies from being abandoned in dangerous surroundings, such as Dumpsters, is the focus of major controversy. Under this system, women who give birth to an unwanted baby can leave it by passing it through a slot in a wall, specially designed for the purpose, and placing it in a crib. These women can remain anonymous. Could the outrage that can greet such an action arise because society places great value on a mother's bond with her child? A woman who chooses to give away her child is clearly demonstrating that she has not bonded—or, at least, that she is prepared to break this bond. And might only women carry this important value for society, not men? This difference could explain why we are not shocked by the men who avoid being part of the lives of children they did not intend to father.

The breach of our belief that mothers automatically bond to their children is starkest and most overt in the surrogate motherhood situation. Unlike the vast majority of women who give up their children for adoption, the surrogate mother becomes pregnant for the purpose of giving away her child to someone else. In adoption we can empathize with the woman who suffers the trauma of relinquishing her child because she believes it is in the child's best interests for her to do so. We cannot do this in surrogate motherhood. The empathy that we feel for the mother in the adoption situation allows us to maintain our belief in the mother's bonding to her child—indeed, this very bonding is the source of the grief she suffers. This means that the societal value carried by mothers that parents bond with their children (and its corollary, that there is something grossly wrong or abnormal about those who do not) is not contravened. The same is not true in surrogate motherhood. Let me be clear here: I do believe that mothers and fathers usually naturally bond to their children. But this natural phenomenon is different from the societal value of which this bonding is the content. This value functions, in our kind of society, to make parents responsible for their children and to ensure that they are not a burden on society.

Yet another group of ethical issues raised by ovarian tissue transplants is likely to be the focus of very substantial disagreement. For instance, this technology makes it possible for young women to store their own ovarian tissue in order to delay childbearing until later in life, possibly even past the usual age of menopause. What are the ethics of doing this? Should post-menopausal women, who are either within the usual reproductive age range or beyond it, have access to donated ovarian tissue, either to reverse menopause or to conceive a child? Would it be acceptable for a post-menopausal woman to act as a surrogate mother for a wealthy man who purchased a model's ovum and had it fertilized with his sperm?

Relevant ethical and legal considerations include respect for women's rights to self-determination and autonomy, and a presumption against interfering with these rights. This presumption means that those who want to prohibit women from using a reproductive technology should have the burden of proving that this prohibition is justified.

Exploring analogies between ovarian tissue transplants and accepted procedures involving the use of technology to intervene in reproduction could provide ethical insights. These analogies can indicate *either* that a new procedure is ethical, because it is analogous to an accepted procedure that is regarded as ethical, *or* that we need to re-evaluate the ethics of an accepted procedure. For instance, many people accept that it is ethical to donate ova and it is not currently illegal. Therefore, we can argue, the donation of ovarian tissue is acceptable within the same limitations. Or are the physical risks to an ovarian tissue donor greater than those to an ova donor, and does this make a difference, ethically? And what if the ovarian tissue or ova are not donated, but sold? Should we prohibit all commercialization of the human body, especially gametes (ova and sperm)?

A variation on the sale of ova has also been the subject of discussion in the media. The situation raising ethical concerns involves women who need to use *in vitro* fertilization to become pregnant but cannot afford to pay for the treatment. They are being offered the treatment "free" (to them) if they will donate one or more of their ova to another woman who needs such a donation if she is to have a child. This second woman pays for the *in vitro* fertilization procedure for both herself and the ovum donor. If we prohibit the sale of ova, should this bartering also be prohibited? If we object to it, what is the basis of our objection? Is it mainly that we believe that since the only way this woman can afford to have a child is to donate ova, her consent is not voluntary? Would she donate if she could pay for her treatment herself? How would we feel if the donor ends up without a child and the other woman gives birth to a child that is the donor's, at least with regard to its genetic heritage?

To return to comparing ova donation and ovarian tissue transplants with currently accepted interventions in reproduction, the freedom to choose to reproduce outside the normal—menarche to menopause—female reproductive age range through use of a donated ovum or an ovarian tissue transplant could be seen to parallel the freedom to choose not to reproduce within this age range through abortion. Or should we distinguish these two situations by focusing on the fact that in one a child is born, in the other it is not, and how this difference affects the ethics of each type of intervention? When we must also consider what is ethical with respect to a child that results from the use of a technology, we could alter our decision about the ethics of the use of that technology. Or should we be less ethically concerned about using technology in a way that results in life than using it to negate life?

Or could a pro-choice stance on abortion reflect, in part, a view of treating men and women equally? Let me explain: We can construct an argument in favour of freedom of choice concerning abortion along the lines that men are not burdened with pregnancy; therefore, women should not be prevented from using technology to intervene in the "natural order" to make themselves "non-pregnant." On the same line of reasoning, the parallel analysis would be that men can father children at an advanced age; therefore, women should not be prevented from using technology to intervene in the "natural order" to become pregnant. If we have reservations about the latter line of reasoning, it could mean that we also need to reconsider the ethics of abortion, at least in some circumstances.

Moreover, men are "compensated" for donating sperm for artificial insemination. Should women be "compensated" for providing ova? If we have ethical difficulties with the sale of ova, do we need to re-examine the ethics of the sale of sperm? My own view is that the civil law of France and Quebec takes the correct ethical approach to the sale of human body parts and tissues, including sperm and ova: The human body is "*hors de commerce*"—outside of commerce—and therefore may not be bought or sold.

Or we could turn to a historical comparison. Some argue that it is not ethical, from the child's perspective, for post-menopausal women, past the normal age for reproduction (which varies between the mid-thirties and late fifties, but is generally around fifty years of age) to have babies. But our life span has been expanded dramatically and older women might, on average, live for as long after the birth of a child as younger women did in the past, especially in relation to their youngest children. Do we have ethical obligations to a future child not to use technology to assist an older woman—let's say a sixty-year-old—to conceive? What counts in assessing this: that the child is likely to have its mother around for a shorter time than the average child in that particular society? Or is there any minimum period during which children have a very strong need for their parent(s) and, if so, should this be taken into account in deciding on access to ovarian tissue transplants? Should older women with a strong family history of longevity (longevity is genetically based in part) be given access? If not, is our alleged concern for the child growing up without a mother concealing some other basis on which we reject childbearing by older women? Do we view older mothers differently from older fathers? If so, why?

To view older mothers less favourably than older fathers raises the question of discrimination on the basis of sex, on the basis of age, and in relation to reproduction—three grounds of discrimination in which the courts apply strict scrutiny. There is, however, an ethically relevant difference between conceiving a child naturally and helping people to do so through the use of technology. Ethically, we have obligations not to interfere with naturally occurring reproduction. In contrast, physicians and others who provide access to reproductive technologies have a moral responsibility to use them ethically. Sometimes they are unsure what this requires, and in recent years a discussion of difficult ethical cases has become commonplace at medical conferences.

I was invited to be a member of a panel at the combined annual meeting of the American Fertility Society and the Canadian Fertility and Andrology Society. (Andrology is the science and medicine of reproduction in relation to men, just as gynaecology is in relation to women.) The conference organizers presented the panel with several quite extraordinary—or so I thought—cases involving the use of reproductive technology and asked us to discuss them. I believed these cases were hypothetical, but I was told later they were real situations that various members of the medical societies we were addressing had faced. One case involved the father of a young single man who had died from testicular cancer and had stored sperm prior to undergoing chemotherapy. The father wanted to hire a surrogate mother and have her bear a grandchild for him. If the young man had not given consent to the use of his sperm after his death, we had an easy answer: It would be unethical to use it. But what if he had given consent and, instead of his father, it had been his partner or wife who wanted access to the sperm? This question is not as easy to answer ethically. Courts faced with this issue have given women access to their deceased husband's or partner's sperm, but is it fair to the children to conceive them knowing they can never meet their father (or mother if it were ova from a dead woman)? What are the psychological risks to the child, in particular from being perhaps some form of replacement for the dead parent?

In other cases, sperm has been recovered from a dying or recently dead man without his prior consent. The approach being taken, in general, to this practice is that sperm may not be recovered or used after the death of the "donor" unless he gave his informed consent prior to his death. But even if consent has been given, we still need to consider whether this practice is ethical with respect to the child who will be conceived.

Perhaps the most famous case in which children could have been born to dead parents involved the Del Rios embryos. This case came to my attention as it was happening. One of the first *in vitro* fertilization units in the world was at Monash University, in Melbourne, Australia. Among others at this unit, Professor Carl Wood and Professor Alan Trounson were pioneers in developing *in vitro* fertilization technology. They invited me to visit Monash. Alan Trounson explained the invitation: "The latest procedures we're using might be raising a few issues you could take a look at." I was happy to oblige. They were, indeed, raising some unprecedented ethical issues. This unit pioneered the preservation of human embryos through freezing them in liquid nitrogen and there was not widespread knowledge of the use of this cryopreservation technology at that time. I first learned of it on this visit. (After one lecture I gave, I was told, "Gosh, Margo, we didn't think we had any problems until we brought you home." [I am Australian.]) A short time after I returned to Montreal, I received a phone call from Alan Trounson. He said, "We have a problem and were wondering if you could help. We have some frozen embryos which we were holding pending their use in *in vitro* fertilization. But both of the prospective parents have just been killed in an airplane accident in South America. Do you have any thoughts on what we should do?"

The fate of the Del Rios embryos became the subject of national and international debate. The parents had not given any instructions regarding what should be done with them, and there was no legislation governing the matter. As Bernard Dickens, professor of medical law at the University of Toronto, succinctly remarked, "If the embryos are persons, they inherit their parents' estate; if they are property, the estate inherits them." The law functions on the basis of two comprehensive, mutually exclusive categories—person or property. We had never before been faced with classifying human embryos. Eventually laws were passed that governed how embryos such as the Del Rios ones should be dealt with. The embryos were donated to a couple seeking *in vitro* fertilization who needed donated embryos. The identity of the Del Rios embryos—as is the case with all donated embryos—was not disclosed to the prospective parents. Because of the anonymity, we do not know what eventually happened to the Del Rios embryos.

In the past, our natural reproductive years have been either shorter than our life span, in the case of most women, or at least limited to it, in the case of men. The question we must ask is whether it is ethically acceptable to expand a person's reproductive life span beyond these parameters and beyond even the gamete donor's death. Does a child have an ethical claim not to be conceived from a dead biological parent? What are the risks to the child, particularly in light of the circumstances of its birth? And what are the claims of a child to have the optimal situation (or at least, not to have this deliberately frustrated) of two living parents?

On a more everyday level, certain practices in sperm donation that used to be common raised ethical concerns and are no longer employed. For instance, it was not unusual to mix an infertile husband's sperm with that of donors, or to mix the sperm of several donors in order to make it impossible to identify the father of the child. This practice would now be regarded as both bad medicine and bad ethics, particularly as it deprives the child of any possibility of learning its genetic identity and also deprives the child of the benefits, particularly medical benefits, that can come from this knowledge.

Keeping adequate records about gamete donors is now generally regarded as ethically required. Children born as a result of these donations may have access to those records. Some of them name the donors, with their consent, others do not. There is also a movement in Canada, among other places, to allow people who use a gamete donation to conceive a child to have access, where possible, to the same donor for subsequent children. This practice allows the children in the family to be full, not half, siblings. Giving parents the opportunity to have fully genetically related siblings can be regarded as a requirement for an ethical system of gamete donation.

In contrast, blood relationship in gamete donation can raise serious ethical difficulties. I was consulted by a family practitioner about a case in which the desired genetic relationship raised an ethical problem. A young woman whose husband was infertile wanted to be inseminated with her husband's father's sperm. This family belonged to a culture in which blood relationship was very important and they believed that this approach would be far more preferable than using an anonymous sperm donor. No law prohibits this procedure. The law against incest would not apply, because incest requires blood relationship and sexual intercourse, neither of which were present in the proposed insemination. The basic presumption that would apply here is that this undertaking is unethical because of the harms it could do to the child, especially with regard to the child's family relationships. I was never advised of what the physician or the family, if the physician was willing to undertake this procedure, finally decided to do.

When we scrutinize the ethics of the uses of new reproductive technologies, we must place the child at the centre of both the decision-making and the infertility business. Recognizing that a child is not a commodity, that the transmission of human life is not for sale, and that a child has the right to know its genetic origins when born from a donation of sperm or an ovum or ovarian tissue, and establishing the means to make this possible, are all steps in this direction.

The most difficult situation that results from putting the child at the centre of decisions concerning reproductive technology is deciding who should have access to this technology—or, more precisely, whether access should be denied to some people because of ethical concerns relating to the child. In particular, do we have ethical obligations to a future child to deny people the use of this technology unless the child would be born into a situation in which both a man and a woman would function as the parents? Often this question is framed as, "Should certain people be refused access to this technology, for instance, single people or those living in a non-traditional relationship, usually as a gay or lesbian couple?" And some very conservative people ask it rhetorically as, "Should everyone except married, heterosexual couples be refused access?"

The danger in addressing this issue is that my comments could be used to reinforce discriminatory attitudes and beliefs. We should all be concerned about such an outcome. Thus, I want to be blunt: We must start from basic presumptions that it is wrong to interfere in people's decisions concerning reproduction and wrong to discriminate on the basis of sexual orientation or family status. Nevertheless, we must ask whether access to reproductive technologies should be an exception to the application of these presumptions. That is the issue I now explore.

When we place the person who wants to have a child and needs to use reproductive technology at the centre of the decision-making, in my view, it is irrelevant whether the person is single, married, heterosexual or homosexual. To deny access on the basis of these characteristics is discriminatory. However, when we place the child at the centre and ask, "Do we have obligations to that child not to intentionally create a situation in which we know the child will not be brought up by a male father and a female mother?" the answer is not nearly as clear.

My basic presumption is that a child needs both a mother and a father, and for society to participate in deliberately creating a situation in which the child will not have both raises serious ethical concerns. (Some people will challenge the presumption that a child needs both a mother and a father. While they will agree that a child needs role models of both masculinity and femininity, they will believe that these role models can be provided in other ways.) Let me be clear as to the issue I am addressing. It is society's participation in providing access to reproductive technology that raises ethical issues. We should never interfere with people's private decisions and actions concerning reproduction. But we have obligations to consider the ethics of what we are doing, in particular in relation to any child that will be born because we are facilitating his or her conception. Some countries have taken a very restrictive stance in this regard. For instance, one policy approach taken in France was to allow gamete (sperm or ova) donation only by a married couple to a married couple. The same result can be achieved by medicalizing the issue of access to reproductive technology: It should only be made available for medical infertility (resulting from some disorder) not for social infertility (lack of a partner of the opposite sex).

Note that in saying that the child needs a mother and a father, I am not specifying that those people should be married. I do believe, though, that they should have a living arrangement that constitutes some form of shared home, in either a physical or a non-physical sense, in which the child will be raised. Nor am I specifying their sexual orientation—they might be heterosexual or homosexual. Nor (although I am less certain in saying this) need they be just one couple. For instance, a shared home of a gay couple and a lesbian couple that includes the parents of the child may provide the child with the kind of access children need to their male and female parents. In other words, I am not necessarily advocating a traditional nuclear family and certainly not for the sake of preserving it. Alternative forms of family could fulfil the ethical obligations we, as a society, owe to the child in facilitating his or her conception through providing access to reproductive technology. We are likely to become more conscious of these obligations as we start to obtain the results of research showing that children in single-parent households, especially boys raised without the presence of a father, do not do as well as those raised in households headed by a man and a woman. To summarize: It may be either the child or the person who wants to use this technology who is placed at the centre of the decision-making concerning access to reproductive technology. Whether it is the child or the prospective user can make a vast difference in deciding who, ethically, should have access to that technology.

The same is true in adoption. Placing the child at the centre of the decision-making and acting in his or her best interests might not, however, result in the same decision in a situation that involves access to adoption and another that involves reproductive technology, even when all other circumstances are the same. The fact that the child already exists when adoption is being considered can make a difference. Placing the child at the centre of the decision-making in adoption again requires starting from a presumption that a child should have a man and a woman as his or her parents. But depending on all the circumstances, this might not be possible or the best option available to the child. Consequently, allowing as we do single people or gay or lesbian couples to adopt children can be to place the child at the centre of the decision-making and is in some children's best interests.

It is sometimes argued that children born to a loving single person or same-sex couple who want them would be far better off than some of the children who are born to single mothers who did not intend to have a child or than children born into abusive heterosexual relationships. It can also be argued that such children may even be better off than children who are brought up in single-parent households as a result of divorce or death. All of this is undoubtedly true. Yet it does not answer the question of whether we have ethical obligations to a future child in giving access to reproductive technology to people whom we know will not bring that child into a family that includes a man and a woman as the father and mother.

Placing the child at the centre of decisions about the ethics of access to reproductive technology also raises an important question about any couple, including male-female ones, who want to use reproductive technology: Should we screen them to ensure some minimally adequate parenting skills or for a history of violence before providing such access? This suggestion raises difficult ethical issues because a justification of "unfit to parent" has been used abusively and discriminatorily in the past to tread on people's most fundamental rights, their rights to have children and found a family. It is an area where we must start from a presumption of respect for people's liberty; that is, a presumption against restricting them. Only in the clearest cases of harm or risk to children should we intervene. And yet I have suggested a basic presumption against providing access to reproductive technology for single people or same-sex couples.

Are we justified in using different basic presumptions for heterosexual couples and single people or same-sex couples who want access to reproductive technology? "Yes, access, but not if…" on the one hand, and "no access, unless…" on the other? Asked another way, the question becomes: Do we have a greater responsibility in providing access to reproductive technology to ensure that the child is brought up by a man and a woman than we do to ensure that he or she has reasonably adequate parenting and is not abused? Many of us, I believe, would consider the latter to be the stronger obligation. There is a difference, however, between these two situations: When single people or same-sex couples seek access to reproductive technology we assume (unless the contrary is proven) that the child will not be raised by a male and female parent. When a man and a woman seek access to the same technology we assume (until the contrary is proven) that they are fit to parent. These basic presumptions are reasonable in each case, but we should be aware of the presumptions we are using and always question the ethics of the choices we make in this regard. This discussion shows the complexity of decisions about access to reproductive technology and how our choice of basic presumptions, which are often linked to our fundamental beliefs, can affect what we decide.

We must also decide how to implement those decisions we do take. There is a difference between using law and using ethics to intervene. I believe that, at present, these issues should, to the largest extent possible, be governed by ethics, not law. Doing so will require establishing codes of ethics that professionals and institutions who provide access to reproductive technology will be required to follow. Whether this will be an effective regulatory system is an open question. Our experience to date is not promising. For instance, a voluntary moratorium by Canadian fertility clinics on certain uses of reproductive technologies—such as not to use them for sex selection—is reportedly not being honoured.

Does this discussion, taken as a whole, provide any insights about how we should treat single people or same-sex couples who want to use reproductive technology? At this time, my own conclusions are as follows: Having a child is life-affirming. It is an inherently right thing to want to do. Prohibiting single people or same-sex couples from access to reproductive technologies will not mean, in most cases, that they will not have a child. Rather, they will do so through means that are less safe for the child and themselves, obtaining sperm from mail order services, from friends or even from strangers. It is much safer for them to have access to established reproductive technology services. Consequently, I believe we should urge people who are considering bringing children into the world by any means, including through using reproductive technology, to consider the ethics of bringing these children into their kind of family, whatever this might be. But I believe we should not, until and unless there is more evidence of harm to children from their being raised in non-traditional families, discriminate on the basis of family status against people in non-traditional families who wish to have access to reproductive technology services that are available to other members of our society.

I recognize that some of my views will be controversial and hurtful to people who are loving single parents or gay or lesbian couples raising children. Some of the most outraged reactions I have ever had directed at me in my professional work have come from gays and lesbians who were appalled that my reservations about what is owed ethically to children would restrict gay and lesbian access to reproductive technologies. The danger in restricting such access, apart from thwarting the deep desires of these people to have their own children—and the suffering this causes—is that we could also reinforce, or be seen to support, discriminatory attitudes towards gay and lesbian people and stigmatization of them. We should also question whether the objections of some heterosexual people to homosexual people having access to reproductive technology have more to do with non-acceptance of homosexuality than genuine concern for the children who would be born as a result. We must be honest in our responses and be careful that we do not base them on unacceptable, hidden agendas, especially political ones.

Whether we are heterosexual or homosexual, we must recognize that some of our most important personal and intimate values will inform our responses to who should have access to reproductive technology when this technology is necessary to have children. We are not necessarily justified in imposing our values on others. But the reality is that at a public policy level, we must choose between conflicting values. Some gay people see present and past choices as having been made as a result of a heterosexual world-view and as being aimed at supporting this view and excluding gay people. Conversely, some heterosexuals see these and some other claims by homosexual people as promoting a gay world-view and political agenda, which they reject. We need to be aware of such deep and broad effects of decision-making in relation to what, at first glance, seems to be only a most personal and intimate matter—bringing children into our own lives and world.

INFERTILITY MEDICINE CAN offer real hope to infertile people and is often used ethically, wisely and well. But infertility is also a major business. And infertile people are eager, vulnerable, often desperate customers, whose personal anguish can be manipulated or exploited for financial gain. For example, infertility clinics have been largely unregulated in most countries. Some clinics, which advertised extensively and charged large fees, had never at the time had a successful pregnancy that resulted in a live birth. Moreover, there has been concern about the way in which statistics demonstrating success are presented. They can be juggled to show much better outcomes than prospective clients can realistically hope for in terms of "take-home babies." Personal characteristics other than infertility can also be exploited. For instance, some potential clients are intensely narcissistic and, as the "ronsangels" Web site shows, this trait can also be manipulated for large financial rewards.

54   While it is individuals who use these technologies, what they do with them affects us all. Some of our most important shared values, attitudes and beliefs relate to human reproduction and what we view as ethical or unethical in the ways in which we seek to fulfil our needs and desires to have children. What ethical limits are we justified in placing on reproductive technologies, if we are to protect both children born as a result of their use and our collective human spirit? It is important to remember that we are more likely to harm our collective human spirit by what we either support, allow or prohibit in the area of human reproduction than in other less ethically and symbolically sensitive areas.

3. Immortalizing Our Genetic Selves

The Ethics of Human Cloning

The ethics of human cloning has been on the public agenda since the birth of Dolly, the cloned sheep. Cloning techniques make possible both the creation of genetically identical human beings and of tissues, organs or cell lines (a homogeneous group of cells derived from a single sample of cells from a tissue or organ) that are genetically the same as the donor. We can clone higher animals and, therefore, humans. Human cloning can be undertaken for two reasons: to produce children who are genetically identical to the cell donor (*human reproductive cloning*), or to produce embryos for research or to manufacture therapeutic products, including tissues or organs for transplantation (*human therapeutic cloning*).

Our ethical reaction to the new genetic technologies often starts with what philosopher and ethicist Professor Arthur Schaefer of the

University of Manitoba has called an ethical "yuck factor." Many people had such a reaction to the possibility of human cloning. But as our familiarity with these new technologies increases and our dread decreases, we may move from ethical rejection and horror to ethical neutrality and ethical acceptance—usually with safeguards—and finally to positive approval of the new technology, especially if we see it as offering major benefits.

This slippery slope to acceptance of ideas we once viewed with disgust starts with familiarity and overcoming dread, factors that can be linked with moral intuition. Therefore, we need to be careful in allowing these changes to occur and not to suppress our moral intuition; we may have to consciously prevent familiarity and the loss of dread regarding scientific developments from dulling our ethical intuitions about these discoveries. And since these intuitions are often manifested as a sense of anxiety, we should not ignore this anxiety.

But some eminent scientists do not agree. They see such anxiety as pathological. They understand the world and human life through science only. They espouse a gene machine or pure science view of human life and a world-view based on it. They do not respect ways of knowing other than reason (although scientific discovery depends on these other ways, especially on creativity, imagination and intuition). Moreover, these scientists tend not to see science's profound impact on our metaphysical reality, especially its human spirit dimension. Indeed, most do not even recognize that this reality exists or, if they do, that it can be damaged. As sociologist Professor Howard Kaye says, the nearest they come to acknowledging the potential for damage is when they admit that the new science raises "reasonable concerns about potential psychological and social harm." They believe, however, that these concerns are counterbalanced by other values supporting individual choice and freedom of scientific enquiry and "the good" that they see their science as being capable of delivering.

These scientists regard people who oppose human cloning as doing so on the basis of "deep cultural prejudice"—to use the words of Professor Richard Lewontin, professor of zoology at Harvard

University—and sheer ignorance of biology. They believe, as Kaye reports, that "the fear that human cloning may prove dehumanizing and therefore ought to be banned is simply the hysterical reaction of the modern-day 'Luddites' held in thrall by 'ancient theological scruples' which must be swept aside so that scientific progress and human liberation may proceed." In other words, they believe that any opposition to their science is largely based on ignorance rather than insight. Consequently, they see the solution to this opposition as better science education.

These scientists would accept, for instance, a short-term ban in order to have time to correct "public misconceptions" about the science and to minimize safety risks, which they see as the only real concern. They see voluntary moratoriums on human cloning as the least threatening way to accommodate what they regard as unreasonable fears on the part of the public. They bolster their approach with statements that the public's fears are based on science fiction and with long litanies of the good that will result from the technology, such as providing infertile couples with children, or saving dying children through the transplantation of tissues or organs.

These scientists dismiss the public's widespread moral intuitions against human cloning. Kaye describes this dismissal as blocking moral judgment and the public's moral opposition. He makes the very important point that

apprehensions [on the part of the public] so nearly universal in expression—that cloning constitutes a threat to the dignity and sanctity of human life—ought not to be dismissed so cavalierly. . . . The claim of cloning's supporters, that the anxieties experienced [by the public] may be safely ignored because they will soon diminish as they always have done before, is . . . profoundly misguided. These anxieties may indeed diminish as panic gives way to temptation or fatalism, but the price of such accommodation may seriously reduce our worth as human beings.

58   Kaye also argues that the scenarios the public construct of the mad scientist who will use cloning or the multiple clones of the mad dictator may indeed be "misconceptions of science but the dangers which they sense so viscerally may be very real indeed." In other words, our anxieties may be needed to guide our moral responses to this science. It is not enough simply to look at the consequences of our actions, we also need "clarity about the ultimate meaning of our actions."

Moreover, we must ensure, as health lawyer and ethicist Professor George Annas warns, that individual scientists do not "act first and consider the human consequences later." In human cloning, society faces the necessity to make moral choices and other important decisions without having had actual experience with this technology and despite a lack of knowledge regarding at least some of its risks. Making these decisions must, therefore, call upon the "other" ways of knowing: intuition, common sense, human memory (history), ethics, imagination and creativity, and "examined emotions," and not just reason as the scientists who want to carry out human cloning propose.

So keeping in mind the general scene just described, in which the human cloning debate is taking place, what are the facts? What is involved in human cloning? In this area, in particular, good ethics depend upon good facts.

How are clones created? We could clone human embryos, or organs, tissues or cells. Even these latter types of cloning can involve human embryos. Human cloning involving embryos could occur in three ways: through the transfer of the nucleus of an adult cell into an enucleated human ovum (the "Dolly technique") to create an embryo; through embryo splitting, which occurs naturally with identical twins, triplets or quadruplets, but which can also be undertaken in the laboratory with embryos that would not have divided naturally; and through cloning from human embryo stem cells (primordial cells capable of forming any part of the human body) taken from embryos. Sometimes, all three procedures are grouped together and referred to collectively as human cloning. There are, however, differences among them, some of which are ethically relevant. The first two methods can result in an identical person; in the last, only organs or tissues genetically identical to the donor of the stem cell can do so. In the latter two methods, the clones are genetically identical; in the first, the clone's mitochondrial DNA, which comes from the donor of the enucleated ovum, differs from that of the person who donated the somatic cell (a cell that is not a reproductive cell, that is, not a gamete—an ovum or a sperm).

The Dolly technique involves taking an ovum (an egg) and removing its nucleus with the DNA (the genes) that it contains—the ovum is then empty except for the mitochondrial DNA in the cytoplasm (the liquid) of the ovum. (The mitochondrial DNA is passed through the maternal line from generation to generation unchanged, it was thought, except by mutation. But some very recent research indicates that sperm might have an effect on it.) Then a somatic cell is taken from the person who is to be cloned. Every cell of our bodies contains all our genes. The genes from this somatic cell are placed into the enucleated ovum. This new cell is then treated in such a way that it starts to function as a human embryo. It will be the clone of the donor of the somatic cell.

Human cloning can be undertaken for one or other of two purposes. Human *reproductive* cloning aims to produce a child. Human *therapeutic* cloning involves producing embryo clones through either the Dolly technique or embryo splitting, then using either the embryos or stem cells from the resulting embryos as "living human tissue generators" or for other research purposes. These stem cells can also be cloned.

What are the facts about human embryonic cells? The cells of the very early embryo are totipotential, that is, they have the potential to function as another human embryo and can each give rise to an entire new being. They are also pluripotential, that is, they can be manipulated to produce any tissue or organ. Although every cell in our body contains all of our genes, at an early stage, the genes in each cell differentiate so that, for example, our liver cells express only the liver genes they contain, or our skin, only the skin genes—the other genes in the liver or skin cells remain silent. After differentiation, a cell can form only the tissues or organs for which it has been differentiated—unless it is de-differentiated using the Dolly technique.

Human embryonic stem cells are taken from a human embryo at about the one hundred-cell stage. They are no longer totipotential but are still pluripotential, that is, they can be caused to differentiate into a certain tissue or organ. Taking stem cells from an embryo necessarily destroys it.

To summarize: Up until a certain stage, each cell of a human embryo can form another embryo; every embryo forms stem cells within it; taking stem cells from an embryo destroys the embryo; stem cells cannot function as an embryo; and stem cells can be cloned.

We must ask: What is the moral status of a human embryo, of embryos cloned from another embryo, and of human embryonic stem cells collected in the way described? Some people believe that the human embryo has full human moral status, others that it has special moral status, and a few that it has no moral status. Those who believe that it has *full human moral status* argue that, from its earliest beginnings, all human life deserves the same respect. Therefore, they believe that we must not undertake any research that is not intended as necessary therapy for the embryo on which it is carried out.

People who believe that the human embryo has *special moral status* as the earliest form of human life, but not (yet) the same status as the rest of us, would allow human embryo research under certain conditions. They would prohibit creating human embryos just to carry out research on them and would permit it only on "spare embryos," those left over from *in vitro* fertilization procedures. And they would limit research on human embryos to the first fourteen days of cell division after fertilization. These people reject the view that it is inherently wrong to carry out research on human embryos, but seem to accept that it is inherently wrong to create them for this purpose—to do so shows a basic disrespect for human life. They might also be objecting to the creation of embryos just for human use or simply as a research tool because to do so harms important values and symbolism attached

to human life, especially the most vulnerable forms of human life, of
which embryos are a prime example.

Other people believe that it is morally acceptable to create human
embryos for research purposes. They usually justify their stance on
the grounds that while human embryos are of human origin and, as
such, have special moral status and deserve respect, this status does
not prohibit research on them. They point out that the embryo is not-
a conscious being who can suffer pain and that great good could come
from the research.

Those who do not believe that the human embryo has any special
moral status would create and use them for research as they would any
other tissue of human origin. This view was forcefully presented by
molecular and evolutionary biologist Professor Lee Silver of Princeton
University at a conference I attended in Squaw Valley, California. I had
given a presentation outlining the case against human cloning, and in
the course of this talk, I argued for recognizing the moral status of the
human embryo. Professor Silver followed me as a speaker to present
the case for human cloning and embryo research. He stood before the
audience, melodramatically took out a tissue and blew his nose into it.
Without saying anything, he held it up to the audience, who were
watching him attentively. He then said, "This tissue has cells on it from
the inside of my nose. I would like Margo Somerville to understand
that I believe that these cells have the same moral status as human
embryos."

To summarize: When we disagree on the moral status of human
embryos, we disagree on the ethics of human embryo research.
Human cloning necessarily involves research on human embryos.
Therefore, the different views on the moral status of human embryos
and human embryo research translate into different attitudes about
the ethics of human cloning, quite apart from any other factors that
might cause us to differ in our views on the ethics of cloning. We
should keep in mind that our approach to human cloning, embryo
research, abortion, and the use of fetuses in research or as a source of
organs or tissues for transplantation are all intimately connected.

We can test the inherent wrongness of human cloning from a secular base by, as I have suggested previously, asking two questions: Does human cloning contravene respect for human life? And would carrying out such cloning damage our sense of the human spirit—by which, as I have explained previously, I mean the essential, intangible, invisible, unmeasurable reality we need to live fully human lives, that "non-physical entity" through which we find a sense of meaning in our lives? If it does either, it is inherently wrong.

Insights about what respect for human life and the human spirit requires in relation to human cloning can come from diverse sources. For instance, Kaye bases his stance against human reproductive cloning on concepts articulated by Emile Durkheim in his book *Suicide*. Durkheim refers to the belief in the inherent dignity and worth of human life as "the religion of humanity" and concludes that it is the only cohesive bond in a diverse and secular world. He regards this belief as the last one that "unites us as a human community and serves as the essential basis of our social and moral order." The famous French philosopher Paul Ricoeur sums up the same approach in a few simple but powerful words: Something is owed to human beings simply because they are human. This religion of humanity is almost certainly the non-negotiable minimum without which we cannot form a viable human society—or at least not one in which most of us would think it was worthwhile living. It requires that we have respect for each individual human life and, I propose, for human life itself and its transmission. Human cloning challenges us on all three bases.

However, even if we were all to agree that we must have respect for human life in all these three senses, we are likely to disagree as to what should be allowed and disallowed if we are to maintain such respect. In particular, we will disagree whether human cloning—reproductive or therapeutic—is inherently disrespectful of human life. For instance, what does respect for human genetic diversity require and does human cloning breach these requirements?

As a society—indeed, as a global community—we must respect the integrity of the human gene pool, which we hold in trust for future generations. Because of our new scientific powers to intervene and change this gene pool, we are faced with decisions no other people have ever confronted. Many people believe that we must not interfere with the human gene pool—or, at the very least, not wrongfully interfere with it—because it is the common heritage of humankind and it would be wrong for us to change that heritage. Such a view reflects a secular-sacred approach to the human gene pool. Just from the perspective of practical survival, genetic diversity is important to ensure the integrity and resilience of the human gene pool and, therefore, of human life. Some people might respond that we would never be able to reduce its diversity to the extent that it would matter in this regard. But even if that is true, genetic diversity is also important for individuals. It is an amazing thought that for every person who has ever lived (genetically identical sibs aside), there has never in the past been anyone genetically identical to that person and never will be in the future unless the person is cloned. This genetic uniqueness is also important in relation to upholding the societal value of respect for persons: It helps to prevent us from regarding individuals as replaceable commodities and losing respect for people, in general, in doing so.

If we decided that human cloning is inherently wrong, it would mean that cloning must not be undertaken no matter how beneficial the consequences of using it could be. Prohibiting a procedure that could be the only hope of saving life or avoiding horrible suffering, or that could help people to have a child and that some do not regard as wrong, can be seen as breaching norms of both compassion and tolerance. These are some of the many forces that indicate it will be difficult to find a strong consensus that we should prohibit human cloning and, if we were to achieve this agreement, to enforce such a prohibition. Let's look at some of these arguments, starting with intense individualism.

Intense individualism is one of the powerful, current trends that favour a situational ethics approach to human cloning. Intense individualism encourages us to focus on individuals' rights to autonomy and self-determination, with societal interests—the common good—if considered at all, taking a subordinate place. Infertile people who want to have their "own" genetically related child can make powerful emotional arguments that they should not be prevented from doing so through cloning. Likewise, desperately ill people or those with diseases that cause great suffering, such as Alzheimer's or Parkinson's, can make it extraordinarily difficult to argue against human therapeutic cloning—to argue that it is inherently wrong—when it could offer them chances of treatment or even cure.

The predominance of intense individualism has given rise to a concern that, as a result, we have lost a sense of community. Lately, another concern has been added to this, that we have also lost a sense of the common good. Philosopher and ethicist Dr. Daniel Callahan has criticized the United States National Bioethics Advisory Commission's report on human cloning precisely on the grounds that the report focuses only on risks to individuals and fails to take into account the requirements of protection and promotion of the common good and the harmful impact that allowing human cloning would have on the common good. The commission proposed placing a moratorium on human reproductive cloning, not a permanent prohibition of it. Callahan believes that this recommendation shows a failure to understand what is needed to protect the common good.

Some versions of *reproductive rights* also favour reproductive cloning. The proponents of these rights claim that reproduction is a private matter involving only individuals and their choices, and these choices must not be interfered with by others. Cloning can be seen as simply another reproductive choice that can be justified by the free and fully informed consent of the person who wants to be cloned. (Although the clone's consent is not obtained, of course.) The basic philosophy behind the doctrine of informed consent is respect for people's rights to autonomy and self-determination. Provided, therefore, that people understand what they are doing—especially the risks involved—they should, as far as possible, the argument goes, be allowed to do what they want. This approach means that consent functions as not only a necessary safeguard, but also as a sufficient one. It maximizes individual liberty, even when this is at the expense of other values.

In making choices about whether to prohibit certain reproductive technologies such as human cloning, we need to keep in mind that we are facing the technological imperative—that is, "have technology, must use it"—in one of its most dangerous forms. I suggest that the most appropriate comparison is with the discovery of nuclear fission and the development of the atomic bomb. In a 1947 speech given at MIT, T. Robert Oppenheimer, one of the scientists who developed the atomic bombs that were dropped on Hiroshima and Nagasaki, said, "In some sort of crude sense which no vulgarity, no humour, no overstatement can quite extinguish, the physicists have known sin; this is a knowledge which they cannot lose."

This statement raises the question: "Could we gain important ethical insights about human cloning by considering whether it is evil?" Professor Upendra Baxi, a distinguished Indian jurist and human rights activist, developed a concept he calls the functionalization of evil, and it is relevant to this enquiry. Baxi argues that one of the dangers in our present world is that we have lost a sense of evil and that, in part, this has occurred because when evil happens we tend to focus only on the good that comes out of it and, in the process, lose a sense of the evil that was involved. We may be in danger of doing this in relation to human cloning. If it is intrinsically morally wrong to clone humans, whether for therapeutic or reproductive purposes, we must somehow maintain a sense that it would be evil to do so, no matter how much good could come out of it.

In two other respects, Oppenheimer's statement also merits thorough consideration in relation to both forms of human cloning: First, is it correct that, as scientists have traditionally argued, science is value-free and that we should never place restrictions on the discovery of knowledge? And, second, can we foresee the harm human cloning would cause and, even if we could, could we control it?

The idea that *science is value-free*, that there is an *absolute right to freedom* of scientific enquiry and it is wrong to restrict scientific research, leads to a conclusion that research on human cloning should not be inhibited. The traditional view that science itself is value-free has been increasingly challenged very recently. More and more people believe that if scientists can see that immense harm would result from their discoveries, they have ethical obligations not to pursue them. For instance, biological warfare research can be regarded as inherently wrong and therefore it must not be undertaken. But not everyone agrees. They argue that science is value-neutral, and it is only when we apply it that ethics comes into play. Scientists are often concerned that ethics will inhibit them in pursuing scientific knowledge, and the split between so-called pure and applied science has been used to avoid ethics being applied to pure science. But ethics must be embedded in science at all stages of discovery and development. When we see the mind- and world-altering power of the scientific discoveries of just the last ten years, it should be piercingly clear that we cannot afford to have ethics simply as an add-on or afterthought. Power entails responsibility, requiring that we embed ethics in every aspect of science. To give just one example of value-laden pure science, using human embryos as research material or making human-animal hybrids to carry out research on them is not a value-neutral activity and must be governed by ethics.

A common argument also put forward is that there is no point in trying to "stop" new and controversial techniques, such as human cloning, because they will go forward regardless of whether they are regarded as ethically acceptable (unless, of course, everyone considered them to be ethically unacceptable and personally refrained from using them). If this view is correct, it reflects our society's moral or ethical bankruptcy—which it is deeply disturbing to think might have occurred. Moreover, just because human cloning is inevitable and uncontrollable does not mean that we should not to try to stop it if we believe it is ethically wrong, any more than, as Annas says, "a recognition that controlling terrorism or biological weapons is difficult and uncertain, [does not justify] . . . making no attempt at control."

A useful analogy to law can be made here. The vast majority of people do obey the law: If they did not, the law would be ineffective. The same is true for ethical rules. Consequently, the fact that some people do not comply with them, as indeed some people do not comply with the law, should not make us despair of the effectiveness of these rules or disregard the necessity for them. Moreover, as is true with law, we usually notice only where ethical requirements are not effective, not the harms they prevent.

We should also be careful that this "impossible-to-stop" argument is not simply one way to argue against placing any restrictions on scientific research. A particular aspect of this argument is encountered when corporations invest very large amounts of money in scientific research, such as human cloning, that raises major ethical problems. This investment creates pressure not to restrict—and certainly not to abandon—the research, even when restriction or abandonment is ethically required. Further complications and difficulties in this regard are generated by the intertwining of universities, industry and government in the research enterprise. This intertwining can result in a situation in which no institution is free of conflict of interest and can ensure that what is done is ethical. In short, ethics is captured by the research enterprise.

Finally, another factor favouring human cloning is that it offers more than the usual *promise of some sort of temporal immortality*—that of one's genome—and, even more so than natural reproduction, of genetic immortality. This promise might be important to some people who no longer believe in the supernatural.

I am not sure we will ever agree as a society that there is a "right" answer about the ethics of human cloning—certainly of therapeutic cloning, although we might agree to prohibit reproductive cloning. The problem is, to return to a previous theme, that for many people the risks and harms they take into account in deciding whether they are ethically justified in running or imposing risks and harms do not extend to damage to our most important human values and our sense of the meaning of human life. Moreover, even were we to agree on what we *should* do ethically, would we actually follow that course?

Let's turn now to consider the ethics of human therapeutic cloning more specifically. Both human embryos and embryonic stem cells can be cloned—that is, multiple copies can be made. Questions this raises include these: If one believes that it is ethically acceptable to use spare embryos for research, is it acceptable to make multiple embryos, as long as one starts with a spare embryo? Do prohibitions or restrictions on embryo research apply to the use of embryonic stem cells? Does the source of the stem cell matter and, even if it does, does it matter once the cell has been isolated? For example, if we believe that it is not ethically acceptable to create human embryos from gametes taken from aborted fetuses, is it ethically acceptable to use a cloned cell line developed from such a human embryo? Or, if we believe that abortion is ethically unacceptable, is it ethically acceptable to collect stem cells from aborted fetuses for use in human therapeutic cloning or to use cells cloned from these stem cells? If we have ethical reservations about abortion, does this mean that research using stem cells derived from an aborted fetus is not ethically acceptable? Morally, can we separate these cells from their origin in abortion?

Is human therapeutic cloning inherently wrong? And, if not, or if we use just a situational ethics approach, is it ethically acceptable?

If using human embryos for therapeutic cloning is inherently wrong, we must not do it, no matter how much good could be achieved. The extraordinary medical benefits that could result would not be a justification for the use of human embryos. To use human embryos just as an instrument for doing good for the rest of us damages respect for both human life and the reality that constitutes the human spirit. We cannot regard a human embryo as wondrous and use it simply as an object on which to carry out research that is not intended to benefit it or to provide it with a chance of life. We lose our sense of wonder and awe at our ethical peril. These senses are very easy to damage, especially if we use our new science in certain ways, and the loss and damage we cause to our metaphysical reality may well be irreversible. The use of just one embryo for human therapeutic cloning presents risks to respect for life and for the human spirit and can harm them.

In the same way, creating multiple embryos from the same embryo damages respect for human life itself—even if it does not contravene respect for any one human individual—and for the transmission of human life. It turns a genetically unique living being of human origin into just an object and one that is replicable in multiple copies. It changes the transmission of human life from a mystery to a manufacturing process. It fails to recognize that we are not free to treat life in any way we see fit, that we do not own life. Rather, we have life and, most importantly, life has us. Recognizing that we owe obligations to life can provide a basis on which to establish respect for life in a secular society. This recognition means that we must ask, "What must we not do because to do it would contravene respect for human life itself?" I believe that one answer to this question is the use of human embryos for human therapeutic cloning. This cloning can, therefore, be regarded as inherently wrong. In summary, I propose that, even leaving aside any questions of the abuse of human therapeutic cloning, the intentional creation and destruction of human embryos it involves could seriously damage important values and the "ethical tone" of our society.

An alternative analysis for those who reject a concept of inherent wrongness is one based on situational ethics: Nothing is inherently wrong—it all depends on the circumstances. Under this approach, in contrast to one based on inherent wrongness, "doing good" through human therapeutic cloning can be a justification for the unavoidable harm to embryos that it involves—and possibly for the harm that it does to respect for human life and the human spirit. Most people who regard human therapeutic cloning as ethically acceptable do not consider these latter harms to be present, however, in the human embryo research that human therapeutic cloning necessarily involves. Could the reason be that to raise such concerns would give them validity and, as a consequence, make it difficult to argue that human embryo research is ethically acceptable? The good focused on in justifying human embryo research and therapeutic cloning includes producing organs and tissues for transplantation, repairing severed nerves, or treating cancer, diabetes, multiple sclerosis, Parkinson's disease, Alzheimer's disease or genetic disorders. It is very hard, and will take great courage, to refuse such extraordinary benefits.

One reason—a paradoxical one—that it is difficult to ensure that the new science is ethically acceptable is that it has the potential to do so much good. There is an old saying in human rights that nowhere are human rights more threatened than when we act purporting to do good. When we focus on the good that we are setting out to achieve, we can be blind to the dangers, risks and harms involved, including ethical harms. This is probably a companion phenomenon to the functionalization of evil.

But could human therapeutic cloning also be considered unethical under a situational ethics approach? To respond requires identifying the harms of this cloning and balancing them against the benefits. (We should keep in mind that we will not necessarily agree on what counts as benefits and harms, and how to weigh them when they conflict, because these decisions are value judgments.)

First, among the harms is the fact that human therapeutic cloning makes human reproductive cloning more likely and more difficult to effectively prohibit—it opens up a slippery slope. But this argument holds only if we believe that human reproductive cloning should not be undertaken. I discuss this issue in the next section. Second, human therapeutic cloning (like human reproductive cloning) opens up the possibilities of genetic enhancement and disenhancement through alteration of the human germ cell line—the units of heredity passed on from generation to generation. If we believe that these types of intervention are wrong, we may not want to make them easier to achieve. Third, even if we do not regard using human embryos for research as showing disrespect for individual human life, it can show disrespect for human life in general. For example, embryos used in therapeutic cloning have been described, as mentioned previously, as "living human tissue generators" or, in stark language, a human manufacturing plant.

Fourth, therapeutic cloning (again, like reproductive cloning) also shows disrespect for the transmission of human life and could affect our sense of wonder about it. Film critic Len Blum, writing about Stanley Kubrick's film *Eyes Wide Shut,* says in relation to the sexual intimacy portrayed in that film: "Because I believed the events were real, I savoured every moment. One isn't aroused—one is sexualised. Made conscious of sexuality. And since sexuality is the transmitter of human life, the feeling was akin to becoming more conscious of life itself." What would it mean to some of our most profound human experiences if we could not only transmit human life asexually, but also do so for the purposes of setting up a basic manufacturing process based on this life? Blum's words should warn us that what we would lose is highly subtle and nuanced, but extraordinarily important. The sexual transmission of human life is integral to our sense, as both individuals and a society, of ourselves and of the meaning of human life. Can we afford asexual transmission, no matter what benefits it promises? Human life is not a commodity. Can we ever afford to make it such?

Ethicists Professor Glenn McGee and Professor Arthur Caplan present a very sophisticated argument in favour of human embryo stem cell research, which involves the destruction of embryos to obtain the stem cells. The same considerations apply to the use of human embryos in therapeutic cloning. They propose that the central ethical question revolves around whether use of the embryo is an acceptable "moral sacrifice" of human life. They point out that the moral imperative of compassion motivates this stem cell research. (In this way, they distinguish it from abortion carried out for superficial reasons.) They assume, for the purposes of argument, that the one hundred-cell human blastocyst from which the stem cells are taken is a "fully human person." They conclude that its only unique characteristic is the recombinant DNA from both parents that it contains.

They point out that this DNA will survive through the creation of cell lines using the pluripotent stem cells derived from the embryo. This DNA could later be used to make a "new nuclear-transfer-derived embryo" (that is, a "replacement" embryo could be created using the Dolly technique) that would have identical DNA to the original embryo. In essence, they are arguing that the destruction of the "original" embryo to obtain stem cells is not necessarily the destruction of the only unique feature of that embryo, which is its DNA, and that this is an answer to those who oppose embryo stem cell research on the grounds that it involves the destruction of human embryos. In other words, they value the genetic uniqueness of the embryo more than the embryo itself, and provided the former can be preserved the latter may be destroyed. (This is a similar approach to that mentioned in Chapter 1, of cloning an embryo from an aborted fetus in order to have the "same" baby at a later date.) They point out that of the needs that merit sacrifice, reducing widespread suffering from disease—the aim of human embryo stem cell research—is an obvious and compelling one.

McGee and Caplan's argument for the use of embryos is constructed in such a way that it would not apply to more developed forms of human life. Those forms that can experience pain or have memory should not be sacrificed for the benefit of others because features such as memory—unlike the unique DNA—are not replaceable. Their argument is an example of sophisticated science being used as a solution to ethical problems raised by sophisticated science. It is a situational ethics approach, but much subtler than most of them and borders on asking whether using embryos as the source of stem cells is inherently wrong. The focus of their enquiry in this latter respect is not on whether it is inherently wrong to intentionally destroy an early human life; rather, it is on whether it is inherently wrong to destroy such a human life if all the unique features of this life can be replicated at a later time. This approach is a highly imaginative combination of philosophy, semantics and avant-garde science. But in using it, would we just be defining away the real ethical issue—namely, are we justified in intentionally destroying a human embryo, in using it as an object to benefit the rest of us?

There may be some answers to the ethical problems raised by human therapeutic cloning on which there could be consensus. With further scientific advances, we might not need to use an embryo to obtain stem cells but could obtain them from the person who needs a tissue or organ or from another person. It might also eventually be possible to cause a somatic cell taken from the person who needs a transplant to de-differentiate and re-differentiate into the tissue or organ that is needed without the creation of an embryo. The problem is that developing this science will take time. Usually doing science in "ethics time" means that we need time to work out the ethics that should govern the science. But here, somewhat ironically, we need time to work out the science in order to avoid ethical problems.

We need thorough consideration of the competing interests that are brought into play by human therapeutic cloning. These are, on the one hand, that we cannot wait for further scientific advances, because those who are suffering or dying and could be helped by human thera-peutic cloning and embryonic stem cell research need treatment now. On the other hand, we will not be able to repair or reverse the harm that we would do to our sense of respect for both human life and its transmission, and of wonder about them, if we unethically use human embryos.

On a personal note, even though I believe that human cloning is morally wrong, I am not sure, if my life or that of someone I loved depended on using therapies developed as a result of human thera-peutic cloning, that I would make the decision I believe is the ethi-cally correct one. We should be very concerned that the cynics might prove to be correct, that no matter what ethical conclusions we come to, human cloning will proceed, especially if people believe that the good that might come from this new science would far outweigh any of the risks or harms we currently perceive it as presenting.

I want to turn now to human reproductive cloning—using cloning technology with the aim of creating genetically identical people. Some of the same ethical issues are raised in all cases of human cloning, whether reproductive or therapeutic—for instance, the ethics of creating human embryos through cloning and carrying out research on them. Indeed, undertaking cloning is, in itself, research. But reproductive cloning also raises different issues and, while some people would prohibit both forms of cloning and others permit both, some people would allow human therapeutic cloning but prohibit human reproductive cloning—in particular, the use of the Dolly technique to clone a baby from an adult human.

A strong argument against creating such clones is that they would be deprived of their unique genetic identity, in a way that is not true even of naturally occurring genetically identical siblings, and to do this is to wrong them. The philosopher Hans Jonas argues that respect for the human person requires respect for human genetic diversity, and this is why human reproductive cloning is inherently wrong. On the basis of Jonas's work, and quoting the philosopher, Annas constructs a powerful argument

> that cloning is always a crime against the clone, the crime of depriving the clone of his or her "existential right to certain subjective terms of being"—particularly, the "right of ignorance" of facts about his or her origin that are likely to be "paralyzing for the spontaneity of becoming himself" or herself. This advance knowledge of what another has or has not accomplished with the clone's genome destroys the clone's "condition for authentic growth" in seeking to answer the fundamental question of all beings, "Who am I?"

Jonas says if we are to act ethically we must never "violate the right to that ignorance which is a condition of authentic action. . . . The ethical command [is] . . . *to respect the right of each human life to find its own way and be a surprise to itself.*" Annas concludes in a similar vein that "through human cloning we will lose something vital to our humanity, the uniqueness and, therefore, the value and dignity of every human. Cloning represents the height of genetic reductionism and genetic determinism."

One of the paradoxes in the debate on human reproductive cloning arises in relation to whether genetic difference matters. In Chapter 1, I discussed the gene-machine view of the human person. Those who adopt this view, particularly the scientists, are relying on a "Genes-R-Us" concept—or, as sociologists Dorothy Nelkin and Susan Lindee describe it, a view that DNA has become the human soul, that is, a DNA mystique. And yet, at the same time, in order to justify human reproductive cloning, these same people argue that creating a child without a unique genetic identity should not be viewed as a problem. They often point out that genes are only partly responsible for who we are. For example, some scientists who do not want to be prohibited from undertaking human reproductive cloning have been identifying and emphasizing the differences between each of the members of two sets of naturally conceived identical quadruplets who live in the United States. Alternatively, or in addition, they argue that in human cloning carried out through somatic cell nuclear transfer (the Dolly technique), the small genetic difference between the person from whom the cell was taken and the clone—as explained above, the clone has mitochondrial DNA different from that of the cell donor— is sufficient to constitute genetic difference to the extent that this should matter. But let's face it, most people who want to have a child cloned from their DNA choose to do so because they want a genetically related child—and some specifically want a genetically identical child. These people are proposing that genes both matter and do not matter, and the position they take in any given circumstances depends on the argument that needs to be won.

An argument against human reproductive cloning—one related to that based on a loss of genetic diversity—is that each person has a right to a *unique genetic identity*. Indeed, it has been proposed by Annas that "the central problem of cloning [is] the devaluing of persons by depriving them of their uniqueness." Again, an argument to the contrary is that we already have naturally occurring identical twins, triplets or even quadruplets, and we do not regard their lives as of less value or less worthy of respect because they are not genetically unique. Why then is this a problem with human cloning? With the advent of cloning technology, these naturally occurring siblings are sometimes referred to as natural clones. Therefore, the argument goes, we are just using technology to do what can occur naturally. However, there are important ethically relevant differences between situations of naturally occurring and artificially created genetically identical people. These include that a different moral order (different ethical concerns and obligations) is involved when we intentionally create such a situation: When we intervene on others, we have moral responsibilities that we do not have if the same situation occurs naturally. Naturally occurring identical sibs are also of the same age and, therefore, their life is, as Jonas says, "a surprise to each of them." And moreover, even if human reproductive cloning's contravention of genetic uniqueness was not a major ethical concern, it is not the only reason that such cloning is wrong.

The further question this discussion raises is whether embryo splitting with the intention of producing identical siblings to be born contemporaneously is also wrong. In my view, it is. Although this situation could occur naturally, the intervention of a human actor who intends to and does cause this result makes it ethically unacceptable. It is human cloning in a sense in which naturally occurring human sibs is not: It is cloning of a human by a human.

We can also argue that human reproductive cloning is inherently wrong because as a general rule each of us has a right to be begotten by chance as far as our genetic inheritance is concerned, not by human choice. This objection would encompass an argument that we have a right not to have another person design us in his or her image, which is precisely what human reproductive cloning involves; it is "playing God" in the most fundamental sense (in the sense that, as the Bible states, God created man [sic] in His image, and we are producing clones in our image) and in a way that other interferences with or manipulation of human reproduction are not. We have a right to come into existence through human reproduction, not, as is the case with human cloning, through replication. One variation on the argument that undertaking human cloning is "playing God" I found very surprising. This approach, suggested to me by a geneticist who favours human cloning, is that deeply religious people believe that God intended them to be His co-creators. Therefore, they can also believe, he said, that God intended people to discover the science of genetic manipulation, including cloning, and to use it to take over more of His creative work.

There must be reverence for the creative forces of nature in the passing on of human life and we need to enquire what limits this requirement would place on us in using our genetic science. Human reproductive cloning—and human therapeutic cloning—contravene the most fundamental requirements of reverence in the passing on of human life.

CONCEPTS SUCH AS DIGNITY are relevant in assessing whether human reproductive cloning contravenes requirements of respect for human beings and human life and, therefore, is inherently wrong. But whether humans are seen to have intrinsic dignity (dignity simply because they are human) or extrinsic dignity (dignity attributed to them by other people) will influence how we would view human reproductive cloning. A concept of intrinsic dignity is more likely to result in a conclusion that human reproductive cloning is inherently wrong than is one of extrinsic dignity.

A concept of extrinsic dignity makes it easier to argue that whether human reproductive cloning is an affront to respect for human dignity simply depends on how we view the cloning process and whether we attribute dignity to the resulting clone. A concept of intrinsic dignity is much less open and flexible in this respect. To explore what respect for intrinsic human dignity would require in the context of human cloning, we can re-phrase Ricoeur's principle: What do we owe to the human beings who would result from cloning—in particular, what does respect for their human dignity require that we not do to them—simply because they are human? Since all humans must be seen as subjects, not objects, we must avoid using technologies in any way that detracts from their being treated or seen as a subject. The obligations we owe to human beings include not to manufacture them; not to make them into objects, things or commodities; and to respect their right not to be designed by another human. Rather, we must allow each person his or her individual and unique ticket in the great genetic lottery of the passing on of human life. Human reproductive cloning contravenes all of these requirements.

THIS VIEW—THAT WE HAVE a right to come into existence through genetic chance, not genetic choice on the part of another human—raises the question whether we would ever be justified in intervening on a human embryo to correct a serious genetic disease. In my view, there is no ethical reason to refrain from undertaking necessary therapy intended for the benefit of that embryo, provided the potential benefits outweigh the risks and the parents provide informed consent. The question becomes much more difficult if what we are doing involves altering the human germ cell line, those genes that are passed on through ova and sperm from generation to generation. If a disease is caused by a defective gene and we correct that gene in the germ cell line of an embryo, all subsequent progeny of that embryo would be free of that disease. But some people think that we should never alter the human germ cell line. This would mean that in order to avoid an embryo inheriting a disease caused by a defective gene, we would need to intervene on each embryo individually. While there is grave danger in allowing any intervention to alter the human germ cell line, the one situation in which this might be justified would be to cure a very serious, genetically inherited disease. We would need to take great care that our definition of such diseases was very narrowly construed, however, and did not open up a precedent for such interventions other than for this very limited purpose.

One danger of allowing alteration of the human germ cell line is that scientists will engage in genetic enhancement or disenhancement of embryos. Characteristics that might be subject to this interference include physical ones of height, eye and hair colour, or build. Lee Silver, in his book *Remaking Eden: How Genetic Engineering and Cloning Will Transform the American Family*, speaks of using the new genetic technologies to make two strains of humans—the "gene rich" (genetically enhanced humans, especially with respect to intelligence) and the "gene poor" (the genetically unenhanced—could we say natural?). He predicts that the gene rich will only want to reproduce with other gene rich persons and, consequently, the inequality will be perpetuated and extended. Many commentators believe that parents who are already willing to sacrifice a great deal in order to provide opportunities for their children—private schools, sports coaching or music lessons—would want to have their children's intelligence, sporting or musical ability genetically enhanced and would be willing to pay for this. They propose that in the long run it would probably be much less expensive than the methods used today. Should we prohibit such interventions? If we allow human cloning, would such interventions become more likely, or easier to carry out, or set a precedent that they are acceptable?

Perhaps the most surprising among the galaxy of astonishing feats that might be accomplished with the new genetic technologies is the possibility that we will be able to create a "disease-proofed child." In the same vein, Ben Bova, a science fiction writer, has recently speculated that the first person to achieve immortality may already have been born, in that this person's genes will be able to be reprogrammed not to age or die. Should parents be allowed to have their children genetically modified in such ways?

The power to enhance intelligence can also be used to disenhance it. This possibility is most often discussed in the context of the need for a labour force for low-level, boring, repetitive jobs that those of natural or enhanced intelligence would not agree to perform. To undertake genetic disenhancement—to deliberately reduce intelligence or other characteristics of a person—would be a contemporary example of pure evil.

There are reasons other than the risks involved for refraining from altering the human germ cell line. A requirement of profound respect for the human germ cell line also flows from at least two other facts: First, it is the common heritage of humankind handed to us by our ancestors and that we hold in trust for future generations; and second, in the past major changes in the human germ cell line have occurred over vast time spans. We can now achieve comparable changes in nanoseconds. At the least, we need to take ethics time to decide what we must not do and may do. It is only now that it is possible to interfere with the essence of human life itself that we are faced with the question of what respect for our very nature requires that we must not do.

ALTHOUGH HUMAN REPRODUCTIVE cloning is not human reproduction, but human replication, it is often referred to as one of the new reproductive technologies. But is there a difference in kind between human reproductive cloning and the use of other new reproductive technologies or simply a difference in degree? We were at first horrified by the new reproductive technologies now widely used, but we relatively quickly came to a "let's do it" stage. Will the same happen with human reproductive cloning? What is so striking is, as health law professor Laurie Andrews points out, that "the time frame from horrified negation to 'let's do it' is so much shorter."

We cannot properly evaluate the impact of new reproductive technologies by looking at each in isolation. Rather, we must consider the effect of connecting them and the effect they will have on the social and cultural context in which they will be placed, and vice versa. We can gain insight about what the future might hold in this regard with

respect to new reproductive technologies, including human reproductive cloning, when we are able to fully integrate them, by looking
at the development of the Internet.

The technologies that now make up the Internet had each been
around for half a century—fax machines since the 1930s, modems
and radio phones since the 1940s—before the Internet became a (virtual) reality. An article in *The* [Montreal] *Gazette* describes it this way:

> The revolution came . . . when we finally figured out how to
> connect them: how to make one fax machine connect with tele-
> phone lines and negotiate with another fax machine; how to let
> one modem talk to another on the telephone and agree between
> themselves how to work; how to take the big, crackling radio
> phones of old and connect them to networks that let you call
> someone who carries a phone tiny enough for his pocket. The
> trend for the future? Look around. "The technologies are
> already here," [U.S. Nobel Prize laureate Arno] Penzias claims.
> "They just haven't been connected yet."

So it was only when the communications and information technologies were combined that they had a massive impact on our world,
including its culture and values. The same is likely to be true for the
new reproductive technologies. What would happen, for instance,
were we to combine the technology for genetic enhancement of intelligence with that which makes possible a half-human half-chimpanzee,
with—what, somewhat surprisingly, is the one missing link—the artificial uterus, which would make ectogenesis (gestation of a child
entirely outside a woman's uterus) possible? While most of us, it is
to be hoped, could not imagine that we would ever accept human-
animal hybrids as an ethical use of genetic technology, it is even more
improbable that we would accept that women should carry them.
It is, however, less improbable to imagine someone setting up an
ectogenesis "manufacturing plant" of such beings—unless, of course,
we are prepared to say that some interventions that the new genetic

technologies make possible are inherently wrong and must never be undertaken.

THE LEAST THREATENING use of human reproductive cloning is to use it to create a family. But, as Annas has pointed out, while many people "love babies and technologies and most . . . applaud the ability of the new assisted reproduction techniques to help infertile couples have children . . . a bad way to protect the children who have been conceived and born with the assistance of the new reproductive techniques is simply to provide the adults involved with what they want." As discussed in Chapter 2, we have shifted the emphasis in adoption practices from the rights of the biological parents to the welfare of the children and we must do the same in relation to the use of new reproductive technologies. Children must be moved to the centre of consideration in decision-making about the use of reproductive technologies, and nowhere more so than with respect to reproductive cloning. Some people who would allow human reproductive cloning believe, however, that it is wrong to argue that this type of cloning should be prohibited out of concern for the resulting child. Such an argument, they say, amounts to asserting the right of nothing to remain nothing.

Philosopher and ethicist Thomas Murray, in his sensitive and humane book *The Worth of a Child,* alerts us to the dangers that unbridled concepts of procreative liberty unmitigated by concerns for values can create: "In the name of procreative liberty, an astonishing variety of arrangements for making and obtaining children have been defended. They are all in the service of making a family and so we should welcome them, say their defenders." Such arrangements include what University of Texas law professor John Robertson refers to as collaborative reproduction, which is often commercial collaborative reproduction—the sale of gametes and of embryos, and paid surrogate motherhood. As Murray points out, the champions of procreative liberty celebrate control and choice on the part of the parents, but with little concern for what this means with regard to harm to the children and to the values at the heart of family life:

> Good families are characterized more by acceptance than control. Furthermore, families are the pre-eminent realm of unchosen obligations. . . .We may choose to have a child but—unless we are "adopting" one of Robertson's cloned embryos—we do not choose to have this particular child with its interests, moods and manners.

It is not possible to explore here all the risks of human reproductive cloning to the cloned child or to important values that govern how we humans bond to each other in our first and predominant intimate relationship, that of the family. Some people who focus on risks to the cloned child as the main reason for prohibiting cloning argue that we would need so much human embryo experimentation, with the risks of injured or handicapped children being born as a result, that human cloning is not justified. And sometimes they add to this that the very large waste of human embryos that cloning would involve means it is not justified. This objection to cloning raises the issue of whether the major reason for prohibiting reproductive cloning is that it involves human embryo research. I propose that even if such research were not involved, human reproductive cloning is not ethically acceptable.

As well as physical risks to the child, there are also risks of psychological harm from a diminished sense of individuality and personal autonomy. Many teenagers have problems with individuation—separating themselves from their parents and seeing themselves as independent persons. Imagine the difficulty in this respect for a clone who has no genetic distance from the parent and, in all probability, looks physically like a carbon copy of his or her "parent." Imagine bringing up a child that was a clone of yourself and correcting the mistakes you thought had been made by your parents or by you yourself. Consider the unrealistic expectations parents would place on the child. Then we can turn to the impact on the family of reproductive cloning. And consider the possibility that we would see a new form of genetic discrimination, between humans regarded as desirable enough to be cloned and the great unclonable masses, or possibly in the opposite direction, between the masses of the cloned and the genetically unique non-cloned people. One of the central problems of cloning, "the devaluing of persons by depriving them of their uniqueness," has harmful consequences well beyond the devaluation itself.

The strongest case for human reproductive cloning is when it is done for compassionate reasons—for instance, to create matching organs or tissues to save the life of a dying child or to "replace" that child. Annas, however, challenges our uncritical acceptance of this justification of cloning. He argues as follows:

> Using the bodies of children to replicate them encourages all of us to devalue children and treat them as interchangeable commodities. . . . The death of a child need no longer be a singular human tragedy, but, rather, an opportunity to replicate the no longer priceless or irreplaceable dead child. No one should have such dominion over a child, even a dead or dying child, as to use his or her genes to create the child's child.

Parents who would clone their children are depriving these children of reproductive choice. They are treating their children as entities that can be split and replicated at their whim. Annas believes this is a stronger argument against cloning children than its biological novelty. It is hypocritical, he says, to argue that cloning expands the liberty and choices of would-be cloners, when it reduces the liberty and choices of the resulting child.

WE CAN ALSO LOOK TO the law that currently regulates intra-familial relationships, to see if it might provide insights on the ethics of human reproductive cloning. For instance, reproduction with blood relatives is prohibited by incest law, certainly for one reason and possibly for two. The certain reason is to avoid dysgenesis, the genetic dangers for children born as a result of close relatives reproducing with each other. It is less certain that the prohibition of incest reflects a concern to maintain important family bonds and relationships that incest would threaten. Dysgenesis is not a problem in reproductive cloning, because it is genetic replication, not reproduction. Moreover, the crime of incest requires sexual intercourse, which is precisely what cloning excludes from reproduction. It is not as clear that the criminal law on incest reflects concern with protecting family bonds and relationships. But to the extent that it does, the use of this law—our most weighty, societal-values-establishing mechanism—to protect these relationships shows how important they are, not just to individuals but also to society. Damage to family bonds is a very relevant concern in relation to reproductive cloning.

In contrast to the law providing a message that human reproductive cloning should be prohibited, others argue that the courts, for instance, in the United States, have held that the state may not force a restrictive paradigm of the "family" on people, and that constitutionally protected reproductive rights should include the right to found a family through cloning. A "Note" in the *Harvard Law Review* articulates this view:

> Cloning should receive constitutional protection because it represents a conscious choice to bring a child into the world and to accept the social role of parenthood, thereby implicating the sort of deeply personal, family-related choices that trigger substantive due process protection. . . . Despite its novelty, cloning would at least ensure a genetic bond between the parent and child, an important component of the social status of parenthood.

It remains to be seen whether the courts' views of what constitutes a family that will be given constitutional protection extends to rights to create one through cloning.

We have no idea how the radical reproductive and genetic departure that reproductive cloning represents would affect bonds and behaviour within the family, and its sense of itself, its past and its future. We often differentiate bonds between intimates and bonds between strangers. A clone's relationship to his or her "parent" and family is so far outside natural human experience, in a sense so intimate, that it is beyond even our human experience with bonds between strangers.

Although laboratory assistance in reproduction can be ethically justified in certain circumstances, I propose that its use should be regarded as an exception to the rule that natural reproduction is preferable. Those who wish to use a new technology such as reproductive cloning should have the burden of proving that to employ it is not inherently wrong, and, if it is not, that the benefits promised far outweigh the risks, and that the risks can be justified. (This is the same approach as that proposed in the previous chapter, in relation to access to reproductive technologies in general. It requires, in particular, that we must place the child at the centre of the decision-making.) Consequently, if we were to decide that human reproductive cloning is not inherently wrong, we must adopt a precautionary ethical principle, similar to that used in international environmental law. This would mean, as Annas explains, that the "proponents of human cloning would have the burden of proving that there was some compelling contravailing need to benefit either current or future generations before such an experiment was permitted (for example, if the entire species were to become sterile)." It merits noting that such a justification looks to the common good, not just the wishes of individuals. Our approach to human cloning—whether reproductive or therapeutic—must reflect societal values, not just the values of individuals or those of scientists and researchers. This raises the need for public consultation. The difficulties inherent in undertaking such consultation and ensuring that it occurs in substance, not just appearance, are discussed in several of the following chapters, including the next one on xenotransplantation.

Śuffice it to say that the issues and problems of human reproductive cloning with respect to the child and the family become even more complex and difficult, and raise additional matters of profound concern, when commercialization is involved—as would be inevitable were human reproductive cloning to be allowed.

NATURE NEVER CONTEMPLATED needing safeguards against science such as human cloning. It was believed that there was a natural barrier to cloning an adult mammal, that genetic material in a somatic cell was irreversibly modified in such a way that you could not obtain a clone from it. Ian Wilmut, a research scientist, and his colleagues at the Rosslyn Institute in Glasgow showed, in creating Dolly, that this was not true. What does this new power require of us in fulfilling our human responsibility to hold nature "in trust," in particular for future generations, but especially that part of nature that constitutes the fundamental nature of us? Perhaps the most profound question that has been asked is: If we were to undertake human cloning, what kind of creatures might we become?

Our anxiety about placing inhibitions on science may arise, in part, from the fact that we think the only way we can truly fulfil ourselves is through unlimited scientific progress. But the opposite might be true: We may need to refrain from certain actions such as human cloning in order to fully realize our humanness and humanity and to protect our human spirit.

If we proceed with human therapeutic cloning or human reproductive cloning, we will irreversibly change the moral or metaphysical reality and, therefore, our sense of the human spirit, which is crucial to our full human well-being. We need this reality to surround human life, and its transmission, with profound respect. And, as often emphasized in this book, through it we also find meaning in human life. Our human spirit is the only means we have to pass on this respect and meaning—our most important and oldest human values—to future generations. Cloning would pass on our physical life, but what would it do to the life of our human spirit?

We will not have the luxury of a trial run; any damage we cause to this moral or metaphysical reality is almost certain to be irreversible. We must, therefore, ask: Are we justified in causing the change in this reality that will inevitably result from undertaking human therapeutic cloning or human reproductive cloning? If not ever, at least, today or tomorrow?

4. Crossing the Animal-Human Divide

The Ethics of Xenotransplantation

odern medical and scientific ethics—bioethics—is often regarded as having been born on the day in 1967 in Cape Town, South Africa, when Dr. Christiaan Barnard carried out the first human heart transplant. When we had dealt with the major ethical, legal and social—and some of the religious and cultural—issues that this event raised, we thought we had solved the problems—at least the serious ones—that organ transplantation would create. But new issues have constantly arisen, and transplantation has remained at the forefront of both our science and ethics.

Xenotransplantation (the transplantation of organs between different species—for instance, from pigs to humans) is the latest challenge. In a very real sense, it is one of the ethical canaries in the societal mineshaft. How we handle the ethical issues raised by the emerging science and technology of xenotransplantation affects not only that area but also our society in general.

In order to address the ethical issues raised by xenotransplantation, we need a general idea of the issues faced in relation to organ transplantation in general. The difficulties we encounter in this broader context and our responses to them are directly and indirectly relevant to the ethics of xenotransplantation.

Xenotransplantation could offer a solution to the shortage of organs for transplantation in many countries. This shortage has been a matter of great concern, and a variety of possible solutions have been proposed. These range from a "donors' honour roll"—for instance, in Canada legislation has been proposed to establish a system for officially recognizing the contribution of those who donate their organs—to setting up a market for organs. Both the shortage and some of the proposals for remedying it, such as the sale of organs, raise ethical problems in addition to those inherent in transplantation itself.

There has been concern, for example, about a black market in organs for transplantation. And very poor people from developing countries sometimes agree, in exchange for the money they desperately need for food, shelter, medical treatment or basic education for their families, to be live donors for extremely wealthy people who need an organ transplant. Yet another concern relates to the choice of live donors of organs for transplant. Some research indicates that the most vulnerable members in a family might be persuaded (or coerced) to become the organ donors. A serious concern in this regard is that women in some developing countries are forced by their husbands to sell their organs. And there has been great concern about carrying out capital punishment on condemned prisoners in such a way that their organs could be recovered and used for transplantation. These "donors" are given a general anesthetic and their organs removed, a practice that is reportedly occurring in China and that some people in the United States have proposed as a method of implementing capital punishment in their country. Capital punishment is one of the most serious breaches of respect for human life. At first glance, it is difficult to imagine how the wrong it involves could be augmented, except if torture were also involved. But the wrong in capital punishment is compounded by treating the condemned person as a commodity to be used to benefit others. There is something profoundly ethically disturbing about people who purport to have respect for human life finding no moral difficulty with capital punishment—indeed, often advocating it. But for them to also agree to using the executed person in this way is horrifying. And yet there might be a coherent explanation. We must disidentify from those we kill. We do this by turning them into monsters, non-humans and perhaps, ultimately, things.

Various reasons are given to explain the shortage of organs. It may be that we are reluctant to think about our own death and, consequently, fail to give consent to the use of our organs. Or perhaps we imagine ourselves hovering over our bodies after death and do not want to witness their mutilation. Another reason given is a reluctance on the part of healthcare professionals to use the organs of a person who has given consent prior to death unless the person's family also consents—and certainly not to take the organs if the family of such a person objects to it. Allegations that the recovery of organs for transplantation tends to be given a low priority when our healthcare systems are short of resources is yet another explanation, as is the fact that recovery of organs is a time-consuming and perhaps a psychologically difficult process for the healthcare professionals involved. It is also pointed out that fewer young, healthy people who would be suitable as organ donors are being killed in traffic accidents because of the use of safety helmets and seat belts.

Some people blame the system used for obtaining consent to organ donation for the shortage. Essentially, there are two such systems. "Contracting-in" is the system used in Canada, the United States, England and Australia: People whose organs are used must have given consent to it before death or, if after death their wishes are unknown, their relatives must consent. "Contracting-out" is used in many European countries: There is a presumption that organs may be taken unless the person who dies has indicated an objection to it. In general, the countries with contracting-out have a higher rate of organ donation than those using contracting-in. It has been suggested that Canada should change to a contracting-out system. Cultural differences, however, make one or other system more or less acceptable to a population.

One study showed that people in France, on the whole, did not object to their organs being taken after their death provided they did not have to think about it beforehand, that is, provided they were not asked to consent to it. On the other hand, people in England were appalled that their organs would be taken unless they had given their consent prior to death. Transplant physicians—especially those who are surgeons—have long been aware that it is important to have the goodwill of the general public towards organ donation and transplantation if the system is to achieve its maximum potential for saving life and restoring the health of those who need transplants. This desire for goodwill probably explains in part why the consent of families is sought even when it is not legally required.

In the same way, a desire to assuage public fear that physicians eager to retrieve organs for transplant might declare people dead when, in fact, they were still alive has caused law reform commissions, legislatures and courts to address the issue of the definition of death (more accurately, the criteria for the determination of death) starting in the late 1960s. This search led to the concept of "brain death," which means that people can be declared dead when they have total and irreversible cessation of all brain function—that is, of the upper brain (cerebral cortex) and lower brain, including the brain stem. People who are brain dead are not able to breathe spontaneously because the part of their brain stem that activates breathing no longer works. Their respiratory system can, however, be kept functioning for a limited time by placing them on a respirator to prevent deterioration of the organs to be used for transplantation. Brain-dead people stop breathing when a respirator is turned off, and as a result their heart very quickly stops beating because heart function depends on respiration. Consequently there is not, in practical terms, any difference between the old definition of death, which was the cessation of respiration and heartbeat, and brain death. The former indicated the latter, but since we were not able to determine brain death directly, we did so indirectly by the absence of heartbeat and respiration. Or, alternatively, cessation of heartbeat and respiration caused brain death. The concept of brain death means that brain-dead people who are on a respirator can be declared dead and their organs can be taken. It also avoids the ethical and legal problems that two definitions of death—one for donors of organs for transplantation and one for other people—would raise. Brain death is death for all people for all purposes.

Some of the most heart-wrenching cases that raise ethical issues regarding organ transplantation involve children—whether as donors or recipients. There is a severe shortage of organs for transplantation into children, especially newborn babies who need very small organs. One of the most contentious debates in this area arose in relation to anencephalic infants—babies born with no upper brain (no cerebral cortex)—who have a very short life expectancy, usually only weeks. It was suggested that they should be classified as "brain absent," and that this classification should be treated as equivalent to brain dead for the purposes of taking their organs for transplantation. In 1994 the Council on Ethical and Judicial Affairs of the American Medical Association accepted this argument, but in 1996 it reversed its position because of objections based on ethical grounds. As the people who raised these objections pointed out, acceptance of the brain-absent concept is a powerful example of regarding a human life as of no value except insofar as it could be used for the benefit of someone else. Its acceptance is also an example of focusing on an individual—the child who needs a transplant—and on doing good, to the exclusion of seeing the serious moral and ethical harms in using the donor babies in this way. Moreover, the larger message given by using a brain-absent concept to justify the taking of organs from an anencephalic baby is that a profoundly mentally handicapped person's life is of no value or is so much less valuable than that of someone who is not handicapped in this way, that the former may be sacrificed for the latter.

Parents of children who are fatally injured in traffic accidents often feel that they face a terrible dilemma in deciding whether to give consent for the use of their child's organs. These situations are, by definition, unexpected, and some parents have subsequently felt they were in such a state of shock that they were not capable of making a considered decision. Ross and Peggy Stone are an Australian couple whose eleven-year-old son was killed in a traffic accident. They gave consent for his organs to be used. As a result of their experience, they founded the Silent Hearts organization to help people in similar situations. Transplantation raises special ethical issues in this regard: Grief can be exacerbated when people believe they have acted wrongly in donating their loved one's organs, and it can be assuaged when they believe the opposite. Which belief they hold can often depend on the interactions they have with the healthcare professionals who are involved in caring for their loved one or who seek consent to organ donation.

The costs of transplantation also raise ethical issues. The only options for people with terminal renal failure, if they are to continue living, are haemodialysis or transplantation. Transplantation is both less expensive overall than haemodialysis and, when successful, offers a much better quality of life. These facts lead to questions such as the following: Would xenotransplantation help us to fulfil ethical obligations to provide the best treatment for people with organ failure? And might xenotransplantation be less expensive than other alternatives and save scarce healthcare resources?

The choice of recipients for transplantation when there is a shortage of human organs also raises serious ethical issues. For example, a task force set up in Massachusetts to advise on organ transplantation concluded that one of the most ethical systems for deciding who should receive a transplant when organs were scarce was a lottery, although they believed that this solution would not be acceptable to the public. The other ethical system was a waiting list of organ recipients constructed on a first-come first-served basis. But even this system was not entirely neutral as to who obtained access, because people of higher socio-economic status tended to recognize their needs earlier and hence were put on the list sooner than those of lower socio-economic status. Such a list must also have emergency provisions for "jumping the queue." The usual provision of this kind is that if somebody farther down the list would die if he or she did not receive a transplant, and the person at the top of the list would almost certainly live until another organ for transplant became available, then the person lower on the list may jump the queue.

The legal concerns that arose initially with respect to live organ donors focused on the fact that the surgery was not therapeutically necessary for the donors—therapy is the usual justification for the wounding involved in surgery. Therefore, the organ retrieval surgery could constitute a crime, one of inflicting grievous bodily harm or aggravated assault. These problems have now been solved by reinterpreting and revising the law. The informed consent of a competent adult is now seen as an alternative justification for non-therapeutic surgery that is not contrary to public policy. The donation of tissues or organs for transplantation that does not present a serious risk to the donor's life or health is not contrary to public policy.

Now that we have some idea of the issues raised by organ transplantation, the scene has been set for a discussion of the ethical and legal issues raised by xenotransplantation. Many of the issues of human organ transplantation do not apply to xenotransplantation, or could be eliminated by making xenotransplantation available. Xenotransplantation would create an unlimited supply of organs, and we would not need to be concerned about consent to cadaveric donation or taking organs from live donors. There is an ethical principle that requires that we should use the least invasive, least restrictive alternative that is reasonably available and likely to be effective to achieve a justified goal. If our organ transplant system were currently adequate or could be made adequate, we would definitely not be justified in taking the risks that xenotransplantation presents. However, the system is far from adequate, and it does not seem it will become adequate in the reasonably foreseeable future. We must, therefore, examine the possible alternatives, one of which is xenotransplantation and the ethical dilemmas it both raises and solves. (Other alternatives are artificial organs or biotechnology advances that would allow an organ such as the heart to repair itself, or creating new organs through cloning.)

What does xenotransplantation involve? When an organ is transplanted from one person to another, the recipient's body will, to a greater or lesser extent, reject that organ because the donor's genetic makeup (genome) does not exactly match the recipient's (unless they are identical twins). The recipient's immune system recognizes the transplanted organ as foreign tissue, which it tries to reject. The rejection reaction for human-to-human transplantation takes several days to a week to manifest itself. People who receive transplants are given immunosuppressive drugs to prevent or reduce the severity of this reaction.

When we transplant an organ from an animal to a human, there is an additional, very powerful rejection reaction—a hyperacute rejection reaction—that occurs within minutes to hours after the transplant. In order to overcome this reaction, scientists have been modifying the genome of the pigs that will be used as a source of organs for transplantation to humans. One approach is to use recombinant DNA technology (the technology that allows us to rearrange, delete or insert genes in the pigs' genome) to transfer one or more human complement inhibitor genes—that is, human genes (how these work is explained below)—to pig embryos. These embryos or their progeny, when adult, will be used as a source of transgenic organs (organs that contain human complement inhibitor genes). These genes trick the organ recipient's immune system: They overcome the hyperacute reaction— that is, the recipient's immune system reacts more as though the organ comes from a human than a non-human species. When the organs from these transgenic pigs are transplanted into humans, the immune system of the person who receives the organ does not reject the organ hyperacutely. It might also be possible to manipulate the pigs' genome in other ways so that the hyperacute rejection reaction is reduced or eliminated. The pigs whose genomes have been altered might also be cloned to provide an increased organ supply.

A range of ethical concerns are raised by this new xenotransplantation technology. They fall into two major groups: those relating to the animals used as the source of the organs; and those relating to the risks to organ recipients, their contacts, and the public as a whole. In November 1997, the Therapeutic Products Programme of Health Canada sponsored a meeting under the title "National Forum on Xenotransplantation: Clinical, Ethical and Regulatory Issues." This forum, which I co-chaired, and subsequent events related to it can, I believe, provide valuable insights into the ethical issues raised by xenotransplantation.

The forum was not open to the public and was not a public consultation or consensus conference. However, participants represented a broad spectrum of interests and involvements in xenotransplantation—from animal rights activists to xenotransplantation scientists and representatives of pharmaceutical companies involved in developing this technology. There was no proportional representation; my impression was that those in favour of xenotransplantation greatly outnumbered those with serious reservations about it. Consequently, while most of the participants in the forum might have agreed on any given issue, the Canadian public would not necessarily divide along the same lines.

Let's start with the issues raised in relation to the use of animals. Questions we must explore include the following: What are the ethics of the use of animals as a source of organs for human transplantation, and, in particular, what are the ethics of how we must treat these animals in order to make them suitable as organ donors? What are the ethics of modifying the genome of animals to include human genes? What are the risks to animal populations or even species of doing this? Could the use of animals reduce some ethical problems? For instance, is the use of animals more ethical than using a living human donor? Or does consent of the human donor make the use of human donors more ethical than the use of animals when we consider the totality of what is involved for the animals?

Many participants in the forum believed that to use animals for xenotransplantation and to treat them to make them an acceptable source of donor organs can be justified, provided certain ethical requirements are fulfilled. These include making sure that everything reasonably possible is done to reduce the animals' suffering; providing the animals with as high a quality of life as possible; and reducing the number of animals to the minimum—for example, by using as many organs and tissues as possible from the one animal. This attitude can be contrasted with that of other participants in the forum who were concerned primarily about animal welfare and the ethical treatment of animals. Some of these participants believe that it is inherently wrong to use animals as organ donors for humans, and that to treat them in the way that is necessary to make them acceptable for use as donors breaches our obligations to respect animals.

Pigs used as a source of organs for transplantation to humans live a completely unnatural life. Because they must be as germ-free as possible, they are kept in sterile, secure facilities. Piglets are born by Caesarean section, they are not suckled by their mothers, and their diet is strictly controlled to ensure that it is germ-free. These animals have no access to a life that could be regarded as normal and natural for a pig—they certainly never, either literally or metaphorically, come anywhere near to being "as happy as a pig in mud." The same seriously deprived life circumstances have been true for other animals kept for medical research purposes, and considerable concern has been raised about these conditions. For instance, Health Canada recognized relatively recently that its colony of Macaque monkeys, which are kept for vaccine testing and development programs (for instance, for developing vaccines for polio and HIV) and for testing the health impact of environmental toxins, deserved a far better life than they had had. The department asked the Royal Society of

Canada to report on what was required. The Royal Society recommended—recommendations that have been followed in large part—that the monkeys not needed for research should not be killed simply as a convenient way to dispose of them and to avoid further costs of their upkeep. They also said that all the monkeys should be provided with more space, access to more natural settings, and more opportunities for socialization and play.

We have become increasingly aware of what we ethically owe to animals used in medical research. Concepts that articulate our indebtedness to animals for the benefits they provide, including in medical research, are important moral and ethical advances. I believe that the use of animals in research can sometimes, under certain conditions, be justified, even though the use of animals in some forms of research—for instance, for biological warfare research—cannot be ethically justified, even if it were not profoundly cruel to the animals on which it is undertaken, which much of it is. We must heed concerns about animals if, in the future, we are to act more ethically towards them than we have, especially in the recent past. And we must not dismiss, as some people try to do, those who raise these concerns by labelling them simply as a lunatic fringe.

People who support the use of animals for xenotransplantation often point out that we use animals as a food source, and it is surely at least as acceptable to use them to save a human life. While many of us would agree with this conclusion, our use of animals as a food source is not necessarily a justification for using them for xenotransplantation. Sometimes new scientific developments can cause us to revisit situations that have not in the past raised serious ethical concerns. Here, the ethical concerns relate to the way in which we treat animals used as a source of food.

We should be deeply concerned about the way we treat animals that are bred and raised as a food source. We have serious obligations to provide animals with a reasonable quality of life, even if we do decide at a certain point that those animals may be killed for food. The fact that we eventually kill them cannot be used as a justification for treating them cruelly. There is a vast difference between recognizing that we have ethical obligations to provide an animal with the conditions for a reasonable animal life, but believing that we are justified in humanely killing it for food, and treating animals used for this purpose as, at best, inanimate, unfeeling objects. The latter is evil. We should not be able to watch without horror some of the documentaries about the factory farming of animals or their treatment in slaughterhouses. Although, sadly, traditional farming also sometimes involved unethical treatment of animals, any cruelty involved was not systematized and institutionalized in the way it is today in factory farming. We might have lost some of our ethical sensitivity in this area, rather than gained it. We, as well as those who directly treat animals in these ways, are responsible for this violence to them and its consequences. We are complicit when we choose not to know, think or do anything about what happens to animals in order for them to end up as steak, ham or chicken on our dinner plates. We do not have to join the animal liberation movement to do something effective. We can use our power as consumers. We can refuse to buy meat when we know that its production involves the cruel treatment of animals, or when the meat is not labelled in such a way that we can know the animal was treated humanely. We should also recognize how we can dull our moral intuitions against the cruel treatment of animals, or define these intuitions away, by using sanitized language to describe what we do to animals: We euthanize them and they become steak.

We cannot compartmentalize the emotions that cruel treatment of animals elicits, whether for good or evil. If we are insensitive to these situations, that insensitivity can and will be transferred to an insensitivity to respect for life in general and human life in particular. Many people who commit crimes of horrific violence have a history of maltreating animals. One foundation of a respect for human life is a respect for all life, even though we may have justifications for treating some forms of life differently from other forms.

We must, therefore, carefully assess the ethics of our treatment of pigs used for xenotransplantation. Those who want to use animals as an organ source should have the burden of proving they are justified in doing so. In assessing any such justification, we must be aware of our biases. For example, psychology students who completed a questionnaire aimed at determining when they would approve the sacrifice of an animal to save a human life gave the lowest priority to laboratory animals and "bad guys [humans]," and were less willing to sacrifice a pet than any other type of animal. They felt it was least acceptable to sacrifice a pet for a bad person. Moreover, high school students were less accepting of sacrificing animals than first-year university students. Post-secondary education seems to contribute to valuing medical research over animal rights. Are our moral intuitions about our treatment of animals being dulled by familiarity and self-interest?

Which animal species should be chosen as a source of organs for transplantation to humans also raises ethical issues. Although primates are our closest genetic relatives, they have been rejected as donors on several counts. Chimpanzees, for instance, are members of an endangered species. Participants at the forum felt that the suffering that primates would experience as a result of the living conditions required to make them suitable as organ donors was unacceptable. People (including scientists) who wanted to exclude the chimpanzees as donors did not apply this same reasoning to pigs. Primates were also felt to be more difficult and much more costly to care for than other animals, again, in particular, pigs. There was also, it seemed, greater personal identification with primates than pigs (perhaps because the former look more like us, leading to a degree of anthropomorphism) and different cultural attitudes to primates as compared with pigs, both of which weighed against using primates and in favour of using pigs. The use of primates would also, forum participants believed, be unacceptable to the general public. And the likelihood of the transfer of infective agents—that is, zoonosis, the transmission of disease from animals to humans—is more likely between more closely related species, that is, between primates and humans, than between pigs and humans.

In summary, many of the participants at the forum believed that if
it was ethically acceptable to use animals, pigs (which were often
referred to by the more derogatory and distancing term "swine"—one
xenotransplantation industry advocate referred to them simply as "the
manufacturing plant") were the animals of choice. There was little discussion of whether this choice reflected ethically relevant and justifi-
able differences between primates and pigs. Rather, the differences
relied on, as mentioned, were those of the relative cost, convenience
and safety—especially to humans—of using one or the other species.

In the subsequent report on the forum, ethical requirements for
the use of animals as a source of organs for transplantation were put
forward; they include that animals should be considered only if suitable alternative therapies are not available and the number used must
be minimized by using as many organs as possible from each animal.
An international registry of transgenic strains should be created to
reduce the total number of pigs needed and to eliminate the duplica-
tion of establishing "founder strains in several locations." Interestingly
and importantly, the report states that efforts should be made to
"improv[e] the equity and availability of donor tissues and organs
from human cadaver donors." In other words, we would be ethically
justified in using live pigs as an organ source only if it was not reasonably possible to use dead humans.

The participants at the forum also considered some ethical questions regarding mixing human genes and those of other animals:
Quite apart from the physical risks involved, is it ethically acceptable
to transfer human genes into animals in order to decrease the likelihood of organ rejection by the human recipient? And, again apart
from physical risks, is it ethical to transplant animal organs into
humans? The participants did not seem to regard either of these cross-
species transfer procedures as inherently wrong. Neither was viewed
as raising ethical difficulties that could not be overcome. It was, however, recognized that mixing human and animal genes and using animal organs in humans could affect important societal values, in
particular those related to maintaining respect for both human and

animal life. How we view transferring human genes to animals and animal organs to humans will, after all, depend on how we view our bodies and identities. Moreover, these views could be affected by undertaking these transfers.

The broadest and deepest level at which we must consider the impact that xenotransplantation technology will have is on our societal-cultural paradigm—our shared story. As was also true for human reproductive cloning, xenotransplantation raises issues related to our sense of identity. Does xenotransplantation take us yet one more step away from an integrated theory of personal identity and towards a modular theory of human identity—away from seeing ourselves as the unique, indivisible human beings that we are and towards seeing ourselves as simply a series of interchangeable parts? Or could the "miracle" that this technology makes possible deepen our awe and wonder about ourselves, our world, and life in general? In xenotransplantation, as is true of so many areas related to the new science, we need genuine, collective moral thinking and ethical exploration.

The second category of ethical issues raised by xenotransplantation relates to the risks it poses to transplant recipients, their sexual partners and families, and possibly the public as a whole. Are these risks, especially possible unknown risks, of such a nature and seriousness that we ought not to run them? The major risk usually considered is that an animal virus or other infective agent might be transferred across the species barrier to humans with potentially tragic results not just for the person who received the organ but for other people, including the community at large, who could subsequently be infected. Such concerns about xenotransplantation have been raised by some eminent scientists. For example, an article in *Nature Medicine*, written by one of the world's leading immunologists—Professor Fritz Bach of Harvard University—and his colleagues, surprised many people with the strength of its suggestion that given the risks to the public of performing xenotransplantation, there should be a moratorium until the public has been better informed and has been consulted. The authors stressed, however, that this suggestion was not intended to be anti-xenotransplantation or anti-science in any way. In deciding whether xenotransplantation is ethically acceptable, we must clearly balance harms, risks and benefits to individual xenotransplant recipients against not only the harms to them if they were denied access to these transplants but also against the risks to the close contacts of the transplant recipients and to the community.

A major current ethical issue on which people are seriously divided is whether, given the risks of infection, clinical trials of xenotransplantation should be allowed to commence. The argument in favour of proceeding with a limited number of sentinel cases is that xenotransplantation is a life-saving intervention for people with no other medical alternative, and that developing it requires research on human subjects. The argument against is that it could put the health and lives of others at risk.

In addressing this dilemma, we must start from a position that the ethics of xenotransplantation must be "embedded in the science," that is, from the very beginning of any xenotransplantation research, especially in clinical trials, we must do the science and the ethics together, not the science first and the ethics later. In undertaking xenotransplantation research, ethics cannot just be an add-on after the science has gone forward. Second, ethics requires that people who are put at risk by medical research must give their informed and voluntary consent to those risks. Consequently, before proceeding with any human trials of xenotransplantation, an informed public debate must first be undertaken, and, ultimately, Canadian society must decide whether xenotransplantation will proceed and, if so, under what general conditions. To reiterate, these decisions must be taken by all the people who are affected by them, not just the scientists or industries involved in xenotransplantation.

One reason that people are concerned about the infective risks presented by xenotransplantation is that "mad cow" disease has given us a very dramatic example of the potential disasters. In Britain, cattle, which do not in nature eat meat, were fed a food prepared from the offal of sheep. The sheep from which this product was made had been affected by a neurological disease called scrapie. This infective agent was transferred to the cattle, and those that developed bovine spongioform encephalitis (BSE) died as a result. Some of the people who ate the meat from infected animals developed a fatal neurological illness called new variant Creutzfeldt-Jakob disease and now called variant Creutzfeldt-Jakob disease (vCJD), sometimes referred to colloquially as mad cow disease. The cause of this disease is a prion, an infective protein. Until very recently it had never been recognized that a protein could transmit an infectious disease. (Dr. Stanley Prusiner, who made this discovery, won the 1997 Nobel Prize in Medicine for his work.) The vCJD prion had been passed from the sheep to the cattle and, subsequently, to the humans who died as a result.

The extent of the vCJD tragedy is still not known. In February 2000 in the West Midlands of England, a baby was born to a mother with vCJD. The mother has since died from the disease. There is concern that the baby contracted the disease from her mother. This is called vertical transmission of a disease, and if it occurs with vCJD—as it does in cattle—the number of cases would be vastly increased. The medical staff who attended the birth also have been endangered because the placenta contained high levels of prions. There is no reliable test to find out if the medical staff are infected, and they could face years of not knowing. They are all reported to be still working in the same jobs. Should there be any concern about their infecting other patients? And because normal sterilization techniques do not destroy the prion, could medical equipment that has been used on people with vCJD infect subsequent patients? Scientists are now working to perfect a blood test for humans that will enable public health authorities in Britain to gauge the potential size of the vCJD epidemic. The numbers could be high, especially if the disease can be passed from mother to child. Countries such as Canada have large banks of stored lymphatic tissue taken from patients who have had their tonsils or appendices removed. Should this tissue be screened for exposure to the prion that causes vCJD when a test becomes available? What would be the ethical requirements for doing so? Would each person's informed consent be needed? If not, should those who test positive be informed that at some time in the future—possibly twenty to thirty years hence—they might die of vCJD?

People who oppose xenotransplantation often cite vCJD as an example of the dangers of "tampering with nature." Other concerns include pig retroviruses being introduced into the human population, and such novel possibilities as sequences of viral DNA in the pig genome (which are harmless to the pig) combining with sequences of viral DNA in the human genome (which are harmless to the human) to form a totally new, as yet unknown, virus. (These viral sequences come from the pigs' ancestors and our ancestors, respectively, who survived their exposure to the viruses whose remnants remain.) Recent research has also indicated that as few as three hundred genes may form a new living organism. Could the inactive viral sequences from the pig and from the human combine to form such an organism? Infectious agents in the pig organs might combine with innocuous human retroviruses to form chimeric agents. (Such a combination is believed to have caused human influenza epidemics.) We cannot know in advance what the mortality and morbidity of such new infectious agents would be in humans. Humans might develop serious illnesses from an infective agent that the pigs are immune to or which causes them little trouble. This is the case with the human immunodeficiency virus (HIV) in some primates. Moreover, research on HIV indicates that it may be a virus that crossed from animals (green monkeys) into humans with the disastrous results we have seen in the AIDS pandemic.

We tended to become nonchalant about infectious diseases in the early 1970s. Many articles in public health journals stated that with the eradication of smallpox, the world would never again see a fatal infectious pandemic. Just a few years later, AIDS proved us wrong. It forcefully and tragically reminded us that we are still part of nature and subject to it. Today infectious diseases are the third leading cause of death in the United States and the leading cause worldwide. And human behaviour is the leading cause of the emergence of new epidemics. It can also contribute to the emergence of new diseases. Could the development and use of the new science one day be regarded as among these behaviours?

One response to people, such as myself, who express fears about the infectious risks of using pig organs in humans is summed up in the title of an editorial in *The Globe and Mail*: "The Frankenpig that wasn't. Genetically engineered hogs aren't a health risk to humans." The editorial goes on to explain that we have lived with pigs "pretty safe[ly] . . . for thousands of years" and, therefore, should not fear xenotransplantation from them. But cows and sheep have also lived pretty safely with each other for a similar length of time. It was only when we used products made from the sheep as food for the cows that we saw the emergence of mad cow disease. Transfer of an unknown infective agent through one animal eating another, even if that animal is not naturally a carnivore, would seem less likely than an infection occurring through xenotransplantation of organs, which involves crossing the species barrier. The degree of risk is likely to be even further augmented when those pig organs have been modified, especially by the insertion of human genes, to make the human recipient's body less likely to recognize them as foreign. Moreover, some of the genes that have been inserted into the pigs' organs to prevent their rejection can serve as receptors for viruses.

If at some point it is decided it is ethically acceptable to proceed with human trials of xenotransplantation, all the usual ethical and legal requirements governing medical research on human subjects would apply, including research ethics committee approval. Some additional requirements would, however, be unique to this form of research, since it poses risks to others, including the public at large. For instance, recipients would be required to agree to long-term—indeed, lifetime—surveillance and monitoring, and to autopsy after death. Informed consent would be required both from the transplant recipients and their sexual partners not only to the physical risks they each could run, but also to risks to their rights to privacy, confidentiality, autonomy, self-determination, inviolability and liberty, all of which would or might need to be curtailed. For instance, they would be required to give blood or other body fluids for testing for infectious agents; their medical records would be used for epidemiological research; and restrictions on their liberty might need to be imposed if infectious risks later manifested themselves. As well, informed consent might be required from other family members because they also could find their rights curtailed. We must also consider whether the recipient's informed consent to xenotransplantation might be considered free (voluntary) only if the recipient was offered a choice between a human organ and a xenotransplant.

In answering the question whether we are ethically justified in creating unknown risks with xenotransplantation, the allocation of the burden of proof and standard of proof required will be crucial. I suggest that those who wish to undertake xenotransplantation have the burden to show that, at least on the balance of probabilities, and possibly to the standard of clear and convincing evidence, it is both reasonably safe and ethical. If there is equal doubt in these respects, for instance, there is a 50 percent chance it is safe and a 50 percent chance it is unsafe, xenotransplantation research on human subjects must not proceed until this doubt has been resolved in favour of proceeding. Resolving this doubt could require, for example, undertaking transplantation between different species of animals and monitoring the long-term consequences before humans are involved. Because there are unknown risks that could be potentially very serious and, moreover, might not appear for long periods of time—ten, twenty or even thirty years—the question arises whether, if we decide to undertake clinical trials on xenotransplantation, there should be a limited number of them, involving relatively small numbers of people, until we can be reasonably certain that serious risks do not result.

Another risk raised by xenotransplantation, identified in Health Canada's "Proposed Canadian Standard for Xenotransplantation," is that we might eat the remains of the pigs raised for this purpose. The Standard recommends that there should be a prohibition on human consumption of these animals because of health risks: "Natural species barriers which might protect humans from porcine derived zoonosis may be compromised in transgenic herds." Is it less safe to eat these animals than to be a recipient of their organs? Eating such meat also involves a very unusual—might we say bizarre—metaphysical risk: We would be eating meat containing human genes.

What might it mean, in practice, to involve the public in decision-making concerning xenotransplantation? In exploring what might be required and the difficulties that could be encountered, I want to turn again to the forum on xenotransplantation. As explained, this forum was not intended to be a public consultation, rather a setting in which people with a wide variety of interests and involvements in xeno-transplantation could debate their views. Nevertheless, it is a relevant and useful example of a broad-based consultation regarding new science and its risks. We should welcome such efforts, especially on the part of all those engaged in the new science, whether government, researchers or industry.

The forum was hosted by the Therapeutic Products Programme of Health Canada and was funded, in part, by Novartis Pharma Canada Inc., the Canadian arm of Novartis Pharmaceuticals Inc. Novartis has a major interest in the development of xenotransplantation, and its sponsorship, with others, of the forum was disclosed to participants. However, each of us, as participants, might not have made other participants aware of our possible conflicts of interest. It can make a difference to how one views the input of a highly respected scientist, for example, to such an event if one knows that his or her research is funded by a pharmaceutical company that is developing xenotransplantation, even if that scientist is not involved in xenotransplantation. (It is noteworthy in this regard, and to be commended, that Health Canada, in sponsoring a follow-up consultation in April 2000, attached to its invitation a detailed disclosure-of-conflict-of-interest form. This form reflects one insight that we gained from the previous forum.)

The forum addressed both the question of whether we were justified, at that time, in undertaking clinical trials of xenotransplantation in humans and, if we were, what the ethical requirements were for conducting such trials. The second question is relevant only if the first is answered affirmatively. The first was not answered affirmatively at the forum, but was assumed to have been simply for the purposes of discussion of the second question. The requirements for these clinical trials were debated in detail. They included adequate risk assessment; informed consent (especially patients' informed consent to surveillance and autopsy after death); the practicalities of surveillance (including establishing registries of patients and sample banks of tissues and bodily fluids); and record-keeping.

About six months after the forum, a staff member from Health Canada telephoned me to say that the report on the forum would be released later that day. I was surprised and said that, as co-chair, I would like to review it prior to its release. She agreed and e-mailed me the document. I was immediately concerned that it did not make it nearly clear enough that the question of whether it was ethically acceptable to proceed with clinical trials of xenotransplantation had not been decided at the forum. I believed that it was especially important to make this clear to readers who had not participated in the forum in order not to confuse them. In fact, the report read as a set of guidelines setting out what was required to proceed with clinical trials of xenotransplantation. I communicated my concerns to Health Canada.

Health Canada agreed not to release the report immediately and to review it in light of the strong reservations I had expressed. A short time later, I was invited to write a section for the report, providing an overview of the forum from my perspective. My co-chair, Dr. Michael Gross, was given the opportunity to do likewise. On seeing the final report in October 1998, I still found it unclear about the fact that it had not been decided that it was ethical to proceed with clinical trials of xenotransplantation. I did not, however, do anything about it, in part because I believed that it was too late. The letter from Health Canada accompanying the copy of the report sent to me made it seem that I was receiving the report in the course of its public release. In fact, the report was released to the public in December 1998.

In January 1999, I was returning to Canada, having spent Christmas with my family in Australia. When I boarded the Air Canada flight in Hawaii, the cabin attendant gave me a copy of *The Globe and Mail*, the first Canadian newspaper I had seen for over a month. On the front page was an article by Carolyn Abraham that described how transgenic pigs—pigs whose genome included human genes and which could be used as breeding stock for pigs to produce organs for transplantation to humans—had been imported "last year" from Cambridge University in England to the University of Guelph in Ontario. The English unit from which the pigs came was supported by the British-based biotechnology company Imutran Ltd., which is a subsidiary of Novartis Pharmaceuticals Inc. Novartis Pharma Canada had established an alliance with the universities of Guelph, Western Ontario and Toronto, as well as with their affiliated hospitals, to proceed with pre-clinical (animal-based) xenotransplantation studies. The article quoted Dr. Gary Levy, director of the transplant program at the University of Toronto and Toronto Hospital, as saying that Novartis was willing to invest up to $1 billion (U.S.) in this Canadian project.

I was, of course, interested to learn this and wondered what further steps had been taken for public consultation, because it would be highly improbable that Novartis would be investing this amount of money unless it felt reasonably confident that eventually it could proceed to clinical trials. It was now fourteen months after the forum and six months after I had objected to the first version of the report. Not having heard about any public consultations, I simply assumed that I was outside the loop. This was not surprising because there was a Xeno-transplant Expert Working Group, which had been set up by Health Canada well before the forum and which was continuing to advise them. It was chaired by my co-chair at the forum, Dr. Michael Gross, and had two well-known ethicists as members. I expected that this group would have been involved in ensuring that ethical requirements, including public consultation, were being fulfilled in taking these further steps to proceed with xenotransplantation in Canada.

Just over two weeks later, I answered the telephone in my office and a very British voice introduced himself as David Cook, the producer of a program for BBC Radio-5 Live, called *Ed Hall Investigates* . . . He had seen my name in an article in *Nature* that dealt with the ethics of xenotransplantation and recent Canadian developments in this area and wanted to interview me for a segment for their program entitled "This Little Piggy Went to Canada." They had been looking into international trade in pigs containing human genes and, under access to information laws, had obtained a document from the Secretary of State for the Home Department of the United Kingdom that showed that twelve transgenic pigs were exported to Canada in April 1998 and eight in September 1998. At the time of the pigs' importation into Canada, there was strong public opposition in Europe, including in the United Kingdom, to undertaking clinical trials of xenotransplantation on human subjects. As a result, the Council of Europe declared a moratorium on all clinical xenotransplantation trials. The BBC also had evidence that five transgenic pigs had been imported into the United States in June 1997, but Cook said the FDA (the United States Food and Drug Administration) had told him that these pigs had been ordered to be deported or destroyed. This information as a whole caused me to wonder whether plans to import transgenic pigs into Canada were in progress prior to the forum being held. Had an agreement been signed with any of the participating universities or were facilities to receive the transgenic pigs being prepared at the University of Guelph at the time the national forum took place in Ottawa only five months before the first importation?

On February 15, 1999, I spoke by telephone with André La Prairie, the project manager for "Blood, Tissue Organ and Xenograft Policy" for the Health Protection Branch of Health Canada. Later that same day he sent me a fax that began as follows:

Glad I had the chance to speak with you today. Clearly there were as many different opinions on xenotransplantation as there were attendees at the Forum in November 1997. But I did want you to know that we were not aware that *Novartis had definite plans to import their pigs to Canada at that time.* To be even more honest, I think most of us believed the first research efforts would involve animal cell transplants [to human subjects], as they do not have the same immunologic challenges as solid organs and may not require transgenic technology. [emphasis added]

I wrote to the forum's organizer, Dr. Peter Ganz at Health Canada, asking whether at the time the forum was held anyone in Health Canada or any other government department knew that steps were being taken to import transgenic pigs to Canada in connection with xenotransplantation involving human subjects. I concluded my letter as follows:

I hope that you can confirm that, at the time the conference took place, the carrying out of xenotransplantation in Canada was no more than a theoretical possibility, that is, no decision to proceed with xenotransplantation in Canada had been taken by Health Canada or recommended by the Expert Working Group on Xenotransplantation and no practical steps aimed at having animals available as the source of organs for transplantation to humans had been taken (for example, there were no arrangements or agreements to import transgenic pigs whose organs or whose progeny's organs could be used for transplantation to humans; no facility to accommodate such animals had been planned or set up, etc.). I wish to be very clear here: My concerns are not based on any allegations that such activities are inherently unethical. . . . Indeed, we may decide in the future, that it is ethical to proceed with clinical trials of xenotransplantation in Canada. Rather, the issue is whether or not there was an ethically adequate disclosure at the Xenotransplantation

Forum of the relevant facts relating to xenotransplantation as they then were in Canada.

Dr. Ganz replied in early March 1999 that at the time of the forum his staff at Health Canada did not have knowledge of any plans to bring transgenic pigs into Canada. He said he could not speak for members of the Expert Working Group or other government departments. These pigs had, in fact, been inspected on their arrival by Agriculture Canada in the same way that pigs to be used for food products such as ham or bacon would be inspected.

Dr. Ganz also pointed out in his reply to my letter "that there was no moratorium [on the] . . . transplantation of tissues and organs from one animal species to another." This statement puzzled me. Would tissues or organs that had been modified to contain human genes be transplanted to a non-human animal as the letter implied? Dr. Ganz went on to say,

> Apparently, decisions by industry to import transgenic pigs for pre-clinical research appear to have been made after the forum. There are currently no Health Canada requirements stipulating that industry must request permission to engage in a program of pre-clinical research. We are, however, following developments at this apparent pre-clinical stage with some interest and I wish to reassure you that industry is well aware that clinical research in the area of xenotransplantation cannot proceed without Health Canada approval.

So at the time the forum was held, Health Canada did not know about any steps that Novartis might have taken to import transgenic pigs. Moreover, in March 1999 they believed that Novartis's decision to import the pigs was "made after the forum." But were they mistaken in believing this?

I tried to obtain the facts. I telephoned the Communications and Public Affairs office at the University of Guelph, which had issued a press release announcing the pigs' presence at the university and the xenotransplantation research project with Novartis. I asked for two dates: that on which the University of Guelph entered the agreement with Novartis and that on which they started to prepare the facilities to house the transgenic pigs. The woman to whom I spoke promised to get back to me with this information. After several phone calls, I was told that the university was not able to answer my questions and that the matter "was being handled by Novartis."

Novartis faxed me a copy of a press release dated December 21, 1998, and left a telephone message that if I had any further questions, I should contact them. My original questions were not answered by the press release, so I telephoned Rhonda O'Gallagher of Novartis as instructed. She told me that the press release was "pretty much the only information [concerning the agreement with the universities of Guelph, Toronto and Western Ontario] that the company is prepared to provide publicly" and that she could not give me the information I had requested. She said that the project was being run by Imutran Ltd. (the U.K. Novartis company), and Novartis Canada was just "overseeing the research here in Canada." She said I would have to contact Imutran if I wanted more information and gave me the name and telephone number of an Imutran employee in the United Kingdom. I asked Ms. O'Gallagher whether they had asked the University of Guelph not to provide me with the information I sought or whether the university had signed a confidentiality agreement that would limit their freedom to do so. She said that she "couldn't say," but she "didn't think they would be willing to speak to me." I remarked rhetorically that "didn't she consider it worrisome that a researcher [me] from one Canadian university could not communicate with another Canadian university and learn the dates on which events in which that university had been involved, that were matters of public knowledge, had taken place?"

Certainly Novartis did not breach any law in importing these pigs or failing to disclose to the forum any plans and arrangements that it might have had to do so. But as a sponsor of the forum, did it act ethically? To answer this question, we would have to know all the relevant facts. But on the basis of what we know, it would have been ethically reassuring to have had a greater openness, both to the forum participants and in general, about any actual or potential plans for importing the transgenic pigs. And if (as seems to be indicated by André La Prairie's fax to me) plans existed at the time of the forum, who among the participants knew about them and, even more importantly, who knew about any steps to implement them and when those steps had been or would be carried out? My concerns as to the ethical adequacy of the disclosures of information made at the forum were increased by the way in which my subsequent enquiries were handled. The public is often mistrustful of large corporations and sometimes of government, and perhaps increasingly of universities and academics, including scientists, as they collaborate with both government and industry. Events such as the ones I have described are antithetical to earning the public's trust; they harm all of us, not the least because earned trust is the basis on which we must now form our society.

I raise my experience as co-chair of the forum and the subsequent events not to cause difficulties for anybody involved, but rather to point out the problems that can arise in doing ethics in the context of broad-based consultation—including consultation of the public— when there is inadequate disclosure, especially a failure to disclose conflicts of interest and, perhaps, when a government acts as both a regulator (whose primary aim should be the health and safety of Canadians) and a promoter (whose primary aim is economic benefit to Canada) of new technologies. The Canadian government is playing this dual role with respect to much of the new biotechnology. The series of incidents surrounding the xenotransplantation forum, although in themselves trivial, raise important ethical issues that we must sort out in a calm, open, non-confrontational and honest manner. Are these events an ethical canary warning us of related—and possibly much more serious—matters to which we should be paying close attention?

5. Dealing with Death

The Ethics of Euthanasia

As I was starting to write this chapter, my assistant, Eileen Parle, knocked and entered my office. She said there was a woman on the telephone who was asking to speak to someone at the Centre for Medicine, Ethics and Law who could tell her how she could gain access to euthanasia. She was enquiring, in particular, whether if she went to Holland she could obtain euthanasia. I took the call.

The woman sounded calm and lucid—and had a young-sounding voice. She had, she told me, widely metastasized bowel cancer and was in terrible pain; she could not go on in this state any longer and wanted to die. I asked her whether she had been referred to a pain specialist. She had not, and we talked about her seeking such a referral. I gave her the names of some pain specialists that she could suggest to her treating physician and said that if she thought I might be able to help further not to hesitate to call me again. She expressed her gratitude and said that she would let me know what happened. I have not heard from her in the few weeks since.

In many ways this incident is an everyday occurrence for those of us who work in medical ethics—desperate patients who do not know where else to turn call us seeking help. It is noteworthy, however, that this woman wanted advice on access to euthanasia. Seeing euthanasia as a possible practical alternative to going on living is an option that I have only recently heard terminally ill people articulate—other than those who are advocates of the legalization of euthanasia and use their own last illness as a final opportunity to promote it.

Death, the final event in each human life, provides some of our most profound ethical challenges. Among these challenges are those concerning euthanasia. What is euthanasia? Why are we now debating it? What insights might exploring it provide about us and our society? How does the euthanasia debate relate to our search for a new societal paradigm? And which world-views do the different positions on euthanasia reflect?

Until very recently, with the exception of the Third Reich, the laws of all countries have prohibited euthanasia, although in the Netherlands since the early 1970s it has been legally tolerated (that is, neither legalized nor prosecuted, provided it complies with certain conditions). Over the past decade in many Western democracies, there has been an unprecedented rise in calls to legalize euthanasia, with some of these calls coming from within the profession of medicine itself. Numerous referenda, legislative committees and commissions have dealt with euthanasia. A law has been enacted in the state of Oregon authorizing physicians to prescribe lethal doses of medication for their patients. And, in a so-far unique example, in 1995 the Northern Territory of Australia enacted a bill to legalize euthanasia and made world history in doing so, although this legislation was later overruled by the Australian Commonwealth Parliament.

The euthanasia debate is a momentous one. It involves issues ranging from the nature and meaning of human life to the most basic principles on which our societies are and should be based. The fundamental issue the debate raises is whether we should change the rule that we must not kill each other—which is arguably the most basic rule on which our societies are founded—from an absolute rule to one that states we may do so in certain circumstances for reasons of mercy and compassion.

We must consider the impact of legalizing euthanasia not only at an individual level (which has been the focus of the debate in the media), but also at institutional, governmental and societal levels, and not only in the present but also for the future. We need to consider not only factual realities such as the possibility of the abuse of euthanasia, but also the effect that legalizing it would have on important values and symbolism that make up the intangible fabric of our societies, and on some of our most important societal institutions, especially medicine and the law.

Whatever our personal position on the acceptability of euthanasia, it is essential, first, that we are clear what we are discussing. Euthanasia is a deliberate act that causes death and that is undertaken by one person with the primary intention of ending the life of another person in order to relieve that person's suffering. Refusals of treatment, including of life-support treatment and artificial hydration and nutrition, and the provision of necessary pain-relief treatment or treatments for other symptoms of serious physical distress are not euthanasia, even if these actions shorten life. In respecting refusals of treatment, the primary intention is to respect the person's right to inviolability—the right not to be touched, including by treatment, without one's consent. In giving pain-relief treatment, the primary intention is to relieve pain, not to inflict death. In euthanasia, the primary intention is to inflict death in order to relieve pain and suffering. It is this primary intention that makes euthanasia unacceptable to those who oppose it.

The term "physician-assisted suicide" is often misused to describe what is really euthanasia. In euthanasia, the physician is the one who

120   causes the death of the patient. In true physician-assisted suicide, physicians give patients the means to kill themselves, with the intent that patients so use them. Legally, there is a difference between physician-assisted suicide and euthanasia. Euthanasia is homicide, not suicide, which means that it is either murder or manslaughter under the criminal law in the United Kingdom, Canada and each of the states of the United States and Australia. Criminal liability for physician-assisted suicide would lie in aiding, abetting or counselling another person to commit suicide, in those jurisdictions in which such actions are criminal. Unless in a particular context some relevant distinction needs to be made, in this chapter I use the term euthanasia to include physician-assisted suicide. I am against the legalization of both for reasons that the rest of this chapter will make clear.

WE MUST ASK OURSELVES why we are considering legalizing euthanasia now, when our society has prohibited it for almost two millennia. Some people point to the fact that our populations are aging, and modern medicine has extended our life spans. As a result, it is more likely now than in the past that we will die of chronic degenerative diseases and not an acute illness. Also, many countries do not have adequate palliative care, and some physicians are either ignorant about treatments for the relief of pain and suffering, or fail or refuse to provide them. The practice of medicine has also changed. A lifetime relationship with a family doctor is largely a relic of the past, and the isolation that people experience when seeking help from healthcare professionals can be seen as a reflection of the wider isolation that individuals and families encounter in our societies. But our capacity to relieve pain and suffering has improved remarkably, and none of the bottom-line conditions that are usually seen as giving rise to a need for euthanasia—that a person is terminally ill, suffering, wants to die, and we are able to kill the person—is new. These factors have been part of the human condition for as long as we have existed. Why, then, are we considering such a radically different response to this situation?

I suggest that the principal cause is not a change in the situation of individuals who seek euthanasia; rather, it is the profound changes in our postmodern, secular, Western, democratic societies, which I outlined in Chapter 1. My aim here is to provide a rough map of how these societal factors have given rise to and are influencing the movement to legalize euthanasia.

First, intense individualism favours euthanasia for several reasons. The loss of community that individualism breeds can leave us feeling alone and often abandoned when we face death and bereavement. A highly individualistic approach, especially in a society that gives pre-eminence to the values of personal autonomy and self-determination, is likely to encourage the belief that euthanasia is acceptable for those who want it. Moreover, while legalizing euthanasia can be seen as a result of intense individualism, individualism is also likely to further promote euthanasia. There is a complex relationship between a lack of belonging, intense individualism and calls for the legalization of euthanasia: Each augments the other and each might be a response to or consequence of the others.

The dominant message of intense individualism is that only individuals and their needs and desires matter. Therefore, it is not surprising that almost all the justifications given for legalizing euthanasia focus on the individual who wants it. Indeed, those who advocate the legalization of euthanasia usually consider it unacceptable to promote their case by arguing, except possibly as a secondary gain, that euthanasia could benefit others or society itself, by, for example, relieving them of the burden of caring for a terminally ill person or saving limited healthcare resources for other uses. This unacceptability may, however, be changing. In the American case of *Lee v. Oregon*, the trial court noted in its judgment the defendant's argument that the Oregon Death with Dignity Act 1994, which permitted physicians to prescribe lethal doses of drugs for their terminally ill patients, should be found to be constitutional (that is, legally valid), because allowing physician-assisted suicide would reduce the financial burdens caused by terminal illness.

Intense individualism is sometimes expressed as a belief that we each own our own life—a property concept. This belief can be linked with seeing our bodies and those of other people as objects, and, in turn, this can also be linked with euthanasia. If we regard our bodies primarily as instruments for pleasure or for taking control, and if we value ourselves (or other people) only for what we (or they) do, not simply because we (or they) exist, euthanasia is arguably a rational response when we (or they) become weak and no longer experience pleasure or are of use. I hasten to add here that I strongly advocate pleasure, but experiencing pleasure should be distinguished from seeing ourselves and others and life as having worth only to the extent that we or they experience pleasure. In other words, there is a vast difference between valuing pleasure and seeing it as the only thing worth valuing. We might also confuse pleasure with happiness, which we can experience independently of pleasure.

To the contrary, if we see ourselves (and others) as having worth and dignity just because we (and they) exist, euthanasia is not acceptable because it contravenes this intrinsic worth and dignity. We might, however, be able to perceive this worth and dignity only when we can see ourselves as part of a community—as part of the past, present and future human family. Intense individualism interferes with this perception. Put another way, recognition of the inherent worth of an individual—as opposed to his or her attributed or extrinsic worth—might flow only from having a very deep sense of the worth of all people.

There is yet another sense in which individualism might be giving rise to calls for euthanasia. In postmodern Western societies, death is largely a medical event that takes place in a hospital or other institution and is perceived as occurring in great isolation; the person is seen as being alone, separated from those she loves and the surroundings with which she is familiar. Death has been sterilized, institutionalized, depersonalized and dehumanized. It does not occur in a community and surrounded by tradition, ritual and ceremony. Dying people are often isolated, even to the extent that they can suffer, to use Yale University professor, psychiatrist and ethicist Jay Katz's deeply insightful words, intense "pre-mortem loneliness." Intense individualism and seeking to take control, through euthanasia in particular, are predictable and even reasonable responses to such circumstances. If we are to avoid legalizing euthanasia, we must, therefore, give death a more human scale and face.

The fact that we are media societies has also, I believe, contributed to the emergence of the euthanasia debate. The arguments against euthanasia that are based on the harm it would do to societies both present and future are very difficult to present dramatically and effectively in the media. Only if euthanasia were legalized and there were obvious abuses—such as proposals to use it on people who wished to continue living—would there be images as riveting and gripping as those of the terminally ill people who seek euthanasia that are used to communicate the case for euthanasia. Among the latter images is a young man dying of AIDS who is facing death with great courage, who wants euthanasia for himself and advocates the legalization of euthanasia in order to help others who will die of AIDS in the future. Doing this can also help the young man to find some meaning in his death.

At present the only examples we can find of people being in situations that could be used to make the case against euthanasia are in literature. P.D. James in her novel *The Children of Men* gives a chilling description of death by euthanasia in the year 2025. Old people in the community described, most of whom are women, are taken by bus late at night to a beach. A small band is there, playing old-time songs that they know. Some start to sing. They change into long white robes in beach huts and, holding posies of flowers, they board barges, to which they are shackled. One old woman tries to escape but is beaten by a guard. The barges are towed out to sea, then the plugs are pulled out and the barges sink. The people drown. The event is called a "Quietus." Although this is an extreme example and those who support the legalization of euthanasia are likely to criticize my use of it, it does carry an important message. I have read James's

124   description several times—the last time as I was writing this book. The horror I felt at my initial reading has not decreased.

Ironically, probably the most powerful way in which the case against euthanasia has been presented on television is through Dr. Jack Kevorkian's efforts to promote euthanasia and the repulsion the style of this advocacy has evoked in many people, including many of those who support euthanasia. Similarly, when a documentary film of a Dutch physician providing euthanasia to a terminally ill patient who requested it was screened on prime-time North American television, many people were shocked and condemned it as an exploitation by the media of the patient and of euthanasia itself. It has also been suggested that if the carrying out of capital punishment were to be televised, people would be so horrified they would demand its abolition. Disturbingly, it has also been pointed out that the opposite could occur, that people would be as fascinated as they were by public executions in the past. It also depends on how capital punishment is administered. One reason for introducing lethal injections as the means of carrying out capital punishment was to make it less repulsive to juries.

Our personal closeness to the infliction of death and the means we use to do it can make a difference to how we view the act. In considering the impact of the media on the euthanasia debate, a relevant question is whether seeing euthanasia on television brings us closer to it or distances us from it. Dr. Kevorkian videotaped himself helping Thomas Youk, a seriously ill fifty-three-year-old man, to take his own life by lethal injection. The film was shown on CBS's "Sixty Minutes." While many of us were shocked, did we, at the same time, have a sense that it was just another "death on the tube" or have to remind ourselves that it was a real death we were witnessing? (The outcome of this [media] event was that Dr. Kevorkian was charged with second-degree murder, convicted and sentenced to ten to twenty-five years in prison, a sentence he is now serving.)

Personal closeness is also a relevant difference between euthanasia and physician-assisted suicide. Except for the person who dies, everyone, including the physician, is more distant from the infliction of death in the case of physician-assisted suicide. It is noteworthy that in the Northern Territory of Australia during the approximately twelve-month period when euthanasia was legal, physicians did not directly give lethal injections to the people whose deaths were authorized by that legislation although it was legal for them to do so. Rather, the patients euthanized themselves with a computer-activated "suicide machine." The physician attached the patient to this machine by an intravenous line. The machine was triggered by the terminally ill person to deliver a lethal dose of drugs. Likewise, the Dutch Medical Association issued a statement advising physicians that providing patients with the means to commit suicide could be less emotionally traumatizing for the physicians than administering euthanasia. But placing a "medical cloak" (medicalizing a situation that has roots and effects far outside medicine) on euthanasia—or, for that matter, capital punishment—and using physicians as the means to carry it out, dulls our moral intuitions and alters our perception of what we are doing.

People also seem to react differently to the theoretical possibility of implementing euthanasia as compared with its practice. Consequently, depending on whether we see euthanasia on the media as "theory" or practice, our reactions to it in this context could vary. The greater inhibition about implementing euthanasia in practice, as compared to agreeing with it in theory or as a hypothetical possibility, should sound a grave ethical warning. This difference might explain in part why polls on euthanasia show that even when over 75 percent of people polled say they approve of it, when these same people vote on the legalization of euthanasia, except in the case of passage of the Oregon Death with Dignity Act 1994, less than 50 percent of them have given their approval.

We are death-denying, death-obsessed societies. People who no longer adhere to institutionalized religion have lost their main forum for engaging in death talk—namely, their places of religious worship. We have to engage in death talk to accommodate death into the living of our lives, as we must if we wish to live fully and well. Keep in mind, moreover, that today we create our shared story—our societal-cultural paradigm—through the media and that death has always been a primary focus of this story. But are we engaging in too much death talk and too little life talk? We can be most attracted to that which we most fear, and modern media provide an almost infinite opportunity to indulge our fear-attraction reaction to death. As the editor of a leading American newspaper expressed it at a conference on media ethics that I attended: "If it bleeds, it leads."

Our extensive discussion of euthanasia in the media is part of our contemporary death talk, which instead of being confined to an identifiable location and an hour a week (as it was in our churches, temples, synagogues or prayer houses), has spilled out into our lives in general. This situation makes it more difficult to maintain our denial of death; it makes our fear of death more pervasive, present and real. One way to deal with this fear is to feel that we have death under control. The availability of euthanasia can give us this feeling of control. Euthanasia moves us from chance to choice concerning death. Although we cannot make death optional, we can create an illusion that it is a matter of choice by making it possible for us to choose its timing and the conditions and manner in which it occurs. The availability of euthanasia helps to support this illusion.

We are frightened of death not only as individuals, but also as societies. As societies, has our fear of death increased with the separation of church and state—we no longer see our society as having a religion that deals with death and thereby symbolically keeps it under control? Could it be that calling for the legalization of euthanasia is a way in which as a society we seek to symbolically tame and civilize death and reduce our fear of it? If euthanasia converts death by chance to death by choice, might it not also give us a feeling of increased control of death and, therefore, decreased fear, not just as individuals, but also as a society? Could legalizing euthanasia, therefore, be a terror-reduction mechanism operative at the level of our societal psyche?

In post-modern, secular societies, we also tend to use law as a response to fear, often, as explained elsewhere, in the misguided belief that it will increase our control of that which frightens us and hence will augment our safety. The reasons ours have become legalistic societies are complex and include the use of law as a means of ordering and governing a society of strangers, as compared to one of intimates. In the past, euthanasia would have been largely the subject of moral or religious discourse, but in recent times it has been extensively explored in our courts and legislatures. The euthanasia debate might also be a debate about more than euthanasia itself, important as this is. It is generally true that those who advocate the legalization of euthanasia have a different set of values from those who oppose it. On the whole, those who oppose euthanasia are more conservative and traditional. The euthanasia debate and the legalization of euthanasia, if it results from the debate, could be seen by some people as an opportunity to change some of society's values and symbolism to an even more liberal stance with a strong emphasis on individuals' unfettered rights to autonomy and self-determination, especially with respect to one's own death. In contrast, but for the same reason, namely the impact that legalizing euthanasia would have on values in general, those who wish to uphold the values that euthanasia would threaten would strongly oppose its legalization.

Many of our societies' features that have contributed to the search for ethics are also highly relevant to the emergence of the euthanasia debate. Our societies are highly materialistic and consumeristic, with a loss of any sense of the sacred, even just the secular sacred. These features, especially in combination, favour a pro-euthanasia position because, as mentioned previously, the loss of a sense of the sacred creates a danger that worn-out people can be equated to worn-out products and both can then be seen primarily as "disposal" problems.

Such an approach is consistent with our societies' intolerance of mystery. We convert our mysteries into problems. If we convert the mystery of death into the problem of death, euthanasia (or, even more basically, a lethal injection) can be seen as a solution to that problem. As can be seen in the descriptions of the deaths of some people who die by euthanasia—for instance, in Marilynne Seguin's description of the death of a young man with AIDS in her book *A Gentle Death*—euthanasia could also function as a substitute for the loss in our secular societies of the death rituals, which we have abandoned, at least in part, in our efforts to avoid any sense of mystery. Seguin—a nurse who worked for the legalization of euthanasia—describes a young man terminally ill with AIDS, who plans a last party with his partner and daughters from his former marriage, before, later that night, taking a lethal dose of drugs. One cannot help but be struck by the features Seguin chooses to describe: The "exceptionally brilliant day . . . the garden paraded its best and brightest blooms . . . feathered friends that came for treats to the garden bird feeder . . . everyone was happy . . . [and the last meal] a little tea and a few Jacob's water biscuits (his favourite)."

C.S. Lewis suggests in his book *A Grief Observed* (which inspired the movie *Shadowlands*) that a sense of mystery might also be required to "preserve...room for hope." Our approval of euthanasia could also be based on a loss of faith in what life may still have in store for us, especially a loss of trust that people will care for us if we are seriously ill. If our approval of euthanasia is based on such a loss, a complex interrelationship between this approval and being uncomfortable with mystery and losing hope and trust—and, as well, a complex relation between these three latter features—can be postulated. The possible connections lead to two questions: Could the loss of a sense of mystery and, therefore, of hope, and also the loss of a certain kind of faith and of trust be generating nihilism in both individuals and society? And could calls for the legalization of euthanasia be one societal-level expression of this nihilism?

In a study of people with Lou Gehrig's Disease (amyotrophic lateral sclerosis) published in the *New England Journal of Medicine*, researchers used a methodology that allowed them to distinguish between research subjects who were clinically depressed and those suffering from a condition that the researchers called hopelessness—which simply meant that they had nothing to look forward to that day, or the next, whether a visit from a loved one or seeing the sun rise the next morning. The research subjects were asked whether they would consider ending their lives through euthanasia, if it could be legally carried out. It was those who had no hope who wanted euthanasia. Hope is our connection to the future, and that future need not be distant to play its essential role in allowing us to experience hope. Hope is our connection to life and to the continuation of life, even when we know that we will die shortly. As both individuals and societies, we might have been insensitive to the need to generate and maintain hope for dying people.

Finally, as is true of so many changes in our societies, our extraordinary scientific advances are contributing to the emergence of the euthanasia debate. When science and religion are viewed as antithetical, as they have been in recent times, science is likely to contribute to a loss of the sense that we, as human beings, are sacred in any way. New genetic and reproductive technologies have given us a sense that we understand and may manipulate the origin and nature of human life. Applying these same sentiments to the other end of life makes euthanasia seem acceptable. Thus, the new science is also indirectly contributing to the emergence of the euthanasia debate.

I TURN NOW TO THE euthanasia debate itself and the arguments behind it.

First, because it is not possible to argue against euthanasia from an empirical base, opponents of its legalization, such as myself, are open to the criticism and challenge that our arguments are purely speculative and lacking in scientific rigour. Another difficulty in making the case against legalization is that the burden of proof has somehow shifted from those who promote legalization to those who oppose it. This leads to the irony that the norm that we must not kill must now be defended more vigorously than its opposite—that we may take human life in certain circumstances.

The problem of producing evidence is not as severe for those who are pro-euthanasia, because they base their case on respect for individual autonomy, the failure of palliative care to relieve all suffering, and often the allegation that physicians are secretly practising euthanasia. They can use polls and surveys that have the appearance at least of being "hard" data to support their case by showing that many people believe that they should have a right of access to euthanasia, that the suffering of some terminally ill people cannot be relieved, and that some physicians admit to carrying out euthanasia.

Not just the substance of our arguments for or against euthanasia matters but also how we carry out the euthanasia debate. Much of the debate is undertaken in the media. Consequently, journalists' values, media ethics and the messages that are conveyed to the public are relevant and important considerations. As we have seen, the reasons giving rise to calls to legalize euthanasia are complex, but the euthanasia debate is itself also complex. We need therefore to be aware of the ways in which the case for one side or the other is promoted. The case for legalization has been promoted, for instance, through confusion with other acts or situations that do not, in general, raise ethical and legal difficulties. This confusion needs to be identified and carefully explored. Doing so can make us see some of the arguments for legalization differently.

The definition of euthanasia is one source of confusion. Many people who support euthanasia, under the global category of "medical decisions at the end of life," lump physician-assisted suicide and euthanasia together with decisions concerning palliative care, pain-relief treatment, refusals of treatment, including life-support treatment and especially artificial hydration and nutrition. They argue that all decisions that are aimed at trying to ensure the patient experiences a "good death" and that could or will shorten the patient's life are decisions that involve euthanasia. While they are correct in a broad sense—the term "euthanasia" comes from *eu* (good) and *thanatos* (death)—this very broad definition of euthanasia can give rise to serious confusion. It can also be used to promote the legalization of euthanasia. For instance, physicians and nurses who accept such a broad definition and are asked in survey research whether they have ever been involved in euthanasia are likely to state that they have been. This, in turn, can be used as evidence that many physicians and nurses are secretly carrying out euthanasia and that it would be safer for individuals and society to legalize euthanasia in order to bring it out into the open and ensure it is not used abusively. Sometimes the proponents of this argument add that those people who oppose euthanasia fail to understand the safeguards that this approach offers compared to one that continues to prohibit euthanasia.

The primary objection to euthanasia of many people who oppose it is, however, that to kill another person is inherently wrong. The fear of abuse of euthanasia, were it to be legalized, is a secondary, although important objection. Those who are anti-euthanasia believe that physician-assisted suicide and euthanasia are different in kind, not just degree, from other decisions about medical treatment at the end of life. They object to lumping all of these together, because to do so is to assume what needs to be proven, namely, that physician-assisted suicide and euthanasia are morally the same as the other forms of end-of-life medical care that could or will shorten life, and euthanasia, therefore, should—as its advocates argue—be treated in the same way by the law. Rather, if physician-assisted suicide and euthanasia are to be justified, it must be done on the basis of their own ethical and legal acceptability, and not by false association with other interventions viewed as ethically and legally acceptable.

Within a narrower context, the term "physician-assisted suicide" is also confusingly used. Often it is incorrectly used to refer to situations in which the physician intervenes with a primary intention of killing the patient, most often by giving a lethal injection. These are not cases of physician-assisted suicide. They are euthanasia—which is homicide, not suicide. The term is sometimes changed to "physician-assisted death," which can mean euthanasia or physician-assisted suicide, but also connotes a very broad range of procedures that physicians undertake—indeed, have ethical and legal obligations to undertake—to help dying people. We all want physician assistance that will help us when we are dying, but this does not mean we agree with physician-assisted suicide and euthanasia.

The euthanasia debate is too important to be based on a confusion over terms. The most honest and clearest approach is to debate the question of whether we agree that the law should be changed to allow physicians to give lethal injections to terminally ill, competent adults who request and give their free and informed consent to it. This is not the only question we need to answer about euthanasia, but dealing with it first should help us eliminate the current confusion surrounding the definition of euthanasia, which is bad for all of us whether we are for or against euthanasia.

As is true of most ethical issues, our choice of language also matters in the euthanasia debate. For instance, a vastly different emotional reaction is evoked when we describe euthanasia as "a merciful act of clinical care" than when we describe it as killing. When I interviewed Dr. Roger Hunt, an Australian palliative care physician who was influential in the legalization of euthanasia in the Northern Territory of Australia, I asked, "Tell me why you think doctors should be allowed to kill dying patients who want this." He strongly objected to my use of the word *kill*. He said that we should talk of "voluntary euthanasia, rather than ... killing. *Kill* is a broad word which includes murder, manslaughter, and various other types of killing. We [advocates of the legalization of euthanasia] are about VAE [voluntary active euthanasia]."

The term "passive euthanasia," or less often "voluntary passive euthanasia," is used by people who are pro-euthanasia to describe withholding or withdrawals of treatment because the patient, or if the patient is incompetent, the family, refuses treatment, and death results. They then argue that if these decisions that they characterize as "voluntary passive euthanasia" are morally and legally acceptable—as most people agree that they are, provided certain conditions are fulfilled—then euthanasia is acceptable and, they contend, it should make no ethical or legal difference whether it is carried out through passive or active means. To the contrary, those who are anti-euthanasia base their case on the proposition that there are long-established, well-understood, profound and important differences between allowing a person to die and making that person die—that is, putting that person to death. Consistent with this position, they oppose the use of the term "passive euthanasia" to describe justified withholding or withdrawals of treatment that will result in death.

There can also be confusion about what a dying person means to communicate in using certain language. For instance, at a certain stage of terminal illness, many people express the wish to die; indeed, to come to an acceptance of death may be an important part of our human dying process. This is very different from wanting to be killed. We must keep such distinctions in mind in assessing whether people are really asking for euthanasia. Moreover, even if they are, we have to take care that they are not asking some other question or seeking reassurance that, for example, they are not an unbearable burden to their caregivers or that they will not be abandoned.

Describing euthanasia as simply the "final stage of good palliative care" and thereby associating it with such care can also affect our impression of euthanasia and reaction to it. Although not everyone agrees on all aspects of what constitutes the best palliative care, few disagree with its underlying objectives of relief of pain and suffering and the provision of humane and compassionate care for dying people. Indeed, if, as the pro-euthanasia argument goes, euthanasia is simply another example of good palliative care, why would anyone be opposed to it?

Proposing that euthanasia is just one part of good palliative care puts a medical cloak on euthanasia and makes it a medical issue concerning primarily individual patients, their families and physicians. We ignore or bury the fact that euthanasia is an equally important philosophical and societal issue.

One way to identify the effects of the confusion caused by viewing euthanasia only under a medical cloak is to ask whether we would allow a group of specially trained lawyers to carry out euthanasia. The reason for choosing lawyers is that they would ensure that the rules governing euthanasia, were it to be legalized, would be followed, because lawyers—unlike physicians—are trained to interpret and apply rules. Some of the same people who strongly object to my describing euthanasia as killing are appalled at the suggestion that lawyers should be authorized to administer euthanasia. "You would let lawyers kill people?" they ask in astonishment. It may be that what we decide about euthanasia outside the medical context will be the same as what we decide about it under the cloak of medicine, but we cannot afford simply to assume that this will be the case.

Another confusion arises when questions asked in surveys inextricably link euthanasia and the provision of adequate pain-relief treatment. For example, people are asked whether they agree that a terminally ill person in great pain and suffering should be allowed to request a lethal injection. There are at least three problems here. First, respondents' emotional response to the thought of leaving people in pain can colour their response to euthanasia and make them more favourable to it than they would otherwise be. Second, sometimes the only response provided for in questionnaires is to agree or disagree. There is no way to record agreement with pain-relief treatment and rejection of euthanasia; one must accept or reject "the package." Third, this approach confuses euthanasia with pain-relief treatment that will shorten life.

Yet another confusion is that between religion and an anti-euthanasia position. Those who are pro-euthanasia frequently say that those who are opposed to euthanasia hold this position essentially on religious grounds. While it is true that some people do oppose euthanasia because of their religious beliefs, there are good secular-based reasons to oppose euthanasia, and the anti-euthanasia stance of many people is founded on these reasons. Conversely, being pro-euthanasia can be confused with being anti-religion. Even some members of the clergy in some religious denominations are pro-euthanasia. I do not intend to deny that one's religious stance can influence one's views on euthanasia; however, we must be careful about making automatic assumptions in this regard. Even more importantly, we must avoid devaluing or dismissing certain views just because they are associated with religious beliefs. We are usually sensitive today to religious bigotry, but we may not be as sensitive to anti-religious bigotry.

Still another confusion that might be relevant to the euthanasia debate is that between individualism and a sense of personal identity. It may be that when we are dying we need a sense of personal identity to assure us that our life has had meaning and to allow us to die peacefully. Currently, as a result of intense individualism, we are likely to seek a sense of personal identity through feeling in control. Euthanasia is a powerful expression of seeking control. Most people, however, probably cannot find a sense of personal identity in intense individualism; rather, hermits aside, they need to interact with others in order to do so. They find personal identity in a structure of complex human relationships that include those that can be created only through feeling that one is a member of a community. As the philosopher Isaiah Berlin says, "I am [at least in some important respects] what I see of myself reflected in the eyes of other people." Paradoxically, we might be able to find full individual identity only through participation in community, that is, through the immersion of our individuality in the greater whole. This issue again brings us face to face with the major problem of the loss of a sense of community in many of our societies, which, in turn, raises the question whether euthanasia is yet another response to this loss.

There is also confusion in the euthanasia debate between the ethical and legal acceptability of certain outcomes and the ethical and legal acceptability of the means used to achieve those outcomes. The strongest version of the pro-euthanasia argument in this respect is that if death is inevitably imminent for a person who wants and consents to euthanasia, then to provide it is no different from withdrawing life-support treatment from a person who refuses it and dies as a result. In both cases, the argument goes, death is the outcome, and the means used to achieve this end are not morally distinguishable and should not be legally distinguished; it is inconsistent to support the ethical and legal acceptability of certain withdrawals of treatment that result in death and not likewise to support euthanasia by lethal injection. The proposition is that in these situations there is no ethical or moral difference between death resulting from a refusal of treatment and death resulting from a lethal injection and there ought to be no legal difference. Applied to physician-assisted suicide, properly so-called, this argument becomes that, in refusing treatment that results in death, a person commits suicide and there is no moral or ethical reason to distinguish this from physician-assisted suicide and, therefore, these two situations should be treated in the same way by the law.

Another version of this same approach is to argue that the courts have recognized the almost absolute right of competent adults to refuse treatment, even if death was the result. Since the law recognizes a legal right to die, it is argued, it should not matter whether death is implemented through passive means (withdrawal of treatment) or active means (a lethal injection). Moreover, those who refuse to recognize this right to die discriminate against those who are not on life-support treatment and, therefore, cannot die by requiring its withdrawal. The error here, in my view, is equating the right to refuse treatment with a right to die. (The basis of the right to refuse treatment can make a difference with respect to whether this right can, in turn, be used as a basis for a right to die. This point is discussed shortly.)

In contrast, those who are anti-euthanasia argue that there is a moral and ethical difference between accepting a patient's refusal of treatment, even if it results in death, and giving the person a lethal injection or assisting the person to commit suicide; therefore, the legal difference between these situations should be maintained. In other words, the means by which death occurs is a morally relevant issue, and the law should continue to reflect the fact that some of these means are morally and ethically acceptable and others, namely, euthanasia and physician-assisted suicide, are not.

People who are against legalizing euthanasia explain that the right to refuse treatment does not establish a right to die. They point out that it is important to understand the legal basis of the right to refuse treatment, because, depending on this basis, the right to refuse treatment may or may not lead to a right to die and, therefore, may or may not be open to being used to support the legalization of euthanasia. This basis of the right to refuse treatment can differ, as can be seen by comparing Canada and the United States.

In Canada, with the exception of some of the dissenting Supreme Court judges in the *Rodriguez* case, the right to refuse treatment has been consistently interpreted by the courts as being founded on the person's right to inviolability—that is, the right not to be touched without one's consent. Such a right is of only negative content (that is, it is a *right against* having treatment imposed without one's consent) and cannot be used to found a positive content right (that is, a *right to* have assistance in committing suicide or access to euthanasia).

In contrast, in the United States the courts have interpreted the right of privacy, which the United States Supreme Court has found is protected by their country's Constitution, as including a right to personal autonomy. This right has been held to have both negative and positive content limbs, that is, to encompass not only a right to refuse treatment, but also a positive content right to determine what happens to oneself. The latter right includes a right to be free from state interference in decisions about what should happen to one's body. This right was interpreted in two cases, one heard by the United States Ninth Circuit Court of Appeals and the other by the Second Circuit Court of Appeals. These courts ruled that legislation that prohibited physician assistance in committing suicide was unconstitutional. These cases were appealed to the United States Supreme Court, which reversed the decisions of the appeals courts and ruled that state laws prohibiting assistance in suicide are constitutionally valid. But state laws allowing assistance in suicide could also be constitutionally valid. We can understand the co-existence of these two possibilities through an example: Just as one state may validly choose to pass legislation to ban the use of pesticides, another state may validly choose to allow but regulate their use.

With its Death with Dignity Act, Oregon is the only American state that has legislation allowing physician-assisted suicide. The constitutional validity of this statute was challenged in *Lee v Oregon*. The trial court held that the legislation was unconstitutional. The appeals court reversed the trial court's judgment and rejected the plaintiff's claim to have the act declared unconstitutional. It ruled that the plaintiff had not suffered any harm from the passage of the legislation and, therefore, had no "standing to sue"; that is, the appeals court's ruling was based on technical legal grounds not the substantive issue of the constitutional validity of the act. This ruling was allowed to stand by the United States Supreme Court when it denied a writ of *certiorari*, that is, it refused to hear an appeal from the decision of the appeals court. The Oregon legislation is presently being used by physicians and patients to give the latter access to lethal doses of drugs. It remains to be seen whether it will be subject to further legal challenges.

MY PROFESSIONAL INTEREST in the topic of pain and suffering has a personal component. In 1983, my father, who lived in Australia, was terminally ill with widely disseminated prostatic carcinoma. One day I received a phone call to tell me that he had developed brain metastases and would die within a few days. I flew from Canada to Australia to find him largely incoherent and in great pain. I insisted on a pain specialist being called in. The specialist discovered that he had aspirin poisoning—he was being given an aspirin and morphine mixture in increasing doses to try to control his pain. His treatment was immediately changed, the pain brought under control and he became entirely lucid. He lived almost pain free for another nine months. He said two things to me: that he wanted to live as long as he could, but not if he had to endure such terrible pain, and that I must do something to help others who were in the same situation as he had been—as he put it, probably not many of them had daughters who, as we say in Australia, "would go berserk" as I had done, in order to obtain essential pain-relief treatment for him. The situation in which I had found my father brought to mind Albert Schweitzer's words: "Pain is a more terrible lord of mankind, than death itself."

Dying people—especially those with diseases such as cancer or AIDS—often experience horrible pain. They can require massive doses of drugs—especially morphine or other narcotics—to control their pain. If a healthy person were given such a dose, it would kill him or her. But usually it does not kill the terminally ill person—in fact, it could prolong life, because the person does not need to devote all his or her strength to struggling with the pain. Sometimes, however, the amount of treatment necessary to relieve the pain could or probably would shorten the person's life. Many people who do not agree with euthanasia or physician-assisted suicide do agree that it is ethical and legal to give such treatment. Indeed, there are ethical and legal obligations to offer it to patients who need it.

Some people who favour legalizing euthanasia use this agreement of anti-euthanasia people to the provision of pain-relief treatment that would shorten life as the basis of an argument for their case. In an article, "Slow Euthanasia," physicians J. Andrew Billings and Susan Block state that physicians frequently "hasten death slowly with a morphine drip," which they describe as "slow euthanasia." They argue that it would be more honest and better for everyone—patients, families and physicians—to accept "rapid euthanasia." To reach this conclusion, they downplay the physician's intention in giving treatment that could, or even would, shorten life. For instance, they equate pain-relief treatment, which is given with the primary intention of relieving pain but which could shorten life, with an injection given with the primary intention of killing the person. They do this by proposing that in both cases the physicians' intent is the humane, ethical treatment of dying patients, and the means used—a drug that causes death—are the same, and that in both situations the same end—the death of the patient—results. They propose that euthanasia is already being widely practised, and we just need to recognize it and legitimate it.

As many who responded to their article pointed out, Billings and Block failed to appreciate the important ethical and legal distinctions that inform not only the law concerning euthanasia but also the law in general, especially the criminal law. For instance, if a doctor uses a morphine drip with the primary intention of killing the patient, not of relieving the patient's pain, this act would be euthanasia and prohibited as such. If, on the other hand, such a drip is needed to relieve pain and the primary intention is "to kill the pain not the patient," the law would not regard this as euthanasia. Likewise, when a physician withdraws life-support treatment with the patient's informed consent, the physician does not intend to kill the patient, but rather to allow nature to take its course. The patient dies from the underlying disease, not an act of the physician.

Legal immunity for administering necessary pain-relief treatment that is given to relieve pain but that might also shorten life is implemented through what is called the "doctrine of double effect." Although this doctrine has multiple requirements, its essence can be summarized in the following way: Provided the physician primarily intends to relieve the patient's pain, not to kill the patient, and provided a reasonable physician would agree that the treatment given was necessary to relieve the pain (that is, it is objectively justified), the physician will not be legally liable for giving this treatment even if the patient's life is shortened as a result.

Those who are pro-euthanasia have two responses to this approach. First, they say it is hypocrisy to accept pain relief that could shorten life but to reject euthanasia, because accepting the former is to agree with inflicting death. But the law has always recognized that while physicians must never intentionally inflict death, sometimes they can justifiably undertake medical interventions that they know are likely to result in death. For instance, an operation that might save the life of someone who would otherwise die can be justified even if it has a 95 percent chance of killing the person who undergoes it.

It is also argued that since some pain cannot be relieved, for instance, some deep neuropathic pain, euthanasia is necessary for the relief of pain. But, even in these extreme cases, pain relief can be achieved through means that do not involve killing a patient, for instance, through total sedation. Some people who are pro-euthanasia have decried the willingness of those who are anti-euthanasia to approve of people dying in a state of "pharmacological stupor," while being unwilling to permit lethal injections. Although we may not agree with the substance of the arguments that such criticisms reflect, they do contain valid warnings. All of us, including those who are anti-euthanasia, need to constantly question the essential nature, ethical integrity and consistency of our actions, values and beliefs concerning end-of-life decision-making about medical treatments.

The second argument against those who would allow pain-relief treatment that could shorten life but not euthanasia is that even if pain is relieved, suffering is not. According to this argument, euthanasia is needed for the relief of suffering. We can distinguish between suffering and pain. Physician and ethicist Eric Cassell has described suffering as a sense of our own disintegration and an inability to prevent it—it is a sense of a loss of control over what happens to us. Difficult as it can be to accept, there is some suffering we cannot eliminate and we should not seek to do so through inflicting death.

To summarize, some of the confusion between euthanasia, on the one hand, and pain-relief treatment and refusals of treatment that could or would shorten life, on the other, is caused by focusing on the outcome, namely death, and arguing that if a person is terminally ill, what brings about this outcome is morally and ethically irrelevant and should be legally irrelevant. The central issue in the euthanasia debate is not, however, the outcome of death; that is, the issue is not *if* we will die, because we all eventually die. The issue is *how* we die, and some means of dying, namely physician-assisted suicide and euthanasia, I believe, ought to continue to be legally prohibited if we are to maintain respect for life and to protect the human spirit, as well as society.

The criminal law is an important value-forming, value-upholding institution for society. Changing the criminal law to legalize euthanasia would, therefore, have important effects on societal values. The present legal approach to pain-relief treatment, outlined above, means that society can maintain its most important fundamental norm, that we must not kill each other, while still allowing physicians to administer all necessary pain-relief treatment. It is essential that we can both give such treatment and uphold this norm, which we cannot do if we legalize euthanasia.

But even though physicians should not hesitate to offer patients all necessary pain-relief treatment, they do not always do so. To leave people in serious pain has been described as "cruel and unusual punishment or treatment" and compared with torture. And physicians' failure to treat their patients' pain is a serious breach of ethics. Why then is this failure so common and difficult to correct? This is an important enquiry when euthanasia is being promoted as the only alternative to leaving people in unbearable pain.

Sadly, it is still not uncommon to hear healthcare professionals state that a person in pain is "just a complainer" or that "I do not want my patients to become addicted." A physician who consulted me told me the following story: She was on night call at a major hospital that accommodated a large number of old and chronically ill patients. She was called to see a man who had very advanced metastatic carcinoma of the prostate. He was in severe pain, and when she examined his chart, she found that the only pain-relief treatment that had been ordered was Tylenol. She changed the order to morphine, brought his pain under control, and gave instructions that morphine was to be used in a way that would keep the pain suppressed. She said that the man took her hand and tears rolled down his cheeks as he expressed his gratitude to her for relieving his pain. The physician did not work at the hospital the following night, but was again working there the night after and was again called to see this same man because he was in pain. On her way into the room she commented to the nurse that obviously they needed to increase the dose of morphine. The nurse replied that the man was not on morphine, he was on Tylenol. The attending physician, during the day, had changed the order, noting in the patient's record that he would not have his patients becoming drug addicts. The physician on night call made a formal complaint to the director of professional services at the hospital. He said he was aware of this attending physician's attitude, but he was having great difficulty in convincing this particular physician to provide adequate pain-relief treatment. The physician had argued that he had the right to exercise professional autonomy to decide what pain-relief treatment should be given.

This case is shocking as an isolated incident. It is even more shocking to learn that another similar case involving a different attending physician in the same hospital occurred a few weeks later. A man who was dying of cancer of the larynx was suffering from such severe abdominal cramps that he had barely slept for three days. He was likewise given only Tylenol by his attending physician. If these examples are typical of the institution in general, they say a lot about its ethical tone. And since a very few people at the highest level of authority in an institution are usually the ones who set that tone, these people have serious and important obligations in this regard and must recognize and fulfil these responsibilities.

Healthcare professionals' fear of legal liability can inhibit the provision of adequate pain-relief treatment, especially if the treatment could shorten life. Such side effects are, however, becoming less common, as more sophisticated pain-relief treatments emerge. Indeed, as noted before, failure to treat pain can shorten life because a person's physical and psychological resources are depleted sooner than they would otherwise be, from trying to deal with the pain.

Although there are no cases in which legal liability has been imposed for the provision of reasonably necessary pain-relief treatment, and authoritative bodies such as the U.S. President's Commission for the Study of Ethical Problems in Medicine, the Law Reform Commission of Canada and the House of Lords in England have all stated that the provision of necessary pain-relief treatment is *not* a matter of potential legal liability, many physicians still seem to believe that it is. One reason, which has been especially prevalent in the United States, is that narcotics-control authorities have, as part of the "war on drugs," legally pursued physicians whom they perceive as possibly "over-prescribing" narcotics. The resulting prosecutions have professionally and often financially annihilated physicians forced to defend themselves. I am not saying that some physicians do not wrongfully prescribe narcotics, but some who rightfully prescribed them have been seriously harassed for doing so. The fear this generates in physicians has led to the medically unacceptable underuse of narcotics in many cases. In some American states, new legislation dealing with pain-relief treatment will help to give a general message that we have ethical and legal obligations to offer adequate pain relief, but we must also deal with the individual physicians who fail to treat pain.

For physicians to leave people in avoidable pain should be regarded as a breach of fundamental human rights. It should be viewed not only as unethical, but also as medical malpractice—that is, negligence (one is tempted to say criminal negligence). It should also be regarded as unprofessional conduct and a basis for disciplinary action by the relevant professional licensing body that can result in a physician's loss of his or her licence to practise medicine. This approach is not out of line, rather, it is consistent with that taken in relation to the legal liability of physicians and other healthcare professionals in general and to disciplinary action involving them. Leaving people in pain can be regarded as equivalent to other culpable omissions by physicians in relation to treatment—for example, failure to remove an acutely inflamed appendix in a situation in which no reasonably competent physician would fail to act. But not only the acts of individuals can be regarded as negligent; systems can also be guilty of negligence. Negligent systems can lead to pain not being adequately treated.

A report in the Montreal press well illustrates a negligent system for the delivery of pain-relief treatment. A young physician was attending a young man dying of AIDS who was in terrible pain. At midnight no more morphine was available in the hospital ward, and the physician was told that the pharmacy did not open again until nine o'clock the next morning. In desperation, the doctor gave the dying patient a lethal injection of potassium chloride (which has no

pain-relief properties and causes cardiac arrest), since, unlike morphine, it was available on the ward. The doctor was not criminally
prosecuted but was censured by the Quebec College of Physicians
and Surgeons for unprofessional conduct. As a disciplinary measure,
he was ordered to undertake training in a palliative-care unit.

Unreasonable failure to establish a system of access to pain specialists, which is reasonably available to referring physicians and to
patients, should also constitute "systems negligence." This failure is
probably the most common way in which such negligence occurs—as
the story that opens this chapter shows.

To the extent that people's fears of pain and being left in pain are a
contributing factor in eliciting calls to legalize euthanasia, it is imperative to change any reality that provides a basis for such fear. We
should regard ourselves as having the strongest of ethical obligations
to achieve such change. We must ensure that we seek ways to relieve
suffering and to kill pain, not people with pain and suffering.

ONE ASPECT OF EUTHANASIA that has been underexplored is what
broad impact its legalization would have on physicians and the institution of medicine. Richard Foot, a journalist, reports that recent
research has shown that a substantial percentage of cases of euthanasia undertaken by physicians in the Netherlands are botched. People
do not have painless or peaceful deaths or they do not die from the
drugs that are meant to cause their death, but regain consciousness at
some time after their administration. It has been proposed that if
physicians are going to carry out euthanasia, they should be taught to
do it well. Can we really imagine standing before a class of medical
students and teaching them how to administer euthanasia—how to
kill their patients? In medical schools, which give woefully inadequate
time to teaching pain-relief treatment, would we devote time to teaching the medical students how to administer death through lethal
injection? What impact would physician role models who carry out
euthanasia have on medical students and young physicians?

A fundamental value and attitude that we reinforce in medical students, interns and residents is an absolute repugnance to killing patients. It would no longer be possible to teach that if we were to instruct them how to carry out euthanasia. The practice of maintaining in physicians this repugnance to killing—and, arguably, an intuitive recognition of the need for it—is demonstrated in the outraged reactions against physicians carrying out capital punishment. We do not consider their involvement acceptable—not even for those physicians who personally are in favour of capital punishment. As a society, we must powerfully, consistently and unambiguously say that killing each other is wrong. And physicians are very important carriers of this message, partly because they have opportunities (not open to members of society in general) to kill people.

It is sometimes pointed out that many societies do justify one form of killing by physicians: abortion. This was justified, traditionally, on the grounds that it was necessary to save the life of the mother. We now have liberalized abortion laws, which reflect a justification that hinges on the belief that the fetus is not yet a "person." It can be argued that abortion is aimed, primarily, not at destroying the fetus but respecting women's reproductive autonomy—we focus on the woman, not the fetus. Indeed, as explained previously, when destroying the fetus is the primary aim—as it is in sex selection— even those who agree with abortion on demand often regard it as morally unacceptable. And the rarity of third-trimester abortions in Canada, and other countries like ours, shows that once we view the fetus as a "person" (or, perhaps more accurately, as looking like us), we do not find killing it acceptable. Euthanasia clearly involves taking the life of a person. Having physicians carry it out would, therefore, seem likely to affect their attitudes and values, and those of society, in ways that, arguably, abortion does not—at least as long as physicians and the rest of us do not see the fetus as a person like us.

We cannot afford to underestimate the desensitization and brutalization that both teaching medical students and physicians-in-training how to carry out euthanasia and their implementing the teaching would have on them. The response of one well-known Dutch physician, Dr. Pieter Admiraal, when asked how he could have carried out over one thousand cases of euthanasia (as he told a conference audience he had done), is relevant in this regard. He said that it was not difficult for him because he was an anesthetist, and euthanasia simply required him to give the first half of a general anesthetic—that is, to render the patient unconscious with sodium pentothal, a quick-acting barbiturate, and administer curare, which paralyzes all the patient's muscles, including the respiratory muscles—and then simply not do the second half of the anesthetic, which would be to artificially maintain the patient on life-support systems until the patient's natural life-support functions recovered. That which we see as a normal and regular part of our professional activity and which we are accustomed to doing may not raise ethical concerns for us.

Natural inhibitions against killing other people would almost certainly be reduced in those physicians who carry out euthanasia. How broad this impact would be we do not know. We know, however, that the range of persons on whom euthanasia is performed in the Netherlands, under the legal immunity given to the practice in that country, has progressively expanded from terminally ill, competent adults in serious pain and suffering to non-terminally ill, handicapped, very young children, including, fairly recently, a three-year-old child with Down's syndrome.

It is sometimes remarked that physicians have difficulty in accepting death, especially the deaths of their patients. This raises the question of whether, in inculcating a total repugnance to killing, we have evoked a repugnance to death as well. In short, there might be confusion between inflicting death and death itself. We know that failure to accept death, when to do so would be appropriate, can lead to over-zealous and harmful measures to sustain life. We are most likely to be able to elicit in physicians a repugnance to killing while fostering an acceptance of death if we speak of and seek to convey a repugnance to killing (although that is an emotionally powerful word), not to death. Doing so would be very difficult if physicians were undertaking euthanasia.

Teaching physicians to carry out euthanasia takes both the profession of medicine and its practitioners far beyond the roles of caring, healing and curing whenever possible. It involves them, no matter how compassionate their motives, in the infliction of death on those for whom they provide care and treatment. This means, as Dr. Leon Kass, a physician and ethicist, has so powerfully expressed it, that euthanasia places "the very soul of medicine on trial." We need to protect the institution of medicine, not only for its own sake, but also because of the harm to society that damage to it would cause. We must consider whether patients' and society's trust in both their treating physicians and the profession of medicine as a whole depends in large part on an absolute rejection by physicians of intentionally inflicting death. It is a very important element of the art of medicine to sense and respect the mystery of life and death, to hold this mystery on trust, and to hand it on to future generations, especially future generations of physicians. We need to consider carefully whether legalizing euthanasia would threaten this art, this trust and this legacy. These are fragile entities, and if we lose a very finely tuned sense of right and wrong, that is, a sense of ethics, the healing mission of medicine can easily be poisoned. Carrying out euthanasia could, I believe, damage this sense.

THE OUTCOME OF THE euthanasia debate will set the "death tone" of future societies and will have a major impact on the societal-cultural paradigm—the shared story—on which these societies will be based. Consequently, we need to engage in this debate not only with great integrity and courage, but also with clarity, not confusion. This clarity must extend to recognizing that whether we are for or against euthanasia, we all agree on many important points relating to decision-making at the end of life. We must start our debate from these agreements, rather than from our disagreement. This will change the tone of the debate, which, in turn, can change its outcome.

Almost everyone agrees that competent people should be able to **149** refuse treatment including through advance directives (living wills or durable powers of attorney) and that there is no legal or moral obligation to continue to administer medically futile treatment—that is, treatment that has no useful physiological effect for the patient. Likewise, almost everyone agrees that people have a right to adequate pain-relief treatment, even that which could or will shorten life. Where we disagree is whether physician-assisted suicide and euthanasia should be legalized. This issue must be faced head on and not dealt with by confusing it, whether accidentally or intentionally, with rights to refuse treatment or the provision of adequate pain-relief treatment. To do so is to pre-empt the question that needs to be addressed—whether there ought to continue to be a legal difference between refusals of treatment and the provision of adequate pain-relief treatment, on the one hand, and physician-assisted suicide and euthanasia, on the other hand.

The position we take on euthanasia will also vary according to our world-view. People who hold a pure science view will have little or no trouble with euthanasia. Those who see the world through a pure mystery view will reject euthanasia and often go further to say that everything possible must be done to maintain life until this becomes impossible. They do not, for example, believe that it is morally acceptable for competent adults to refuse life-support treatment. And those who hold a science-spirit view usually reject euthanasia but believe that it is morally acceptable to refuse life-support treatment and to have a legal right to treatment that is necessary to relieve pain, even if it could shorten life.

Each country will need to decide whether it will legalize euthanasia, and making this choice will be a complex process, as it should be. It is essential that all of us engage in the euthanasia debate. In doing so, we must ask ourselves many questions about euthanasia, but perhaps three of the most important are: Would continuing to prohibit euthanasia or legalizing it be most likely to help us in our search for meaning in our individual and collective lives? How do we

want our grandchildren and great-grandchildren to die? And in relation to human death, what memes (fundamental units of cultural
information that are inherited by being passed from generation to
generation) do we wish to hand on to those who will follow us to live
in the world of the future?

Euthanasia confirms the power of death over hope, the power of
death over life. It fails to recognize the great mystery that allowing death
to occur, when its time has come, is an act of life. Euthanasia is an act
of death. Thus, there is a vast difference between natural death and
euthanasia. In our often unsubtle, un-nuanced, very physically
oriented, non-metaphysically sensitive world of the beginning of
the twenty-first century, we are failing to recognize how some deaths,
and some forms of death, are compatible with life and hope, and others,
especially those resulting from euthanasia, are not. It might be that in
less sophisticated times, certainly less scientifically sophisticated ones,
we comprehended this through our intuition.

I describe elsewhere how in dealing with ethical issues we often
move from a true simplicity phase, to a chaos one, to apparent simplicity. I believe that we have moved from true simplicity concerning
how our societies should handle human death, to a chaos stage in
which the euthanasia debate has emerged. We must now move to a
situation of apparent simplicity in which we will recognize the complexity and mystery of human death, which exactly mirrors the
complexity and mystery of human life. Our decision, at this third
stage, must be one that respects the mystery of our humanness, while
recognizing the suffering of terminally ill and dying people and our
most serious obligations to relieve it. This respect for the mystery of
our humanness requires that we respect death, which, in turn,
requires each of us to undertake the profound journey of life to its
natural end. In saying this, I do not mean to romanticize or glamorize
death. On the contrary, we need to be realistic, which means accepting that death can be horrible. I am proposing that we need to accept
and respect death, despite the horror and fear it can engender,
because if death has no meaning, life has no meaning. Euthanasia is a

failure to respect death. We do not need to believe in the supernatural or be religious to adopt the concept of respect for human life and for human death proposed here. It does, however, require that we recognize that we have a human spirit, that it can be damaged or even annihilated, and that we have obligations to protect it. We should reject euthanasia because it is incompatible with fulfilling these obligations. Euthanasia is inherently wrong because it contravenes respect for human life and harms the human spirit.

Death is one of the oldest focuses of human fear, curiosity and philosophical debate. It is the last great act of life. It must remain so, if we are to live fully human lives and pass on the capacity and opportunity for this to our descendants. We are not, and never should be, supermarket products to be checked out by others at our best before date. We must not let our justified fear of death overwhelm our sense of the mystery of it and of life. If we do so, the loss and harm to each of us and to society will be beyond our present imagining.

6. Terminating Life Support without Consent

The Ethics of Withdrawing Treatment

One Sunday afternoon in July 1998, CFCF, a television station in Montreal, called to ask whether they could do an interview with me in the next thirty minutes. They had been contacted by the two sons of a man who was in an intensive care unit in one of the large teaching hospitals in Montreal. The physicians wanted to withdraw the respirator that was keeping the father, Herman Krausz, alive, despite his sons' opposition to their doing this. On the previous Friday, the sons had had a lawyer send a letter to the physicians advising them that both they and their father wanted treatment continued. Despite this notice, over the weekend the physicians were proceeding to withdraw the respirator by gradually reducing the assistance in breathing it was providing to Mr. Krausz. The sons had gone to the television station in a last-ditch attempt to prevent this, not knowing where else to turn on a weekend. They hoped that the publicity might stay the physicians' hand. We did the interview and focused on the ethical and legal requirements to have a competent patient's informed consent to the withdrawal of treatment, or, if incompetent, that of the patient's legal representative—in this case, Mr. Krausz's sons. The sons said that neither their father nor they had given such consent. At midnight on that same Sunday, the respirator was, however, turned off and Mr. Krausz died.

At about the same time, Andrew Sawatzky, an elderly man who had Parkinson's disease and had suffered several strokes, was admitted to a Winnipeg long-term-care establishment. His wife, Helene, discovered that the hospital had placed a "do not resuscitate" order on his medical chart. The hospital beleived that undertaking cardiopulmonary resuscitation would be futile. Helene Sawatzky asked the court to suspend this DNR order in her husband's case. The court temporarily did so. Mr. Sawatzky died before a full hearing could be held.

What are the ethics and law governing these situations? Do we have a right to have life-support treatment continued if that is what we or, if we are incompetent, what our families want? Or do physicians and hospitals have the right to withhold or withdraw treatment? The Krausz case and the coroner's inquest that followed provide a good context in which to explore these very contentious questions. In doing so, we must start with the facts.

Who was Herman Krausz? This is an ethically important question. Respect for people requires that we see them as individuals in context. By doing so, we are not just being kind or nice. Ethical and legal concepts such as "substituted judgment"—that is, standing in the shoes of incompetent people and trying to make the decisions they would make if competent to do so—require this knowledge. This knowledge also indicates who is most likely to know the incompetent patient's wishes and even, if the patient is competent, to know how best to interpret what the patient is saying. In the *Krausz* case, the physicians believed that they understood what Mr. Krausz wanted better than his sons did.

Herman Krausz was seventy-six years of age when he died. A Holocaust survivor, he had come to Canada with his wife and two sons from Russia in 1973. When he settled in Montreal, he spoke Hungarian, Yiddish, Russian and Ukrainian but had no knowledge of French or English. He took French courses and learned English by watching television. In 1976 he opened a clothing store, which he ran until he retired at age sixty-nine, when one of his sons took over the store. Mr. Krausz continued to help his son, took care of the house and his wife, who had Alzheimer's disease, worked in the garden, read and attended synagogue. Throughout all the years he was in Canada, he refused to take a taxi and did not own a car; he travelled either on foot or took public transportation. Between 1980 and 1997, he was ill and had surgery on several occasions. In May 1998, he was admitted to hospital suffering from a persistent case of pneumonia. Despite treatment, his condition deteriorated. He was transferred to the intensive care unit and placed on a respirator. He was treated with antibiotics, antifungal drugs and cortisone, but he failed to improve. Mr. Krausz was conscious until very near the end of his life. Because he was connected to a respirator, he could not speak, but he understood what was said to him and could respond to questions by eye or body movements.

After he had been in the intensive care unit for about a month, the physicians decided that further treatment was useless, that the pulmonary disease that was affecting Mr. Krausz was irreversible and that he should be gradually taken off the respirator. Over a period of four days, they ceased giving him antibiotics and other drugs and began to reduce the support given by the respirator on which he was dependent for life. His sons were completely opposed to this and wanted treatment continued. A series of very acrimonious exchanges occurred between the doctors and Mr. Krausz's sons, which brings us back full circle to the night on which Mr. Krausz's case appeared on the evening television news. He died later that night still connected to the respirator, although it had been turned off.

The physicians justified turning off the respirator on three grounds: First, that the respiratory support treatment they were giving Mr. Krausz was futile and, therefore, they had no obligation to provide it. Second, that they were simply prolonging his suffering and his dying with this treatment. And third, that by tugging on the tube that connected him to the respirator, and by his apparent agreement with statements by different physicians and nurses caring for him that he would be more comfortable if the respirator were withdrawn even though it meant he would die, Mr. Krausz had given his consent to this withdrawal. A coroner's inquest was ordered into the circumstances of Mr. Krausz's death. It took fifteen days to hear evidence from the family, the physicians and nurses, and expert witnesses. (I was an expert witness for the Krausz family, which I point out for ethical disclosure reasons.) The coroner's report, which was released in February 2000, found that Mr. Krausz was competent to consent; that his consent to withdrawing the respirator was ethically and legally required; and that his consent had not been obtained.

This case raises many of the difficult decisions we face about medical treatment at the end of life. These decisions can be hard even when everyone is sensitive to one another's needs. The situation is explosive when, as in the *Krausz* case, there is serious conflict between the healthcare providers, especially the physicians, and the family.

How should this situation have been handled? Who should have made the decisions about medical treatment? And what process should have been used to handle the conflicts that arose? The answers to these questions are important for all of us, because the situation in which Mr. Krausz found himself is not rare. Many of us are likely to die of chronic rather than acute illnesses, and we could be in the same situation as Mr. Krausz at the end of our lives. How would we want decisions to be taken? By whom? Which factors would we want taken into account and which would we want not to be taken into account in making those decisions?

In the recent past, many people were mainly frightened of over-treatment at the end of life—of dying, as one person expressed it, "at the mercy of doctors and their machines." This fear has been addressed by the doctrine of informed consent—competent adult patients have an almost absolute right to refuse medical treatment, even if this refusal will result in death. In the past, disputes generally arose when patients refused treatment that physicians wanted to give. The *Nancy B.* case sets out the modern ethics and law of this situation. Nancy B. was a young woman living in Quebec who had irreversible high-level quadriplegia as a result of a neurological disease called Guillain-Barré syndrome. She wanted the respirator keeping her alive disconnected. The hospital and her physician went to court, and the court gave an order authorizing the withdrawal of the respirator. This case is the mirror image of the *Krausz* case, in that Nancy B. wanted the respirator keeping her alive disconnected, whereas while we do not know what Mr. Krausz wanted, his family—and they said he also—wanted it maintained. Physicians have no right to impose treatment and must respect patients' rights to autonomy and self-determination in refusing treatment. People can also give directions regarding both treatment and who should decide for them should they become incompetent, in the form of living wills and durable powers of attorney. These "advance directives" allow people, while competent, to decide what treatment they do and do not want should they become incompetent, and to name the person who should ensure that their wishes are followed and, if these are not known, make decisions concerning their treatment.

Much more recently, there has been a fear of under-treatment—that we will be allowed to die because others regard our quality of life as not worth living, or we are too much of a burden on others or the healthcare system, especially with regard to what we cost it. This fear is especially likely to be well-founded if we are old: Simply on the basis of their age, and even though discrimination on this basis is legally prohibited, old people are denied medical treatment that healthcare professionals would provide to younger people in the same circumstances. Decisions about medical treatment at the end of life were not difficult in the past, because not much life-prolonging treatment could be offered to terminally ill patients. This situation has changed and will continue to change.

The dilemmas we face in making these decisions are what cardiologist Dr. Maurice McGregor, writing in *The New England Journal of Medicine,* has labelled "the costs of our success." These costs can be of three kinds: the emotional and psychological costs of denying treatment or, sometimes, of providing it; the symbolic costs (at the societal level, these decisions will be important factors in establishing the values on which we will base our society); and the monetary costs. Which of these "costs" we will accept and which we will reject demands a thorough public discussion.

Until very recently, we have avoided overt decision-making, certainly at the societal level, about the allocation of healthcare resources at the individual patient level. We have allowed these decisions to be taken by individual physicians—and sometimes nurses—on an *ad hoc* basis and often in a diffuse and latent manner. In other words, until very recently whether or not a patient was offered a certain treatment or given it at the patient's or family's request depended on the views and values of the treating healthcare professionals. These professionals have a very important role to play in such decision-making, but should this decision-making be entirely in their hands?

One way in which physicians justify their decisions to withhold or withdraw treatment is by labelling the treatment as futile. But before dealing with the concept of futility in more detail, some general comments are called for. First, when determining physicians' obligations to provide care or treatment, each item of treatment must be assessed individually. Just because one treatment is medically futile, for instance, does not mean that all treatments are. And while there might be no obligation to offer the patient certain life-prolonging treatments, there is an obligation to offer those treatments needed for palliative purposes. And even if no treatments are medically indicated for the patient, care is always required.

Second, there is no ethical or legal difference between withholding or withdrawing care or treatment. The ethical and legal acceptability of doing either depends on the same justifications. Research has shown, however, that about two-thirds of physicians find it much more difficult to withdraw treatment than to withhold it. Many factors could be at play here. The same research indicated that cases involving withdrawal were less ethically clear-cut than those in which treatment was withheld—there was more of an ethical grey zone in the former as to what should be done. This could mean that the physicians' moral intuition was warning them of ethical difficulties that were not obvious on the surface of some cases. This difference in physicians' feelings about withdrawing as compared with withholding treatment might also reflect the fact that we bond psychologically to people on whom we intervene trying to help them. In withdrawing treatment, physicians might be experiencing these bonds being broken. In comparison, these bonds might never have been established in withholding treatment.

Let's now examine the concept of futile care using the *Krausz* case as an example.

Medically futile treatment or care is treatment or care that would have no useful physiological effect on the patient. Examples would include placing a dead person on a respirator, or giving a blood transfusion to a person who had no need of one. There is a strong consensus that medically futile treatments, as defined here, need not be offered to patients, may be withdrawn and need not be provided in response to patients' or families' requests. The respiratory support that Mr. Krausz was receiving was not medically futile treatment. It sustained the vital function of his respiration; that is, it had a life-sustaining physiological effect for him.

In her report, the coroner agreed that the treatment Mr. Krausz received was not medically futile. She found, however, that it was therapeutically futile; the treatment had some effect but its therapeutic benefit did not merit its continued use. What the coroner meant was that she found that Mr. Krausz's condition could not be cured; that when the respiratory support was given, it was only an interim measure to see if he would recover; and that he would not recover but would die whether or not he remained on the respirator. The difference between continuing the respiratory support and withdrawing it, the coroner ruled, was *when* he would die. If the respirator was withdrawn, he would die soon after. If it was not withdrawn, he might have lived for days, weeks or even months. One difficulty with this definition of therapeutic futility is that many people who cannot be cured receive treatment that prolongs their lives and this is not regarded as therapeutically futile. We need further analysis, therefore, to work out what the coroner meant by this concept in her use of it in the *Krausz* case.

In the past, physicians characterized treatment as futile for a variety of reasons; for instance, in their view, the suffering inflicted by the treatment did not merit the benefits it promised; because the risk of the treatment outweighed its potential benefits; because the cost of the treatment outweighed its benefits; because the cost of the treatment did not merit sustaining the quality of life the patient was experiencing; and sometimes because, for a variety of reasons that involved the physician's own ethical value judgments, he or she believed it was unethical to provide certain treatment and cloaked this judgment with the concept of the treatment being futile.

The characterization of certain treatment or care as futile was used by physicians as a justification for withholding or withdrawing the treatment or care. But as can be seen from the factors listed above, the definition of general futility often takes into account complex value judgments, for instance, about quality-of-life factors, and allows treatment or care to be judged futile if the quality of life of the person who would be kept alive is below a certain standard. But the judgment as to what constitutes a "life not worth living" depends on deep personal values, attitudes and beliefs. Is it appropriate for physicians to decide this, at least alone? And if there is disagreement, as there was in the *Krausz* case, who should decide?

Most ethicists and medical lawyers have agreed that this general concept of futile treatment or care is dangerous because it can be used to cover up a wide variety of value judgments, some of which are acceptable, and some of which are clearly not acceptable, but each of which needs careful, individual analysis and justification. In other words, we must analyze any given situation more precisely to determine whether a decision to withhold or withdraw treatment or care is ethically and legally acceptable, rather than simply labelling a decision to do so as the withholding or withdrawal of futile treatment or care and then assuming that this decision is justified.

A physician is the appropriate person to decide on medical futility because such decisions fall within the physician's professional expertise, and reasonable physicians can agree on what is medically futile treatment. In contrast, a general concept of futility is not simply a medical decision or a values-based decision for the physician. Moreover, decisions made pursuant to a general concept of futility, such as whether it was worthwhile to Mr. Krausz to have an extra period of life, even if short, by remaining on the respirator, are not within any special area of expertise of physicians. We see such situations every day in the lives of dying people: They want to see a loved one who lives far away one last time; to reconcile with an estranged friend; or to see a grandchild graduate or marry.

Another way to capture the distinction between medical futility and a more general concept of futility is to differentiate between *medical decisions* (for example, what was the correct dose of a specified drug to give to Mr. Krausz), which are properly the province of physicians, and *decision-making in a medical context* (for example, whether the respirator may be withdrawn from Mr. Krausz), which is not. This same distinction is captured in the contrasting terms "quantitative (or objective) futility" and "qualitative (or subjective) futility."

Some general points can be made with respect to how one goes about making this latter type of decision. First, decision-making in a medical context has moved from being physician-centred to being patient-centred. The Civil Code of Quebec provides a good example in this regard. It states that the decision rests with the competent patient, or if the patient is incompetent, the decision-maker chosen by the patient, or, if there is no such person, the person's spouse, close relative or person who shows a special interest in the patient. The person making the decision for another must "act in the sole interest of that person, taking into account, as far as possible, any wishes the latter may have expressed." Consequently, the patient's, not the physician's, values must predominate if there is conflict in determining whether care and treatment should be withheld or withdrawn. For example, if Mr. Krausz wanted the respirator maintained in order to continue to live, for no matter how short a period this might have been, it was not open to his attending physicians to decide that Mr. Krausz's quality of life was such that it did not merit the continuance of his life through respiratory support. Labelling respiratory support as futile treatment does not justify withdrawing it. Only if it were medically futile treatment—that is, if it had no physiological effect for Mr. Krausz—could a physician decide to do this on the basis of futility. Whether or not withdrawal is justified on other grounds depends on a careful analysis of all the circumstances. In particular, because the coroner found that Mr. Krausz was competent, his values, his view of his quality of life and his decision about treatment were crucial.

The coroner held that Mr. Krausz was competent and his consent was needed before the respirator could be withdrawn and that the physicians should have presented him with the three options open to him and respected his choice. These options were to have the physicians take out the tube connecting him to the respirator; to be weaned off the respirator (its contribution to his breathing would be gradually reduced to zero); or to remain on the respirator. She ruled that the physicians did not obtain his consent to the course that they adopted—reducing the respirator support to zero over a period of time, as a result of which Mr. Krausz died sooner than he would otherwise have done.

162   One difficulty raised by the coroner's report is that she seems to have treated therapeutic futility and informed consent as cumulative justifications—that is, as though both were required. Usually informed consent and futility are alternative justifications. In other words, the reason that futility is an issue is that it provides a justification other than informed consent for withdrawing treatment. If a treatment is medically futile, there is no need to obtain informed consent to its withdrawal. If it is not medically futile, informed consent to its withdrawal must be obtained. Do the same rules apply to therapeutically futile treatment? The coroner required Mr. Krausz's informed consent to withdrawal of the respiratory support treatment that she ruled was therapeutically futile. Why would she do this if therapeutic futility would justify its withdrawal? And if therapeutic futility does not justify withdrawing the treatment without informed consent, why use this concept at all because informed consent alone justifies its withdrawal? Another difficulty in the coroner's report is that the distinction between medical futility and therapeutic futility is not clear-cut. Neither is that between therapeutic futility and general futility.

The only reason for the coroner designating the treatment Mr. Krausz was receiving as therapeutically futile that I can think of would be to make it acceptable for the physicians to ask Mr. Krausz whether he wanted the respirator withdrawn. Let me explain. Physicians must act ethically in presenting patients—or their families where relevant—with the need to make a decision, especially a decision as momentous as the withdrawal of life-support treatment. The coroner might have been ruling that if a treatment is therapeutically futile, it is ethically appropriate to ask the patient whether he or she wishes to have it withdrawn, and then act on the basis of the patient's informed decision. If the treatment is not therapeutically futile, it would be ethically inappropriate to raise this question. The situation in which a physician raises the issue of withdrawal of treatment, as in the *Krausz* case, is subtly but importantly different from one in which a competent patient initiates the request that treatment be withdrawn—which all competent patients have the right to do at anytime.

One such request by patients that healthcare professionals and families often find difficult to respect—and which some people vehemently oppose implementing—is that to withdraw artificial hydration and nutrition when a person's life is dependent on them. Images of a person dying of dehydration and starvation come to mind. This situation can be viewed differently, however, if we think of the terminally ill person as suffering from a failed alimentary system and the withdrawal of artificial hydration and nutrition as withdrawal of artificial alimentary system support. In short, respecting a refusal of this type of treatment is no different from accepting a person's refusal of respiratory support for a failed respiratory system. We have tended to see these situations differently because of the values and symbolism attached to the provision of food and drink for those in our care, especially babies and young children. We have wrongly equated artificial hydration and nutrition (a medical life-support treatment) with natural food and drink and, thereby, have mistakenly equated the withholding of them. I hasten to add that I am not suggesting we are always justified in withholding or withdrawing artificial hydration and nutrition. Rather, the basis on which this decision should be made is the ethics of the withholding or withdrawal of artificial life-support treatment, not that of food and water.

A situation can arise in which a patient demands a treatment that the physician could provide, but that the physician in "good faith" and on reasonable grounds refuses to provide because the physician believes the treatment is medically futile or, overall, so seriously harmful in itself to the patient that it would be unethical to administer it. Often these situations arise in relation to incompetent patients for whom the family wants everything medically possible to be done and the physician sees this treatment as causing terrible suffering with little chance of success. For instance, some desperate parents want to try powerful, experimental chemotherapy with horrible side effects for their child who is in the last stages of dying from cancer. But assuming that the treatment is relevant to a condition from which the patient suffers, as respiratory support was in Mr. Krausz's case, the burden of proof is on the physician to justify withholding the treatment. Provided that the physician's judgment—that the treatment is either medically futile or it would clearly be unethical to provide it—is objectively correct (that is, in the circumstances, no reasonable person—or, possibly, no reasonable physician—would disagree with the physician), there is no ethical or legal obligation to offer or continue such treatment. To continue respiratory support for Mr. Krausz was not, as explained, medically futile. It seems, however, that the physicians thought it was unethical for them to continue it because of the suffering Mr. Krausz was experiencing; because of their perception of his quality of life; because of their belief that a hospital policy allowed them to withdraw the treatment (the coroner found this belief to be mistaken); and because of their belief that his tugging at the respirator tube and indicating that he would like this removed showed he had consented to withdrawal of the respirator (which the coroner found he had not).

Even assuming that physicians believe they would be acting unethically by continuing a treatment that a competent patient (or, if incompetent, his family) wants, does not end physicians' obligations with respect to the patient's access to the treatment. In most cases, they would have an ethical and legal obligation to transfer the patient to a physician who is willing to continue the treatment. If there is such a physician in the same hospital as the patient, while such a transfer can cause emotional suffering to a dying patient, it is feasible. But if there is no such physician, the only option is to transfer the patient to another hospital or perhaps to send him home. Often in the case of a terminally ill patient such as Mr. Krausz, however, such a transfer or discharge is not feasible, not least because other hospitals might not be willing to take a dying patient who is already hospitalized, or to undertake it would involve so much physical suffering for the patient that it would be unethical to inflict it.

Sometimes patients or their families (as was true of the Krausz family) worry that physicians might place the interests of others—especially with regard to cost-saving—before those of the patient.

Physicians are the end-stage allocators of almost 80 percent of health-care resources and, therefore, exercise considerable power in this regard. But while those concerns may in certain cases be justified, the fact is that ethically and legally the treating physician has a primary obligation of personal care to the individual patient. The physician must not place the interests of others before those of the patient or allow the interests of others to be taken into account, if doing so would conflict with any primary interests of the patient. This is not to say that physicians cannot act to save healthcare resources—they may and, indeed, have ethical obligations to do so. These obligations, however, are secondary to those owed to the patient. Such an approach is essential to maintaining our trust in physicians, whom we must be able to trust when we are sick, that is, when we are most in need, weak and vulnerable.

Recently, the Supreme Court of Canada has been recognizing the major power imbalance between physicians and their patients and has sought to deal with and re-balance this by finding that the physician has fiduciary obligations to the patient. In other words, the physician must act in the utmost good faith and without conflict of interest to protect the patient's interests and to honour the trust placed in the physician by the patient. It is an interesting question whether this more exacting, trust-based legal obligation will be held to extend to the patient's family in any way. For instance, where it is not contrary to the patient's interests or even required by them, could there be an obligation not to emotionally traumatize the family when it is avoidable? This is a relevant question in the *Krausz* case, as became evident in listening to the evidence given by Mr. Krausz's sons at the coroner's inquest.

I would like to summarize what I believe would have been the correct ethical and legal approach for the physicians to have taken in the *Krausz* case or to take in other similar cases involving treatment that is not medically futile: Because Mr. Krausz was competent, it was neither ethically nor legally acceptable to withdraw the respirator without his informed consent. If he had been incompetent, his wishes, as expressed by his substitute decision-makers, in this case his sons, must prevail. If there is doubt as to the patient's competence, a psychiatrist who has the required expertise should make a determination. If there is doubt as to an incompetent patient's prior wishes, and conflict between the substitute decision-maker and the physician about how to proceed, the legal presumption in favour of life should govern, that is, respiratory support should be maintained in the period during which an application is made to a court for a ruling to resolve the doubt. If the patient's wishes are not known, then for the physician or hospital to displace the decision of the substitute decision-maker, it must be shown that the decision-maker was acting either not in the "sole interests" of the patient (that the decision-maker had a serious conflict of interest), or manifestly contrary to the patient's "best interests." Again, a court order might well be required to determine these issues.

The physicians in Mr. Krausz's case repeatedly referred to him in giving evidence at the coroner's enquiry as being "in the process of dying," and they seemed to regard this situation as a justification for withdrawing respiratory support since they believed it was, therefore, futile care. Before we were as comfortable, ethically and legally, as we are today with withdrawing life-support treatment from either a competent patient who refuses it or from an incompetent person whose substitute decision-maker refuses further treatment for the patient, a concept of not unjustifiably prolonging a person's dying was sometimes used to justify withdrawing life-support treatment. But this concept was used only to justify withdrawing treatment that was validly refused (that is, as a justification in addition to informed consent), never to justify withdrawing treatment that a patient or the substitute decision-maker had not refused or, even more so, wanted. It merits noting that the concept of futility was almost entirely developed in the context of withdrawing life-support treatment from permanently comatose patients (who used to be referred to as being in a permanent vegetative state—or PVS patients). It was unthinkable (and for many people still is) that it would be used to justify withdrawing treatment that was not medically futile from a competent patient, who had not given informed consent.

Similarly, there can be a misuse of the quality-of-life concept. Initially, this concept was articulated as a means to provide access to health care. It was argued that since people have a right to a certain minimum quality of life, and since access to a minimally adequate level of health care is necessary to ensure the exercise of this right, people, therefore, have a right of access to that level of health care. Currently, and with the opposite intent, some physicians seek to use a quality-of-life concept as a justification for *not* making certain kinds of care available, by arguing either that the person's quality of life is such that it does not merit maintaining or that the anticipated improvement in the person's quality of life as a result of providing that care does not merit its cost. Recent research has shown that physicians do not assess patients' quality of life in the same way the patients do, especially those who are old. Physicians consistently assessed it as being much worse than the patients themselves did. Patients' values must, therefore, clearly play a prominent role in decision-making about the withholding or withdrawal of treatment.

In the vast majority of cases that involve dying patients, neither the patient nor the family, as substitute decision-maker, want minimally beneficial treatments continued or given. But in the few cases where they do, we do a grievous wrong to them and a serious harm to our societal values by not respecting their wishes. The enormous importance and fragility of the societal fabric that we are necessarily dealing with here cannot be over-emphasized. Some physicians and hospitals feel extremely distressed by being required to continue what they regard as unnecessary or wasteful treatment, especially when it is the family members who want this treatment given. But sometimes a financial cost is attached to the protection of important societal values, and this money is usually well spent. Moreover, unless this treatment is medically futile or unethical, in order to give physicians the right to override the patient's or, where relevant, the family's opposition, and to withdraw or refuse to provide treatment, we would need to change the current law. (As explained, this requires the patient's or, in the case of incompetent patients, the substitute decision-maker's informed consent to the withholding or withdrawal of treatment.) And before we did that, we would need to reach some societal consensus on what treatments may be withheld or withdrawn in which circumstances from whom, and who would decide this in individual cases.

We have now seen that cases such as the *Krausz* case raise ethical issues at the individual and societal levels. They also raise them at the institutional or hospital level. Sometimes, as the physicians believed was true in Mr. Krausz's case, hospitals have a policy that governs decisions concerning the withholding or withdrawal of life-support treatment. These policies can help resolve some difficult situations, including ethical ones, and they are educational for healthcare staff. They also help to set a high ethical tone in a hospital. They can, however, also cause problems.

The first area of difficulty occurs when mistakes are made in deciding whether the policy applies. The coroner ruled that such a mistake was made in the *Krausz* case. The hospital policy used by the physicians in the *Krausz* case was entitled "Resuscitation and Other Critical Interventions Policy." The coroner found that this policy did not apply to the situation in which Mr. Krausz found himself, that of progressive chronic obstructive lung disease, which would cause his death. Rather, she found that this policy covered, as it stated, "a limited number of life threatening events that occur suddenly at unpredictable times. These include cardio-pulmonary arrest, acute hemorrhage, acute sepsis, and acute cardiac arhythmnias." In short, these guidelines were meant to govern decision-making in relation to unexpected critical events that arise in caring for a patient, not decisions about treatment in situations that can be regarded as part of the normal course of the disease. But the physicians caring for Mr. Krausz believed that the policy did apply to decisions concerning his care and treatment and that it justified their withdrawal of life-support treatment. The policy, therefore, merits further analysis.

The principles underlying it reflect some of the same ethical and legal principles that should have been applied in Mr. Krausz's case. These include that the competent patient has a right to decide on treatment and that the incompetent patient's family is the appropriate decision-maker regarding treatment. The policy also required that the patient must be told of the therapeutic plan and it included a provision that the patient "need not be informed of measures that are to be withheld on grounds of futility."

Depending on how these provisions are interpreted, they may or may not be ethically and legally acceptable. If the requirement to tell the patient of the therapeutic plan means that the patient must be advised of the range of treatment options that ought to be offered by a reasonably careful and competent physician in the same circumstances, this requirement is ethically and legally acceptable. If it means that the physician may unilaterally decide which treatments will or will not be given to the patient and simply advise the patient of these decisions, this is not ethically or, in my view, legally acceptable.

Likewise, if the concept of futility referred to is that of *medical* futility, this policy is ethically and legally acceptable: The patient need not be told of treatments that would have no physiological effect. If the concept of futility is a more general one, it would allow the physician, on grounds going well beyond purely medical ones, to simply decide what is futile treatment and withhold it. Such an approach is not ethically or legally acceptable.

The policy also sets out a very important principle that is relevant when there is conflict between a physician and a patient (or an incompetent patient's family):

Questionable quality of life—In those instances where a critical intervention would result in or prolong a questionable quality of life—examples include intractable instances of pain, discomfort, and/or deeply impaired cognition—then discussion concerning critical interventions should be instituted with the patient. *The final decision on quality of life rests with the*

patient (or, if incompetent, with the patient's legal substitute).
[Emphasis added]

In short, this policy rightly recognizes that it was for Mr. Krausz, not his physicians, to decide whether life of the quality he was experiencing in receiving respiratory support was worth living.

A second area of difficulty in relation to policies governing the withholding or withdrawal of treatment is that the ethical and legal acceptability of the decisions made on the basis of these policies depends on how they are applied in a particular case. A policy is not a formula that, if followed, gives ethical or legal immunity. Moreover, because a badly drafted policy might allow unethical or illegal decisions to be taken, reasonable care must be taken in drafting it. Failing to take such care could amount to fault or negligence at the hospital level, which, as mentioned in the previous chapter in relation to hospitals' failing to provide pain-relief treatment, is sometimes referred to as "systems negligence," meaning that the system itself is established or runs in a negligent way. This important concept can sometimes be used to sue for damages on the basis of negligence, which might be the only way to remedy what can appear, at first, to be minor problems that patients face in a hospital setting, but that can be a source of grave suffering for people.

Let me describe two cases brought to me by distressed families. Both involved elderly, dying women. One woman was kept for four days in a busy emergency-room corridor that was lit twenty-four hours a day. She died with no privacy or peaceful or tranquil space to share with her loved ones. In another case, a very elderly woman was placed in a shared room with a man, a situation she and her family found deeply distressing. This woman had never been in bed in a room in which a man other than her husband or a physician was present. She also died without this situation being remedied. Her family is still traumatized by the disrespect they believe was shown to their dying mother, the suffering this caused her and by the fact that they were powerless to correct the situation. In both these cases, cost constraints or aims of maximizing efficiency were almost certainly the reasons the hospital system operated as it did. But we must retain our sensitivity to breaches of ethics—and law—in such circumstances, especially because those breaches become more likely with cost constraints. The individual healthcare professionals in each of these cases were not in breach of any duty to the patient. It is not nearly as clear that the same is true of the hospital in relation to its duty to run a non-negligent system.

In the *Krausz* case, the hospital's clinical ethics committee was consulted by the physicians at the time the conflict with the family arose. These committees are a last-quarter-of-the-twentieth-century phenomenon, and their role in hospitals is still an emerging one. There are two kinds of ethics committees: clinical ethics committees and research ethics committees. These committees are similar in their memberships and the processes they use but advise on different areas of medical practice.

An ethics committee must be properly constituted and use acceptable procedures from both ethical and legal points of view. Among the requirements are that the members have a range of expertise; in particular, there should be at least one member with expertise in ethics. They must not have a conflict of interest with respect to the cases on which they are consulted. People who are not employees of the hospital should be included as members to avoid decisions being taken primarily in the "best interests" of the hospital, for instance, in order to save resources or to avoid potential lawsuits and legal liability. The members must be physically present at the meetings. And adequate records of the discussions and recommendations should be kept.

These requirements might seem so obvious as to not need articulation. But in the past it has not been uncommon for hospitals' research ethics committees to hold corridor or telephone meetings in reviewing research protocols. These are not acceptable for several reasons. First, if the members never meet, they do not hear one another's views. Moreover, decision-making can involve one person telephoning each of the others and reporting, for instance, that so far all members agree with a certain outcome. This approach can result in pressure that affects the outcome. Second, now that modern communications technology makes it possible for us to communicate instantly at great distances, I believe we will learn that face-to-face communication in one another's physical presence has important elements that are not present outside this setting. For instance, in order for our moral intuition and emotional responses to function appropriately, we may need to be in one another's physical presence. Third, the keeping of minutes of ethics committee meetings can affect both the decisions taken at any particular meeting and future decisions. People might decide differently if their views are being recorded, and these records can be used as precedents. Finally, such requirements are not only ethically relevant: If ethics committees act negligently, they can be held legally liable for doing so. Negligence occurs when an ethics committee fails to live up to the standard of care that a reasonably careful and competent ethics committee would live up to in the same circumstances.

The rules governing access to ethics committees can make them more or less available to different people. Mr. Krausz's sons spoke to one member of the ethics committee who tried to diffuse the conflict between them and the physicians. There was, however, no formal consultation. Whether patients and their representatives should have access to an ethics committee has been a contentious issue. Healthcare professionals have been concerned about this complicating both their relationships with patients and their and their patients' decisions concerning care and treatment. These healthcare professionals believe that making decisions about medical treatment is already complex and this would just add to the complexity. They have also worried that the process might become adversarial. Many people believe, however, that patients should be able to have access to an ethics committee and, certainly, if the patient's case has been referred to a committee by a healthcare professional, it would only seem right that the patient could have input to the deliberations and be told of the outcome and the basis on which the committee structured its advice.

In the *Krausz* case, one of the physicians who was in conflict with the Krausz sons was the co-chair of the hospital's clinical ethics committee, and the other co-chair and several members were on holidays. Consequently, no meeting was held. The treating physician telephoned his co-chair at Cape Cod and explained the situation as he saw it and what he proposed to do, and the co-chair agreed. The latter made it clear to the inquest, however, that he did not consider this to be a formal consultation but was trying to be helpful in assisting his colleague to deal with a deeply distressing situation for everyone involved. As the coroner found, in such situations arm's-length, structured and established procedures are needed.

If there is conflict between a patient (or the patient's family, especially if the patient is not competent) and the physician, the ethics committee may be called in as a mediator. The coroner in the *Krausz* case proposed this approach. It is not likely to be straightforward to implement, however. On what basis should the committee mediate? For example, should they give priority to the patient's values or the physician's views? What may they take into account and what must they not take into account? It is also important to understand the usual impact of the outcome of a consultation with an ethics committee. The committee's recommendations are not binding, they are merely advisory. If the committee was to act as a mediator or conciliator, would its decisions be more than advisory? If so, what would be their status?

A hospital needs a clear policy on how disputes between a physician and a patient should be handled, and this policy must comply with ethics and law, especially the requirements of due process (a fair hearing by an impartial person). An ethics committee may fulfil this function. But if the conflict cannot be resolved to the satisfaction of everybody, the appropriate approach is to maintain the status quo with respect to continuing treatment and to ask a court to make a ruling on how the situation should be handled. This, in my opinion, is what should have occurred in Mr. Krausz's case.

The Krausz case involved yet a further tragedy. During the coroner's enquiry, one of the physicians who had treated Mr. Krausz suffered a

174   cardiac arrest and died in the courtroom. In the difficult, conflictual circumstances in which any of us, whether as patients, families or healthcare professionals, can sometimes find ourselves, we do well to remember that we are all human and we are all vulnerable.

7. Pushing Parents to the Sidelines

The Ethics of Imposing Treatment
on Seriously Ill Children

T he case of Tyrell Dueck opens up some of the most difficult issues we face in the everyday practice of ethics and law in a medical context.

In late 1998, Tyrell Dueck, a thirteen-year-old Saskatchewan boy, was diagnosed with osteosarcoma, the same disease that caused the death of Terry Fox. (Fox was a courageous young man who, despite losing his leg to cancer, set out on a run across Canada to raise money to fight the disease and became a national hero in doing so. He died before he could complete his run.) Osteosarcoma has a high mortality rate. Tyrell's parents, who are deeply religious Christians, had serious doubts about conventional medical treatment, including chemotherapy, and refused it for Tyrell. The doctors who wanted to treat Tyrell with chemotherapy went to court in December 1998, seeking an order to authorize this treatment.

Before a court can displace parents as decision-makers for their children, it must find that the child is neglected or abused and in need of protection. Under the Child and Family Services Act of Saskatchewan, failure to provide a child with necessary medical care, when this endangers the child's life or health, is child neglect. The court can then name a person to replace the parents as the decision-maker about medical treatment for their child. The court ruled that Tyrell was a child in need of protection and granted the Minister of Social Services a nine-month supervisory order, and the authority to consent to the treatment and care of Tyrell. The minister was also given the authority to carry out the directions and recommendations given by the healthcare professionals at Royal University Hospital and Saskatoon Cancer Clinic who were treating Tyrell. As would be expected, the Duecks, who are loving and caring parents, were deeply distressed by this order and by the fact that it was based on a finding that they were guilty of child neglect in doing what they firmly believed to be best for their son.

Three months later, after three cycles of a first course of chemo-therapy and two cycles of a second course, the doctors recommended surgery to amputate Tyrell's leg. Tyrell's parents wanted to take him to a centre in Mexico, where he could be treated with diet, herbs and multivitamins. As the court subsequently records in its judgment, Tyrell told the pediatric oncologist "he didn't want any more chemotherapy and he didn't want to have surgery. He believed that God had healed him." The physician treating Tyrell knew that chil-dren may legally refuse treatment, and he was uncertain whether he should abide by Tyrell's refusal of treatment. In March 1999, the physician again went to court, this time asking it to decide whether he should respect Tyrell's refusal of surgery to have his leg amputated.

The court held that Tyrell's physicians were "not required to obtain Tyrell's own consent to or to accept any refusal [of treatment] he may give. The granting of consent lies squarely with his guardian, who in this case is the Minister of Social Services." In other words, the court held that, legally, Tyrell could not consent to or refuse treatment for himself and neither could his parents. Rather, the decision about his medical treatment rested solely with the Minister of Social Services, who had been appointed by the court as Tyrell's guardian for the purposes of making decisions about Tyrell's medical treatment.

Tyrell's cancer progressed and, prior to any surgery, his physicians at the Saskatoon Cancer Clinic decided that further treatment would be of no avail. His parents took him to Mexico, where he was treated. Afterwards, he returned home to Saskatchewan. Tyrell died in June 1999. We cannot know whether the short delay caused by the need for the physicians to obtain the court's authorization before surgery could be undertaken, because Tyrell and his parents had refused it, contributed to his death, but it seems highly unlikely.

There are no more difficult cases, including ethically and legally, than those involving critically ill or dying children. We must approach these cases on an individual basis and analyze them with the utmost care and sensitivity, taking into account a full range of relevant factors. These include the child's age, experience, intelligence, independence from his parents and the reasons he gives for refusing the treatment. We must also consider the nature of the illness from which the child is suffering and whether or not it is life threatening, how likely treatment is to be effective and the suffering that the treatment involves. We protect the lives and health of children, but we must take care not to intervene when doing so would inflict serious suffering not compensated for by the promise of adequate benefits. For instance, in treating children dying of cancer, we can find it difficult to accept that there is nothing that we can do to prevent their death and can sometimes over-treat them. In other words, we can, in these circumstances, lose a proper perspective on the suffering/benefit ratio of the treatment given to the child. We can also lose a proper perspective on the suffering-relief/risk ratio of the treatments we choose not to give to children. For example, recent research has shown that children dying of cancer receive inadequate treatment for symptoms of serious

178   physical distress—such as pain, breathlessness and vomiting—because of a fear that the treatment could "harm" them.

Second, we must start from a presumption that parents have the right to decide matters such as medical treatment for their children, but recognize that this right is not absolute. The right to refuse treatment for a child is not necessarily of the same scope as that of an adult deciding for himself or herself. The scope of what one can consent to or refuse for oneself as a competent adult is much broader than what one can consent to or refuse for a child in one's care and custody. A competent adult's right to refuse medical treatment for any reason at all is almost absolute, and competent adults can consent to non-therapeutic interventions (for instance, cosmetic surgery), provided these interventions do not contravene public policy. (Public policy is a doctrine used by the courts to set limits on the exercise of certain liberties. For instance, in our society while a competent adult's decision to have a nose job is not seen as contravening public policy, the same adult's decision to have their leg or their arm amputated, when there is no medical reason to do so, would be. Consequently, in contrast with the nose job, the amputation could not be validated by that adult's informed consent.) Parents may not, in general, however, consent to non-therapeutic interventions on their children. (This is why routine infant male circumcision, which is discussed in the next chapter, is raising ethical and legal difficulties.)

Parents' rights to decide on medical treatment for their children are derived from their obligation to provide the medical treatment that their children need to protect their lives and health. This right rests on the presumption that parents will protect their children's welfare and act in their "best interests." For a variety of reasons, including religious beliefs, however, parents can refuse treatment for their children, even if medical professionals and others regard the treatment as essential to protect the children's health or life. How should such refusals be handled?

In circumstances where serious harm could result from following a parent's decision, clearly the child must be protected. When such decisions are, from an objective point of view, contrary to the child's "best interests" in a way that would result in serious risk or harm to the child, the presumption that the parents are acting in the child's "best interests" is rebutted, which means that the parents can lose their right to decide for the child. In such a situation, when a court overrides parents' decisions concerning their children, they are fulfilling a responsibility that rests on all of us, as a society, to protect children who are in danger and unable to protect themselves.

But before a court or a government agency acts, it must be certain it is justified in interfering and not simply meddling in the private affairs of citizens, particularly in relation to their most important intimate relationships, which include those with their children. Moreover, even when we are justified in intervening, we have ethical obligations to do the least harm possible, especially in circumstances that are already very traumatic, as is always true in situations that involve seriously ill children.

In cases such as Tyrell Dueck's, an alternative to using child protection legislation, which avoids the stigma this involves, would be for courts to rely on their *parens patriae* power. This very ancient inherent power of superior courts, inherited from the sovereign, to look after those people unable to look after themselves, has been increasingly used of late to deal with some of the challenging dilemmas faced within a modern medical context. In the past, when medicine could do little to help, there was much less need to be concerned about people refusing treatment for those who were unable to decide for themselves. Now there is much more that we can do medically, and we have a much more extensive understanding of the causes of harm—including to fetuses or children—and ways in which this harm can be avoided. As a result, more and more frequently, we must decide whether we should intervene to impose medical treatment in order to protect those who are unable to protect or decide for themselves, when the person who has the authority to decide refuses the treatment.

One of the situations raising the greatest controversy is whether we should ever intervene on a pregnant woman in order to protect the fetus to which she intends to give birth. The case of Ms. G., which was mentioned in Chapter 2, provides a good example. Ms. G., a young Manitoba woman, was five months pregnant with her fourth child and addicted to glue-sniffing, which can damage the nervous system of a fetus. Two of her children had suffered brain damage caused by her addiction and yet she was continuing to sniff glue during this pregnancy. She had sought treatment for her addiction, but was told that all the treatment facilities were full. There was a very public debate across Canada about whether the court could and should order Ms. G. to be compulsorily hospitalized for the duration of her pregnancy in order to protect her unborn child.

The Manitoba Court of Queen's Bench ruled that under its *parens patriae* power, it could order Ms. G. into custody for this purpose. The Manitoba Court of Appeal reversed the trial court on the basis that the existing law did not support the order. The Supreme Court of Canada, with two dissents, upheld the Court of Appeal judgment. The majority ruled that the fetus was not a person in the eyes of the law; therefore, the *parens patriae* power did not apply to the fetus to give the court jurisdiction to protect it. *Parens patriae* was not available in relation to Ms. G. either, because she was not an incompetent person. Thus there was no basis on which the court could intervene in this case.

The two judges in dissent ruled that the *parens patriae* power could be used. These judges held that the rule that a fetus must be born alive before it had any legal rights was simply an "evidentiary presumption rooted in rudimentary medical knowledge." In non-legal language this means that historically the law chose not to recognize the fetus as a person with legal rights because to do so would be to open up many difficulties for the courts. These included difficulties regarding proof of causation and of damage to a fetus that was stillborn, or born injured, as a result of the action of another person who was sued with respect to the injuries the fetus had sustained. But modern medicine can answer questions of what might have caused certain injuries to a fetus. Therefore, it no longer made sense, the dissenting judges reasoned, to retain and apply this presumption that the fetus had no legal rights— **181** and, consequently, could not be protected by the law—where to do so would be to allow serious damage to continue to be inflicted on a fetus.

Not surprisingly, this case generated great public controversy. When, if ever, are courts justified in breaching the rights of a pregnant woman in order to protect the fetus? The answers are neither easy nor simple. Even those who want to protect the fetus recognize that we must assess the overall impact of allowing courts to intervene. Would it mean that high-risk pregnant women would be frightened to seek help, especially medical treatment, for fear they might be involuntarily hospitalized? The case should also make us aware that as a society we have ethical obligations to provide the care—whether medical care, addiction treatment or other social supports—that would make situations such as those Ms. G. faced less likely to occur. Even if we believe in compulsory treatment of women in situations similar to those of Ms. G., ethically this treatment must be a last resort. We are not fulfilling our ethical obligations as a society when—as was true for Ms. G.—treatments for conditions that could harm the fetus are not reasonably available to pregnant women who seek them.

Should challenges to parents' refusals of medical treatment for their children be handled through court cases? Because each case has to be decided on its own facts, taking into account all the relevant circumstances and by an unbiased, independent decision-maker with the authority to implement the decision taken, traumatic as it is for the family and the child, this often requires court hearings. But could the trauma of these hearings be reduced? For instance, Ontario legislation prohibits publication of the name of the child. It also requires that the child have independent legal representation. These restrictions help ensure a full and fair hearing of the issues, especially from the perspective of the child's "best interests."

In a case in Montreal, in early 2000, an HIV-positive mother refused conventional medical treatment for her two HIV-positive minor children. Her wishes were overruled by the Quebec Superior

Court. In order to reduce trauma to the children and their mother as much as possible, in contrast to the Tyrell Dueck case, the court did not reveal the names of either the children or their mother, and the judgment was sealed to protect their privacy. Some details of the ruling were provided, however, through a press release prepared on the mother's behalf by an advocacy group, the International Council for Medical Justice, who had argued against treating the children with conventional medical therapy.

This press release stated that the court ruled that just because the mother refused "combination cocktail treatment for AIDS" for her children did not mean that she was an unfit mother. The judge also ruled that the mother could take into account "dissenting medical thought concerning the treatment of HIV-positive persons" in deciding about therapy for her children. This alternative treatment was also a relevant consideration for the court to take into account in deciding whether to take away the mother's right to make decisions about medical treatment for her children. The judge declined, however, to return the children to the care of the mother, citing her decision to treat the children with homeopathic and natural remedies as opposed to treatment with "strictly Western medicine" as the reason. The mother was allowed to retain legal custody of the two children, but they were placed in the care of their maternal grandparents. Authority for medical decision-making for the children was vested in the Office of Youth Protection Services in Quebec. In this way, the mother's legal rights regarding her children were invaded only to the strict extent necessary to provide medical treatment for them. Several months after this ruling, the mother disappeared with her children after visiting them at their grandparents' home. Although the police issued news bulletins in their search for her and the children, no announcements have been made to say whether they have been found.

One of the most common reasons that parents reject medical treatment for their child is that the treatment is at odds with the parents' religious beliefs. In the *Sheena B.* case, the Supreme Court of Canada in 1995 made it clear that parents cannot, on the basis of their religious beliefs, put the health or life of their child in danger. In that case, the parents, who were Jehovah's Witnesses, refused a blood transfusion for their baby. Sheena B. was born four weeks prematurely and had many physical ailments. When she was a month old her haemoglobin level (the red cells in her blood that carry oxygen) had dropped to such an extent that the treating physicians believed her life was in danger. She might have needed a blood transfusion to treat potentially life-threatening congestive heart failure or during exploratory surgery to diagnose infantile glaucoma. The Ontario Provincial Court (Family Division) found Sheena to be a "child in need of protection" and made her a ward of the Toronto Children's Aid Society, which thereby had the authority to consent to a blood transfusion for her. Sheena received a blood transfusion during the operation for the suspected glaucoma. In both Sheena B.'s and Tyrell Dueck's cases, child welfare legislation was used to take the right to make decisions about medical treatment for their child from the parents.

Sheena's parents challenged this legislation on the basis that it infringed their rights under the Canadian Charter of Rights and Freedoms. The Supreme Court considered the parents' rights to refuse medical treatment for their child under the right to liberty in section 7 of the Charter and right to freedom of religion and conscience as guaranteed under section 2a of the Charter. The judges varied in their reasoning, but all concluded that neither the parents' right to liberty, which includes freedom to raise their children according to their beliefs and values, nor their right to freedom of religion, allowed the parents to refuse the transfusion.

Three of the judges reasoned that an exercise of parental liberty that seriously endangers the life of a child falls outside any liberty right of the parents. The child's right to life takes precedence, and an exercise of parental beliefs that grossly invades a child's "best interests" is not protected by the right to liberty. The judges also held that parents' freedom of religion does not include the right to impose religious practices that threaten the safety, health or life of their child. They made the point that although freedom of belief may be broad, the freedom to act upon these beliefs is considerably narrower. Moreover, although the parents argued that their freedom of conscience was infringed by giving others the power to consent to a blood transfusion for their child, some of the judges made the point that the child's right to freedom of conscience included the right to live long enough to make her own reasoned choice about the religion she wished to follow or to decide that she did not want to hold a religious belief. In summary, the child's right to life and security of her person overrode her parents' right to freedom of religion. The state was therefore justified in infringing the parents' right to freedom of religion in enacting the child welfare legislation that allowed a court to take decision-making authority concerning medical treatment for their child away from the parents and give it to some other person or body who could then consent to the child receiving a blood transfusion. Note that the court does not order a blood transfusion (or other medical treatment) for the child. Rather, it gives someone other than the parents the right to decide about the treatment. The courts almost always adopt such an approach in these cases.

THE SITUATION CAN BE different, however, for competent minors acting on the basis of their own religious beliefs, even when these beliefs are the same as the parents'. Courts have recognized, for instance, the right of a seriously ill Jehovah's Witness teenager with leukemia to refuse a blood transfusion even if the physician considered it necessary to prolong or save his life. But the question of whether children, especially teenagers, can consent to or refuse medical treatment is complex, as Tyrell Dueck's case shows. Historically, in the law, children were the property of their father, and in a patriarchal system, the father made all the decisions for his children. In this same system, physicians often acted as a *pater familias* to their patients. In most cases even competent adults simply accepted the treatment physicians proposed. Now, through the doctrine of informed consent, the right of competent adults to refuse medical treatment is almost absolute in Canada.

The ethics and law that govern minors' rights to decide about medical treatment are derived from the principles and concepts governing the rights of competent adults to consent to or refuse treatment. We must first understand this "adult context" in exploring the borderline situation in which we must draw a line between those minors who may consent to and refuse treatment for themselves and those minors who may not.

The doctrine of informed consent is used to decide whether a person's consent is legally valid. Informed consent has three major elements: competence, information and voluntariness. I will deal with information and voluntariness first, because they were less of a problem in Tyrell's case than competence.

In order to give an informed consent, people must be given all the information that would be material to a reasonable person in the same circumstances. This information must include the harms, risks, benefits and potential benefits of the proposed treatment, of each of its alternatives, and of refusing all treatment. The physician must disclose any other information that he or she knows or ought to know would be material to this patient, including answering all the patient's questions fully and honestly. Many medical malpractice cases involve patients suing physicians because it is believed that the physician failed to disclose all the information to which the patient was entitled and which the physician had a legal obligation to disclose. These patients claim that, as a result, they made decisions about treatment that harmed them, and that they would not have made if they had had all the required information. These malpractice actions allege that the physician's failure to disclose information means that the patients' informed consent to treatment was not obtained and that this amounts to negligence for which they should be compensated.

Voluntariness requires the patient's decision to be free of coercion and what the law calls "undue influence and duress." Voluntariness can raise some difficult issues. It can sometimes be difficult to draw the line between factors that influence all of us and would not be regarded as affecting the voluntariness of our decisions, and factors that are considered unacceptably influential. These unacceptable factors can be either outside the person (extrinsic), or inside the person (intrinsic). For instance, extrinsic coercion would be present and the resulting decision would not be voluntary if someone put a gun to a man's head to make him consent. Could the strong influence Tyrell's father had over him be regarded as an extrinsic coercive factor? Intrinsic coercive factors are more difficult to judge. In Tyrell Dueck's case, we might ask whether the religious beliefs his parents had encouraged him to adopt were an unacceptably coercive factor in his decision to refuse treatment.

Competence is a much-debated, complex and often difficult-to-apply legal doctrine. First, the law recognizes two kinds of competence: legal competence and factual competence. All adults are legally competent unless a court has declared them incompetent; all minors are legally incompetent unless they are emancipated minors. In the past, the decision about whether people were able to consent to or refuse their own medical treatment was based just on legal competence. As we became more sensitive to people's rights to autonomy and self-determination, the law developed a more sensitive and nuanced doctrine of factual competence. People are now considered competent to make decisions concerning their own person if they have the capacity to perform the function to which the assessment of competence is relevant. For instance, people who have been declared legally incompetent can still be factually competent to consent to or refuse medical treatment if they can understand the nature and consequences of a proposed treatment, its risks, harms and benefits and those of its alternatives. The informed consent to or refusal of treatment of such factually competent people is valid. So the law has recognized that, to the largest extent possible, people should be able to decide for themselves what happens to their own bodies.

Treating legally incompetent but factually competent adults as competent to decide for themselves about medical treatment has a parallel in situations involving the rights of minors, who are also legally incompetent but often can be factually competent. The law has increasingly recognized that factually competent minors should be **187** able to make their own decisions concerning medical treatment. Until recently, minors were considered legally incompetent unless they were emancipated—that is, they had married, joined the army or were living independently. The day before the minor's age-of-majority birthday, the minor had no legal rights. The next day the minor was presumed to be competent (as, legally, all adults in Canada are until the contrary is established) and had all the rights of a competent adult. Gradually, with the recognition of children's rights, this black-and-white rule changed, and the approach now taken by both ethics and law is that capacities, competencies and rights gradually accrue to children as they mature, particularly when the decisions to which these are relevant concern the child's person and physical or mental integrity. The law implements this approach through what is called the "mature minor" doctrine.

Until the Tyrell Dueck case, it was on the whole presumed that in taking this approach the law was treating a factually competent minor as a mature minor. The court's decision in that case, however, opened up the possibility that while factual competence is necessary for a child to be judged a mature minor, it may not be sufficient. And minors who are not classified as mature probably cannot decide for themselves about treatment, even if they are factually competent. Let me explain.

Tyrell Dueck's factual competence depended on his being able to understand the risks, harms, potential benefits and benefits of the treatment that was proposed, of its alternatives, and of no treatment at all. The judge heard evidence from two expert witnesses, a psychologist and a child psychiatrist, who had interviewed Tyrell and his parents. On the basis of their evidence, the judge ruled that Tyrell Dueck was not able or entitled to make his own decisions. He did "not appreciate and understand that if he discontinues his chemotherapy and refuses surgery, he will die within a year from the spreading cancer."

What can we learn from this ruling? First, the law sometimes distinguishes between understanding certain information and appreciating that information. Which of these is required to find that a person is competent can make a difference to the outcome. Some people suggest that understanding requires only that we cognitively understand the information; they say, therefore, that our emotional response to the information is irrelevant in determining competence. Others argue that we need to understand and appreciate the information and that the word *appreciate* means that our emotional response to the information is a relevant consideration in assessing whether we are competent. Another way to describe the difference between these two views is that understanding requires only cognitive competence, whereas appreciation requires emotional competence as well. In general, the law looks only to cognitive competence. There are good reasons for doing so. The more demanding we make the test of competence (and requiring emotional competence as well as cognitive competence is a more demanding test of competence), the greater the number of people who will be found to be incompetent, with the result that more people will have their wishes concerning themselves overridden.

To give a specific example, there is debate about the degree to which one has to appreciate the nature of one's illness and the relevance of possible treatments in order to be found competent. A stringent test of competence would require a reasonably high or high degree of appreciation; in contrast, a personal-liberty-favouring test would not. Under the latter type of test, people would be considered competent if they had the mental capacity to understand the required disclosure of information, regardless of how they viewed this information in relation to their illness. Under this test, adults would be competent even if they did not believe that they suffered from the illness with which they had been diagnosed, or that the consequences of refusing treatment might be serious or fatal. The test of competence used by the law is nearer to the one based on understanding than that based on appreciation, at least when one is an adult. Unless the patient's emotional state means that he or she is unable to understand the required information, it is not usually taken into account in determining competence. Certainly, adults are not required to be emotionally mature before they are held to be competent.

Let's return to the judge's holding that Tyrell Dueck did "not appreciate and understand" that he would die within a year if he discontinued his chemotherapy and refused surgery. First, it is not clear if the judge ruled that this lack of appreciation on Tyrell's part arose from Tyrell's lack of capacity or competence, or from his lack of information concerning the treatment or its refusal. But to the extent that she was ruling on Tyrell's capacity and, therefore, competence, the judge seems to have applied a more stringent test than would normally be applied to adults. In other words, she was saying that in order to be held factually competent, a minor, unlike an adult, must not only understand but also appreciate the relevant information. Alternatively, the judge might have been holding that in order to be adjudged a mature minor as compared with just a competent one, the minor must be able to both understand and appreciate the information he is given. I believe that the court was correct in applying this test, even if it would not be applied to an adult. Thus, legally, in order to be able to consent to or to refuse medical treatment, a minor must be both competent and mature. This means that a minor must meet a more demanding standard than an adult. While we should err on the side of respect for liberty when adults make decisions about medical treatment that seem to be clearly contrary to protecting their life or health, we should err on the side of protection when children make similar decisions for themselves.

Sometimes competence and rationality are confused. They are separate factors: Because a patient makes an irrational decision does not necessarily mean that the patient is incompetent. And physicians must respect the irrational decision of a competent adult patient. Physicians are, however, much more likely to question—as they should—the competence of patients who make irrational decisions. Minors who make irrational decisions concerning medical treatment are very unlikely to be characterized as mature and, therefore, their irrational refusal of medical care would not be legally binding. Characterizing a decision as irrational is, however, a value judgment. This means that we must be careful to analyze the values that are in conflict in such cases and to ensure that we are justified in giving priority to the ones we choose to uphold.

When the patient and healthcare providers agree on a treatment decision, competence is not usually an issue. Indeed, physicians' decisions about patients' competence are strongly influenced by whether or not the patient agrees with what the physician thinks should be done. Patients who agree with the physician are usually found to be competent; those who disagree are much more likely to be found to be incompetent. One case on which I was consulted provides a striking example in this regard.

A middle-aged homeless man was admitted to a large university teaching hospital. The physicians found that he had a very advanced cancer eating away the top part of his arm. They wanted to amputate. He refused. From time to time, however, especially when a nurse spent time and effort trying to persuade him to agree to the surgery, he would change his mind and agree. Later he would again refuse. His medical chart showed, in the physician's writing: "Patient refuses surgery: Lacks understanding. Incompetent"; "Patient agrees to surgery: Lucid and competent."

Although children's functional competence gradually increases with age, a court has only two choices in deciding on a child's competence. The alternatives fall at opposite ends of the spectrum: It is clear that young babies are not factually competent; and in the vast majority of cases it is often also clear that young people, months away from their eighteenth birthdays, are factually competent. The judge ruled that Tyrell Dueck, as a thirteen-year-old with his particular life experience, should be classified with the babies. But whether she did this because he was not competent or, rather, not mature or found his refusal of treatment invalid for some other reason is an open question.

The judge found that Tyrell was not a mature minor because he was "a boy deeply under the influence of his father, [and] . . . his father's influence will continue to play a large part in Tyrell's decision-making." Moreover, Tyrell did "not appreciate or understand the medical treatment he requires," because his father was "screening the medical information" and because "the information his father gives him is wrong." While these are all valid concerns in assessing the validity of a minor's informed consent to or refusal of treatment, unless very carefully spelled out and applied, they could lead to confusion in deciding what factors should be considered when assessing the validity of such a consent or refusal. If Tyrell could not understand the information required to be provided, he was incompetent. If he had the capacity to understand, even if he did not use it, Tyrell was competent. But, depending on one's definition of a mature minor—that is, whether it requires only competence or something more—he may not have been a mature minor.

The approach taken by the judge could also cause competence to be confused with the other requirements for a valid informed consent, namely, disclosure of the required scope of information and voluntariness of the minor's decision. Unlike incompetence, these defects can in some cases be remedied by offering information or creating conditions that mean the requirements for voluntariness of the decision will be fulfilled. If these defects in consent are not corrected, the minor's decision will be invalid, just as it would be were he incompetent. If the problem with Tyrell's refusal of treatment was not lack of competence but lack of information, the remedy was to provide the information, not to deem him incompetent. The child psychiatrist who appeared as an expert witness for the Dueck family had, as the judge states in her ruling, "advised the court that Tyrell has the capacity to give his own consent, but is not able to give an informed consent today . . . because [he] . . . does not have the accurate information so that he could provide an informed consent." It is not clear whether the judge accepted this expert evidence, but she did not find that Tyrell lacked the capacity to understand the required disclosure of information.

The judge was also concerned that Tyrell's decision to refuse treatment was not his own, but merely a recitation of his father's decision. If the problem was lack of voluntariness, then that should have been identified as the factor invalidating Tyrell's decision. If this influence could be neither abated nor neutralized, Tyrell's refusal of treatment could indeed be deemed invalid. But such grounds are not the same as a lack of capacity or competence. In other words, it is not clear whether the reason that Tyrell Dueck's refusal of treatment was not accepted by the judge was that she found he lacked competence, or information, or the freedom to make a voluntary choice—or all three. Certainly, however, the judge seems to have decided that these deficiencies kept him from being regarded as a mature minor. It is important for courts to be clear about the reasons for their findings because we must understand them in order to interpret the judgment correctly and because these reasons often form the precedents that we rely on in the future.

Another broader issue is raised by the judge's focus on Tyrell's maturity. She stated that "while Tyrell is age thirteen, he is less mature than average thirteen year old children in Saskatchewan. This immaturity is a result of Tyrell's social experiences being within the context of his family and his church." This raises the question: How should we assess a minor's maturity? Are there requirements, beyond being able to give a free and informed consent, that must be fulfilled before the law will regard a minor as mature for its purposes?

In our turn-of-the-millennium secular societies, a young person's maturity is often assessed by how autonomous, independent, self-determined and individualistic that person is. On these criteria, a child from a family such as the Duecks' is unlikely to be found sufficiently mature to be held competent to consent to or to refuse treatment. As the judge stated: Tyrell never

discussed his illness with anyone other than his family. . . . His father makes all the rules [which] are jointly enforced by both parents, but they are not negotiable. Tyrell said he had never broken a rule, and would not speculate what would happen if a rule were broken....The Dueck family structure was consistent with their Christian principle, that is, parents are to direct the

affairs of the children and children are to obey their parents. Mr.
Dueck . . . [said] that he could control Tyrell's behaviour with
just a glance. Tyrell could not give an example of any occasion
where he disobeyed his parents.

On the basis of this evidence, one might decide that Tyrell had been
highly socialized by his parents, by their family structure and by the
religion to which they belong, and that he was very mature in comparison to children who run away from home, live on the streets,
engage in prostitution and are dependent on drugs. Yet this latter
group of children would almost certainly be held to be mature
minors, able to give their own consent to medical treatment, although
their refusals of treatment might not be accepted in situations where
there was a serious threat to their life or health.

The existence of these two radically opposed ways of interpreting
whether Tyrell's personal and family characteristics show that he is
mature or immature provides two insights. First, it shows that decisions about a minor's maturity are based on values and that sometimes people's values conflict. Second, it should make us aware that
the legal system—like all systems—reflects a certain set of values and
that these values can cause an inherent bias in the system. This bias is
usually unavoidable—at the public policy level we must choose
between different values when they conflict—but it remains important to be aware of that bias.

The question, therefore, is when two sets of values conflict in
tragic circumstances such as those in which Tyrell Dueck and his
family found themselves, whose should take priority? The answer in
the case of minors unable to consent for themselves who are found to
be in need of protection (itself a value judgment) is that the values of
the community—as expressed in legislation passed by our elected
representatives and interpreted by the courts—will prevail. People
like the Duecks caught in these situations experience them as the
application of brute force and feel as though they are David facing
Goliath. Just imagine facing the death of your child; being in court

fighting for what you as loving parents believe is best for him; confronting an absolute media barrage, with discussion of your son's case being covered by national television and radio and featured as the subject of national talk-back programs, and even being raised in the legislature. We have ethical obligations to reduce the suffering of people such as the Dueck parents, as far as we are able, even when we are ethically and legally justified—indeed, obliged—to act in a way that will inflict it. While many of us believe this can require imposing treatment, where ethically should we draw the line on media coverage of such a case? Not an easy question to answer, because discussing cases such as Tyrell Dueck's in the "public media square," is an important part of the values-formation process in our society. But we must never forget that these are not theoretical questions. Real people who can be seriously hurt are at their centre, and these people must be treated ethically.

Concepts such as assent and dissent can help us to act ethically towards individuals who are incompetent to make their own decisions concerning medical treatment. A minor (or an adult) who is incompetent to consent to or refuse treatment still might be able to make his or her feelings about the treatment known by expressing assent or dissent. Ethically and legally, one needs very strong justification for acting against a child's (or an incompetent adult's) objections to medical treatment, even if that child (or incompetent adult) does not have the right to refuse the treatment. Taking an incompetent person's assent or dissent into account can matter. Incompetent people are much more likely to be treated with respect if their wishes concerning medical treatment must be taken into account (even though they are not decisive) than if they need not.

It's worth noting that some provinces have legislation that allows minors to consent to their own care and treatment. In Quebec, for instance, a statutory provision allows minors fourteen years of age and over to consent to their own care and treatment but requires that their parents be notified if the minor is hospitalized or extended treatment is necessary. This provision allows minors who have medical conditions they do not want their parents to know about—for instance, those who need contraceptive advice or require treatment for sexually transmitted diseases or addictions—to obtain treatment without parental consent. Unless this were possible, many of these minors would avoid health care. But does this validation of a minor's consent activate a corollary spectrum of rights to refuse treatment? In interpreting the statutory provision, a court would, probably, as the Saskatchewan court did in dealing with Tyrell Dueck's refusal, take into account whether the decision related to a life-threatening situation for the child, and in situations of doubt as to whether the minor's decision should prevail, decide on the basis of a presumption in favour of protection of the minor's life and health.

IN CONSIDERING THE larger issues raised by Tyrell Dueck's case, we should also look at the potential variations of parental and child consent to medical treatment and its refusal. Tyrell and his parents were in agreement, and the physicians disagreed with them. In other cases, a physician and a child have agreed—one case concerned an abortion for a pregnant minor—and the parents, on the basis of their religious beliefs, refused. It is also not uncommon for parents to consent to treatment and for the minor to refuse. Whose decision prevails will depend, in part, on whether the child is a mature minor. But, as the Tyrell Dueck case shows, how a court will decide, when it is turned to in these cases, will also very much depend on the medical facts of the situation. In this context, it is crucial to keep in mind that good facts are essential for good ethics.

Let's assume that a child has a ruptured appendix and will almost certainly die if it is not removed. His parents believe that surgery is an unacceptable treatment and that prayers are the necessary treatment. It would be extremely surprising if a Canadian court did not order surgery in these circumstances. In contrast, if there was only a remote chance, let us say less than 1 percent, that a very invasive treatment would help a child dying of cancer and both the child and the parents refused it, it would be extremely unlikely, in my view, that a court would order it. The problem with Tyrell Dueck's situation was that according to the doctors who gave evidence there was a 65 percent chance the therapy would save his life. Just as Tyrell's age made it difficult to decide if he should be classified with younger or older children, it was difficult to determine if this probability of success, as opposed to one higher or lower, meant that the treatment should be imposed.

Another medical fact that courts often consider in imposing therapy is its nature—in particular, its physical and psychological consequences for the patient. For instance, an appendectomy leaves very little evidence, but an amputation results in a noticeable mutilation, and we rightly recoil from inflicting an unconsented-to mutilation on a minor. We should, however, bear in mind that our strong reactions depend partly on the visibility of our coercive interventions. Those that result in less visible consequences are less objectionable to us. Some people have suggested that we are willing to take a kidney from a consenting person for transplantation into another because we are not constantly made aware of the loss that has occurred. The same would not be true if we took a consenting person's eye for donation to another, which, these people argue, is one reason that everyone is appalled at the thought of doing so. In short, we must fully assess and justify all coercive interventions and not just those that leave a constant physical reminder of what we did or allowed. In a similar vein, we do not react in the same way when the damage is less tangible or, to us, less understandable—as, for instance, is the emotional and spiritual suffering inflicted on a Jehovah's Witness child and the family when the child is given a blood transfusion.

The phenomenon of dis-valuation must also be taken into account when assessing which medical interventions should be authorized against the wishes of minors despite the refusal of their families to consent. If you ask people where they would place, for example, blindness on a scale of zero to minus ten, with minus ten being the worst thing that could happen to them, most sighted people put it at about minus seven to minus eight. On the other hand, blind people put it around minus two. Likewise, recent research shows that although others judge the quality of life of a group of old people to be very low, those same old people do not judge their own quality of life nearly so negatively. In other words, the anticipation of a dread event can be much worse than the actual experience of that event. Such phenomena might be taken into account, with the utmost care, by a court in determining whether to order treatment against an immature minor's wishes and the refusal of consent by his family.

The range of treatments that should be offered to a patient such as Tyrell Dueck is also relevant to whether a court should authorize a certain treatment against the wishes of a child and his parents. One question that needs to be asked in establishing that range is whether specialist care is required. If so, including this care can extend the treatments that should be offered as possible options. Tyrell Dueck had a life-threatening condition and was faced with mutilating surgery, which he and his parents refused. There is no question that he had a right to be offered the range of treatment that a competent orthopaedic oncologist would offer to him in the same circumstances. We need to ask whether there were any other feasible mainstream medical treatments—such as removal of the tumour, bone grafting or artificial knee replacement—that could have avoided amputation. Consideration of possible alternatives is required, not only legally, but also ethically. Ethically, one is required to act in the least harmful, least restrictive, least intrusive way possible, especially in providing treatment imposed as a result of a court order. In other words, even when there is legal justification for overriding the refusal of treatment by both Tyrell and his parents, ethics requires that we do this in the least harmful way possible.

The court also dealt with the parents' and Tyrell's belief that alternative medicine therapy in Mexico, combined with prayer, would heal him. The court found that this course of action did not constitute "recognized medical treatment," which meant that even if it were provided, Tyrell would continue to be a child in need of protection under the Child and Family Services Act, for whom the Minister of Social Services would decide on medical treatment. Some people who have confidence in complementary medicine believe that this finding is in error. What seems clear from the judgment is that the judge relied heavily on a belief in orthodox medicine and a disbelief in complementary medicine, or at least in the particular alternative treatment that Tyrell and his parents wished to pursue. While judges' own value preferences and beliefs unavoidably influence their decisions, again great care needs to be taken to ensure that decisions, such as those involved in Tyrell Dueck's case, reflect community standards. Community standards was a relatively easy rule to apply in the small, homogenous communities of the past. It is much more difficult in the large, pluralistic, multicultural, secular societies of the present. We have rightly adopted a policy of non-discrimination and tolerance towards the values, beliefs and cultures of others. There are times, however, when our obligations to protect those unable to look after themselves—which is, whether rightly or wrongly, how the court saw Tyrell Dueck—require that we set limits on our tolerance.

In the tragic situation of children faced with life-threatening cancer, we need to be very self-aware. In particular, we must be conscious of how our responses are affected by our feelings that children ought not to die and that we ought to be able to prevent such deaths, especially with our modern miracle medicine; our "do something" reaction—that doing something is better than doing nothing; and our focus on the science of medicine, sometimes to the detriment or even exclusion of the art of medicine. We can and need to be healed in many ways, especially through activating our own self-healing mechanisms. These are likely to be damaged if others do not respect our cultural and religious beliefs.

Recent advances in medical research have shown how closely our physical, mental, emotional and spiritual lives are linked, and how complex our psycho-neurobiology is. We no longer believe there is a clear division between mind and body. We know that what affects one often affects the other. We know so much more about some physiological processes than we knew even ten years ago that we now know how much we don't know about them. Included in these are the mechanisms through which the mind and brain affect physical healing and well-being. Factors that can influence healing range from the effect of a belief in our physician as a healer, to the companionship of a loved cat or dog after a heart attack or coronary artery bypass surgery, to healing touch or the prayer of others even if we are not aware of others' efforts on our behalf. We do not need to be religious—although we probably do need to have a sense of the human spirit—to acknowledge the possible contributions of healing factors such as these. We simply need to be open-minded to the incredible complexity of the ways in which nature works, a complexity that very recent genetic and molecular biology research is demonstrating.

Physicians themselves have an important role in helping us to activate our own self-healing mechanisms. Researchers have sometimes referred to the physician's healing effect on us as the true placebo effect (the word *placebo* comes from the Latin for "'I please") to differentiate it from the false placebo effect, which is the use, especially in medical research, of inactive substances that patients are led to believe is an active drug or other treatment. This false placebo effect has been condemned ethically. It is also likely to be in breach of the law, because when deception is present, it usually means that the patient's informed consent to the treatment has not been obtained. (It should be noted that the false placebo effect does not include research in which research subjects have given informed consent to participation in a trial that includes a placebo arm.)

The true placebo effect might, moreover, be much greater than we thought in the recent past. In the distant past, we tended to have more faith in the innate powers of our healers. With modern medicine, some of this faith was transferred to the powers of technology. While technology will, of course, remain very important in providing the most effective medical care and treatment, we may be seeing new recognition of the intrinsic power of the healer. As is true for powerful new technologies, so too for physicians, both things and people that have the power to do great good often have an equal power to do harm. Consequently, it matters what our physicians' attitudes are, especially towards us as patients.

To speak of activating our own self-healing mechanisms is to straddle the border between conventional and complementary (or alternative) medicine. Practitioners on each side of this border have found it uncomfortable to discover themselves in the other's "territory," and conflict has resulted. This attitude seems to be changing, certainly from the side of conventional medicine. As individual professionals and as a profession, practitioners of conventional medicine, while still affirming the need for rigorous scientific standards, are more open these days to recognizing and valuing the contributions of some forms of complementary medicine. The either/or, black-or-white approach to the relation between conventional and complementary medicine is evolving. We can believe in the contribution of both to the overall healing that we need. Indeed, surveys show that large numbers of people demonstrate just this belief, and use both conventional and alternative medicine.

In situations such as the Dueck family faced, we need to be concerned not to further traumatize an already traumatized family and child. The judge's findings that it "is simply cruelty to Tyrell . . . [that] Tyrell has been misguided by his father into placing his hopes for recovery on a cure that does not exist" may, without intending any disrespect to the court, be insensitive and over-simplistic. This is not to say that the court should not have given an order to allow conventional medical treatment to be administered. Rather, the court might not have given enough weight to the beliefs of Tyrell and his family as important elements in his well-being, and possibly prolongation of his life. For instance, would it have been possible to have given Tyrell access to some of the alternative medical treatment that he and his family wanted, while still providing conventional treatment? The judge ordered that "Tyrell Timothy Dueck is to receive his medical treatment without the presence of or influence of his parents." Whether this order was a sufficiently empathetic response depends upon whether it was the only reasonable alternative open to the court in very difficult circumstances for everyone involved, but especially for the Dueck family.

Tyrell Dueck's case raises many important questions. What is the extent of parents' rights to decide about medical treatment for their child? To what extent should we respect parents' religious beliefs when they impinge on decisions concerning medical treatment for their children? What are young people's rights to decide for themselves on medical treatment? What constitutes competence in a minor to consent to or to refuse medical treatment? Does a minor's right to refuse treatment depend just on competence or on being a mature minor, if this has additional requirements? If it does, what are the characteristics that define a mature minor? What should be the relationship between orthodox medicine and alternative medicine? And what are society's obligations to care for children whose life or health is put at risk by their or their parents' refusal of medical treatment?

These questions do not appear dramatic on their face. But most of the situations in which we must answer them involve the profound human tragedy of parents facing the possible death of their child— the situation in which Tyrell Dueck and his family found themselves. Therefore, our responses to these questions as societies, institutions and various kinds of professionals must always be personal, empathetic, sensitive, compassionate and wise. In particular, we must ensure that we do not place "the law" or "medicine" between us and the people, such as the Duecks, who are caught in such a tragedy. There is a serious danger that our horror at the thought that this could happen to me and could be my child, and our need to dis-identify from that possibility, can sometimes cause us as professionals to act in detached—and consequently inhumane—ways.

8. Altering Baby Boys' Bodies

The Ethics of Infant Male Circumcision

f someone asked you what our reactions to human cloning could teach us about the ethics of infant male circumcision, you might think it was a trick question. I was working on speeches on both these topics at more or less the same time and, with some surprise, recognized there was at least one important lesson that cloning would provide in relation to circumcision. When they first hear of human cloning, most people's reaction is "Yuck!" But as familiarity increases, and dread decreases, they move from this rejection and horror to neutrality to acceptance, usually with safeguards, and finally even to positive approval. In contrast, many people's view of infant male circumcision has gone in the opposite direction: from positive approval to rejection and sometimes horror. This is certainly true of my attitude.

When, in the early 1980s, I learned of the practice of female genital mutilation (FGM), I decided to speak against it. (In the past this practice was often referred to as female circumcision.) In its most severe form it involves infibulation-clitorectomy (the removal of the clitoris) and the removal of the outside parts of the genitalia and the reduction of the vaginal opening to a very small aperture. Bettie Malofie, the founder of ETHIC (End the Horror of Infant Circumcision), heard my comments and wrote asking what my position was on infant male circumcision. I replied that I thought it was a minor procedure, a harmless practice that for some people had important religious significance and for others was a matter of tradition. I said it was not a matter of concern. So how did I end up, in 1997, as the subject of a headline on the front page of the *Ottawa Citizen*, the major daily newspaper of Canada's capital, that stated, "CIRCUMCISING BABY BOYS 'CRIMINAL ASSAULT'. ETHICIST SAYS SOCIETY MUST CONSIDER BAN"?

Over the years I have been patiently and respectfully educated by many people who oppose circumcision or genital mutilation of any children. Many factors have combined to change my view and to lead me to conclude that circumcision of baby boys raises important questions of ethics and of law. A major factor was new facts.

As I have noted elsewhere, good ethics depend on good facts, and good law depends on good ethics. The medical facts about infant male circumcision have changed as a result of medical research. We now know that infant male circumcision is harmful in itself and has harmful consequences. Circumcision removes healthy, functioning, erogenous tissue that serves important protective, sensory and sexual purposes. The surgery also involves risks of further damage—ranging from minor to serious damage to the penis or even its loss or death. In one recent American case a baby died from the general anesthetic he was given in order to deal with the complications that had resulted from his circumcision. Some physicians who continue to support routine—that is, non-therapeutic—circumcision argue that its potential medical benefits—which research shows do exist—justify carrying it out on infants. But these potential benefits do not outweigh its harms when the procedure is not medically necessary, which in the vast majority of cases it is not. Moreover, when we look to the nature of the medical benefits cited as a justification for infant circumcision, such as a reduced rate of urinary infections, we can see that medical problems can be avoided or, if they occur, treated in far less traumatic and invasive ways than circumcision.

The most recent claim of a medical benefit from circumcision is a reduction in the risk of contracting HIV infection or other sexually transmitted diseases. The research on which this claim is based is being challenged, but even if it is correct, it would not justify circumcising infant boys. Even assuming that circumcision gave men additional protection from becoming infected with HIV, baby boys do not immediately need such protection and can choose for themselves, at a later stage, if they want it. To carry out circumcision for such a future health protection reason (assuming for the moment that circumcision is protective) would be analogous to testing a baby girl for the gene for breast cancer and, if it is present, trying to remove all her immature breast tissue in order to eliminate the risk of her developing breast cancer as an adult woman. I believe that most of us would be shocked at undertaking such a procedure on a baby girl, but some of us might not have the same reaction to infant male circumcision. Why is this? Quite simply we value breasts—we see it as a serious harm to a woman to lose them—and we do not value foreskins, in fact they are often devalued—spoken of as ugly, unaesthetic and unclean. Yet both are part of the intact human body and both have sexual and other functions. Consequently, to summarize, routine infant male circumcision cannot be ethically and legally justified on the grounds that it is medically required.

A common error made by those who want to justify infant male circumcision on the basis of medical benefits is that they believe that as long as some such benefits are present, circumcision can be justified as therapeutic, in the sense of preventive health care. This is not correct. A medical-benefits or "therapeutic" justification requires that *overall* the medical benefits sought outweigh the risks and harms of the procedure required to obtain them, that this procedure is the only reasonable way to obtain these benefits, and that these benefits are necessary to the well-being of the child. None of these conditions is fulfilled for routine infant male circumcision. If we view a child's foreskin as having a valid function, we are no more justified in amputating it than any other part of the child's body unless the operation is medically required treatment and the least harmful way to provide that treatment.

Another reason to reject infant male circumcision is the pain it causes. In considering their obligation to "first do no harm," physicians must give great weight to one of the most immediate harms of circumcision—it causes pain. Research has shown that we have been insensitive to those who are unable to verbalize their pain, that is, to put their suffering into words. We have carried out procedures on children that would never be carried out on adults without adequate and full anesthesia; as recent research on infant male circumcision has shown, traumatic pain experiences in very young children heighten their pain sensitivity, possibly for life. Research also shows that newborn babies have a unique nervous system that makes them respond to pain differently from adults. As journalist Victoria Mac-Donald, describing the recent research of Maria Fitzgerald, professor of neurobiology at University College, London, reports in London's *Sunday Telegraph*:

Reports in clinical and psychological literature indicate early injury or trauma can have long-term consequences on sensory or pain behaviour that extend into childhood or beyond. . . . Because the spinal sensory nerve cells worked differently in babies, even a simple skin wound at birth could lead to the area becoming hypersensitive to touch long after the wound had healed. By studying these sensory nerve cells in infants the scientists discovered that their reflex to pain or harm is greater and more prolonged than that of adults. The sensory nerve cells are also linked to larger areas of skin, which means they feel pain over a greater area of their body.

People have a fundamental human right not to have pain intentionally inflicted on them and, where pain is unavoidable, to have fully adequate treatment for the relief of that pain. These people include babies and children. Breach of this fundamental human right should be regarded as very serious wrongdoing. Recent medical research, people's own observations and our own experience and common sense show that circumcision is an intensely painful procedure. It is therefore in violation of human rights unless it can be justified in particular cases. One issue is whether adequate pain relief can be obtained with local anesthesia, even a dorsal penile nerve block, or whether general anesthesia would be required to make the surgery involved in infant male circumcision pain-free. In my opinion, a physician would not be ethically or legally justified in administering a general anesthetic for a non-therapeutic intervention on a child who could not himself consent. There is also the question whether adequate pain relief can be obtained after the effects of the anesthetic have worn off. It takes approximately a week for the wound to heal, during which time, apart from other causes of pain, the open wound is in contact with the child's urine. It is, indeed, a harsh welcome to the world.

It is very difficult to believe that a person, especially a physician, could understand the new knowledge about circumcision and believe that it did little or no harm to the baby boys on whom it is carried out. And yet my experience has been that many physicians, especially those who are older and have performed very large numbers of circumcisions, are unwilling to accept this evidence or, it seems, even to give it open-minded consideration. In by far the majority of cases, this resistance is not connected with physicians' own religious beliefs, although it could, of course, be connected with concern that recognizing the harms involved in infant male circumcision could interfere with others' religious beliefs or traditional or cultural practices. This concern probably influences politicians and leaders of medical professional societies. When approached about the ethics and legality of infant male circumcision, they frequently fail to respond. If they do respond, either they state that the practice does not raise any ethical or legal issues or, if they recognize that it does raise these issues, they often justify the practice with statements that are ethically and legally wrong. I have spent many hours replying to letters signed by ministers of justice or of health, or presidents of colleges of physicians and surgeons. In these letters, I give the same arguments that I discuss in this chapter to explain why, in my opinion, they are ethically and legally wrong. Sometimes, I do not receive any reply, but I have found that when I do receive a response, it rarely addresses the ethical and legal issues I have raised and often simply repeats the same statements as those in the letter to which I replied that I argued were wrong. I assume that these statements are made in good faith. Probably the people making them are acting out of a concern not to distress their constituents or members of the colleges who would be deeply dismayed by recognizing the harms involved in infant male circumcision that are not compensated for by medical benefits, and therefore the practice's ethical and legal unacceptability. No doubt they are also dismayed to realize that as parents who consented to routine circumcision, they may have inflicted harm on their sons or, as physicians who carried it out, on other people's sons.

Infant male circumcision is certainly not the first procedure that was once thought to be medically beneficial but was later shown to be harmful. Everything from blood-letting to lobotomies was once considered a standard practice. As medical knowledge about infant male circumcision and, therefore, its medical justification changed, the ethics changed. In future, the application of the law may well change.

SOME PEOPLE BELIEVE THAT in order to make routine infant male circumcision undertaken for other than religious reasons illegal, we would need to change the law. This is not correct. The Criminal

208   Code already prohibits assault, aggravated assault and sexual assault. An assault is any touching of another person that is more than what the law calls *de minimis* (a trifle) without that person's consent. (*De minimis* touchings include those involved in normal social interaction, unless the person touched has objected to them.) Aggravated assault is assault that involves a wounding. Legally, a wounding is constituted by any breaking of the full thickness of the human skin. Consequently, all surgery, including infant male circumcision, could potentially fall within the definition of aggravated assault. Under our present interpretation of the Criminal Code, surgery does not do so, however, in two situations. Surgery is ethically and legally justified when it is necessary therapy undertaken by a competent physician with the informed consent of the patient or the incompetent patient's legal representative. And non-therapeutic surgery that is not contrary to public policy (for example, cosmetic surgery or donation of a paired organ for transplantation) is justified if undertaken with the fully informed consent of the competent adult undergoing it. But some history of how we arrived at this current interpretation of the law is relevant to the debate on the legality of infant male circumcision.

In 1980, I published an article entitled "Medical Interventions and the Criminal Law: Lawful or Excusable Wounding?" in which I looked at the traditional legal justification for surgery—namely, that it was intended to be therapeutic, that it was necessary for the preservation of the health or life of the patient, and that its promised therapeutic benefits outweighed its risks and harms. The article also explored how we could justify cosmetic surgery and surgery carried out on live organ donors, both of which are non-therapeutic. I argued that the informed consent of a competent adult on whom such surgery was carried out could by itself legally justify it, provided in any given case the proposed surgery was not contrary to public policy. (For instance, a person cannot consent to having their leg amputated unless it is required for medical reasons; absent of therapeutic necessity, such an intervention, even if requested and consented to by a competent adult, would be contrary to public policy.) But the justification of "a competent adult's personal informed consent" cannot, of course, by definition apply to an infant or a child. The other legal justification for some non-therapeutic interventions was that they were *de minimis*, that is, a trifle. For instance, piercing the earlobes of girls might fall within this category. According to the old saying "*De minimis non curat lex* (the law does not concern itself with trifles)," such interventions do not give rise to any legal liability.

When I was writing that article, it never occurred to me to consider whether infant male circumcision could be legally justified. If I had done so, I probably would have thought, in keeping with my understanding at the time, that it was either therapeutic and therefore justified, or a *de minimis* intervention. But routine circumcision cannot be classified as therapeutic, and everyone, including people who undertake infant male circumcision as a religious obligation, agree that it is not a *de minimis* intervention. Therefore, the issue is whether infant male circumcision can be legally justified in some other way than by regarding it as therapeutic or *de minimis*. Such an analysis must take into account that respect for the person, respect for the person's rights to physical and mental integrity, and, when the person is competent to decide for himself or herself, respect for the person's rights of autonomy and self-determination, are founding principles in most of our Western societies. They are often expressed in our most important legal instruments, such as constitutions or codes of human rights, and at the international level in treaties, declarations and conventions. Can we reconcile the routine practice of infant male circumcision, other than for reasons of absolute religious obligation, with these fundamental norms? Clearly we cannot. Whether we can reconcile infant male circumcision undertaken for religious reasons is a more complex question that is discussed shortly.

The assault provisions in the current Criminal Code could be used to stop infant male circumcision, but this route is probably neither the most ethical nor the most effective way to approach a situation that involves long-standing, deeply held social, cultural and religious beliefs. In particular, we have to start from a basis of deep respect for religious belief and a requirement of very strong justification for any interference with the expression of this belief.

In May 1997, the Canadian Parliament amended the Criminal Code to include as a specific offence any interference with the genitalia of a female child or adult, except when it was clearly necessary for medical reasons. This provision was aimed at stopping the practice of female genital mutilation. Outside the traditions or cultures that practise female genital mutilation, there is widespread agreement that it should be prohibited, on minors in particular. Unlike some American states, Canada has completely prohibited it, even on consenting adult women. But not everyone agrees with this prohibition. Some people argue that if women can consent to breast augmentation or reduction because they believe that it makes them more sexually attractive, why should they not be allowed likewise to consent to certain alterations of their genitalia? They argue that there is a cultural bias in prohibiting genital mutilation (they also argue that to use the term "mutilation" is to pre-judge the issue) but not breast augmentation. I was once consulted by an obstetrician who had a patient who had previously undergone female genital mutilation. The woman's vaginal opening needed to be cut for the delivery of her baby, and she was extremely upset that the physician was unwilling to restore the infibulation after the delivery. He correctly believed that the medical ethics guidelines governing him prohibited him from doing this, and that probably (unless we argued that the reinstitution of the infibulation was required for the woman's mental health) the new Criminal Code provisions would prohibit it.

Under the Canadian Charter of Rights and Freedoms—as is true under most codes of human rights—discrimination on the basis of sex is prohibited. Legislatures must not pass laws that protect people of one sex but not the other when both are in similar situations. People who oppose infant male circumcision argue that the provision in the Canadian Criminal Code that specifically prohibits genital mutilation only on females is discriminatory in that it protects the "right to security of the person" of girls but not of boys and that this failure to protect boys is unconstitutional. In all likelihood, we will see this issue addressed by the courts in the not too distant future, probably in the context of a man suing a physician on the grounds that in circumcising him as a child, a legal wrong was done to him, and that governmental action, in either formulating or applying the law in such a way that he was not protected, was unconstitutional.

When I spoke out against infant male circumcision, one response that I encountered was an angry reaction from some feminists. They accused me of detracting from the horror of female genital mutilation and weakening the case against it by speaking about it and infant male circumcision in the same context and pointing out that the same ethical and legal principles applied to both. It is true that the harm caused by female genital mutilation is, in most cases, vastly more serious than that caused by infant male circumcision. But the fact that the harm of infant male circumcision is less than that of female genital mutilation does not justify our inflicting this lesser harm.

Using the criminal law to prohibit certain conduct is the strongest statement we can make in our society about the unacceptability of that conduct. One reason we have criminalized female genital mutilation but do not view infant male circumcision in the same context is that we do not perceive the actions and cultural practices with which we are familiar and which we ourselves engage in with the same cultural eye as we view those that are foreign to us. All these practices should be examined through a lens of "first do no harm" and respect for all persons, and we must act ethically in either allowing or prohibiting them.

Physicians who undertake infant male circumcision could be legally liable for medical malpractice (civil liability in battery or negligence), which can result in an award of damages simply for carrying out the circumcision even if it was competently performed. They could also, as explained, be charged with criminal liability for assault. In both ethics and law, a physician has a primary obligation

212   of personal care to the patient. This obligation requires the physician both to place the patient first and to first do no harm. Physicians who undertake surgery on patients must prove that it is justified. The usual justification is that the surgery is necessary therapy and that the patient—or if incompetent, the patient's legal representative— gave informed consent to the surgery. In general, parents cannot authorize non-therapeutic interventions—that is, routine circumcision—on their children. A competent adult man could consent to non-therapeutic circumcision on himself, but this does not mean he may consent to it on his son. If the parents' consent to the circumcision of their son was held to be legally inoperative, the physician would be liable. Moreover, if, in the light of new medical evidence, a reasonably careful and competent physician would not consider it medically necessary to undertake circumcision on a child, to do so could result in legal liability regardless of the parents' consent. Such liability is even more likely if a reasonably careful and competent physician would consider it not just unnecessary but contrary to a reasonable standard of medical care to undertake circumcision on a particular child in given circumstances. A long-recognized example of such a situation is when the child suffers from haemophilia, a condition that could cause him to bleed to death from circumcision. But as our knowledge of the risks and harms of circumcision expands, the range of circumstances in which undertaking routine circumcision on any child is a breach of a reasonable standard of medical care also expands. To summarize, it seems to me clear that, certainly outside the religious context, recent medical research on routine infant male circumcision shows that this operation cannot be ethically or legally justified on the basis of its potential medical benefits.

There has been some confusion about the ethical and legal effect of this lack of a medical justification for routine infant male circumcision, particularly on the part of medical associations who seem to be concerned not to speak out against the practice. For instance, the American Academy of Pediatrics recognizes that the potential medical benefits of this procedure do not outweigh its risks to a degree that it can be recommended to parents as a routine procedure. But they then conclude that the decision about circumcision should be left to the parents in consultation with their physician. In my opinion, this conclusion is wrong both ethically and legally. Unless the potential and actual medical benefits of a surgical intervention on a child unable to consent for himself clearly outweigh its risks (and the academy has found that in the case of routine infant male circumcision they do not), then it cannot be ethically or legally justified just on the basis of the parents' consent and, therefore, the physician must not undertake it unless he or she has some other justification for doing so. The question therefore is how should we balance respect for baby boys' rights to physical integrity and parents' responsibilities and rights with regard to their children and to their freedom of conscience and religion?

Paradoxically, the more global, pluralistic and multicultural our world, the more we need deep respect for religious, cultural and traditional beliefs. As pointed out often in this book, we humans need to feel that we belong, to see ourselves reflected in the eyes of other people and to form community. Although our modern travel and communications technologies have connected us, we feel disconnected; we have lost a sense of community even in our own local area; the extended family has broken down; and new scientific discoveries have left us with a feeling that we are so small and finite in the larger world or vast universe.

When considering infant male circumcision carried out for religious reasons, we must recognize people's rights to belong to a community of faith and to bring their children into this community. Some special factors must also be given great weight. After I first spoke publicly against infant male circumcision, some people in the Jewish community accused me of being anti-Semitic. Other people, including some rabbis, were appalled by these allegations. Much as they did not agree with my position, they were adamant that people must be able to discuss an issue such as infant male circumcision without being accused of anti-Semitism. We must, however, always be able to justify the harm that we inflict on others, and just because we are well-intentioned, as I believe I have been in criticizing infant male circumcision, we do not necessarily have justification for doing harm. It is with such competing claims and concerns in mind that I have been struggling with the issue of infant male circumcision in a religious context.

In my view, the only way to justify the practice would be on the basis of rights to "freedom of conscience and religion" and respect for the religious beliefs of the parents as set out, for example, in the Canadian Charter of Rights and Freedoms. But as the Supreme Court of Canada has ruled in the *Sheena B.* case, in which, as explained in Chapter 7, the court authorized physicians to give a blood transfusion to a baby who needed it, despite the refusal of this treatment by her Jehovah's Witnesses parents, there are strict limits to what parents may decide with respect to medical treatment of their child on the basis of their freedom of religion and religious belief. They may not withhold medical treatment necessary to protect the child's life or health and they may not inflict harm on their child. Therefore, it is far from clear that the parents' right to freedom of religion would validate infant male circumcision carried out for religious reasons.

The law sometimes allows individuals to refuse to comply with certain laws when compliance would contravene their religious belief. These exemptions are implemented on the grounds of conscientious objection. For example, Quakers, who have a fundamental belief in pacifism and believe that to fight in a war is morally wrong, can be granted exemptions from laws that authorize conscription into the services. But in these cases, the beliefs are those of the person granted the exemption. In the case of infant male circumcision, the parents are using their beliefs to justify an intervention on their child who is not yet capable of holding any similar belief.

It also merits noting that an exemption based on a conscientious objection is much less likely to be recognized if the intervention that is permitted involves harm to another. If we assume that carrying out infant male circumcision is technically a criminal assault, the legal question is whether the parents' conscientious objection to the prohibition of this practice could provide a defence to undertaking it. Conscientious objection is more likely to exempt a person from doing something they object to than to grant them legal immunity for having participated in prohibited conduct. In other words, the law is more likely to allow conscientious objection to validate a failure to do something that the law requires to be done than to justify an action that is prohibited. Consequently, an exemption based on conscientious objection might not be available to excuse those who undertake infant male circumcision from legal liability for doing so.

HOW THEN ARE WE TO deal with infant male circumcision undertaken for religious reasons? First, we must have great respect for people's religious beliefs, especially when these beliefs are long-established and by interfering, not only do we harm the people whose religious beliefs we interfere with, we also harm society. Respect for religious beliefs that differ from our own, or simply respect for others' religious beliefs if we are agnostic or atheist, is central to a general climate of ethical tolerance. We must consider whether the harm involved in prohibiting infant male circumcision could so far outweigh the harm that infant male circumcision does to the child that it should not be prohibited when undertaken for religious reasons. That is, in this situation of competing harms, should the claims of the community ever be given priority over those of the child? If they should, a further question is how could such an approach be legally implemented. This is addressed shortly.

Second, the people opposing a practice based on religious beliefs should have to justify any interference with this practice. Therefore, when infant male circumcision is carried out as an absolute religious obligation, the burden of proof, which is usually on those carrying out infant male circumcision to show that the surgical procedure is justified, would shift to those opposing it to show that it should be prohibited.

Third, we should not use coercive methods to interfere with the religious practice of infant male circumcision unless we can show that the practice involves serious harm to the children that cannot be avoided in any other way than by prohibiting the practice.

Fourth, ethics requires that, even when we are justified in interfering with others, we do so in a way that is least restrictive—here, of their practice of their religion—and least invasive of their rights. With respect to those people who undertake infant male circumcision for religious reasons we should therefore first attempt ethical conversation, especially with religious leaders, not legal intervention. A change from within a religion is vastly preferable to one that is imposed from the outside, and is more likely to accomplish real change than a facade of change. Legal intervention could be justified only if the harm involved were sufficiently serious, if other means of avoiding this harm had failed, and if the use of the law would be reasonably likely to prevent the harm. But we also have serious obligations as a society to protect children, to ensure respect for their human rights and to use the law when necessary to fulfil these obligations. Therefore parents' rights to freedom of religion must be interpreted in the light of the rights of the child and society's obligation to him.

Fifth, only those who believe they have a fundamental, absolute religious obligation to carry out infant male circumcision should be exempt from a prohibition on it. Those whose religion allows them any choice or for whom circumcision is only a matter of tradition, custom or culture should not be exempt.

Sixth, if an exemption for the "religious obligation" practice of infant male circumcision is allowed, harm-reducing measures must be adopted to the degree that it is possible. Harm-reducing measures would include fully adequate local anesthesia and pain relief; the least harmful and invasive form of circumcision that would fulfil the religious requirements; and both parents' fully informed consent. Some people believe that such a consent is possible only after the parents have witnessed the circumcision of another child.

Finally, because the present law, at least technically, prohibits infant male circumcision, if we want to allow an exemption only on religious grounds, the law would need to be either interpreted or changed to permit this. One alternative is a more limited version of the current practice of prosecutorial discretion, in that prosecutors do not charge people carrying out infant male circumcision with any offence. This prosecutorial practice could continue to apply, but only to those infant male circumcisions that are carried out for religious reasons, and that also comply with all the other conditions outlined above.

Not everyone agrees with the idea of a religious exemption. After I first spoke out against infant male circumcision, I was presented with the International Symposia on Sexual Mutilations 1998 Human Rights Award. As I accepted the award at the symposium held at Oxford University, approximately one-third of the audience stood to boo me. Almost all the participants at the symposium were strongly against infant male circumcision, and some of them were appalled that I would argue, as I had in my award acceptance speech, we should consider an exemption on the grounds of profound religious belief and obligation. Someone remarked that I had managed to make everyone furious with me: the anti-circumcision movement; Jews and Muslims who felt that I was attacking their deep religious beliefs; feminists who were outraged because I had made comparisons between female genital mutilation and infant male circumcision and argued that both were ethically wrong; physicians who carried out circumcision and believed that I was accusing them of medical malpractice for having done so; parents who had had their baby boys circumcised and who interpreted my arguments against circumcision as accusing them of child abuse; and one young man who was an anti-circumcision activist from Tel Aviv who accused me of being anti-Semitic because my proposal for a possible exemption for religious belief meant that I was willing to protect all newborn baby boys in the world except Jewish ones.

Back from Oxford, at home in Montreal, I received a call from a woman telling me that she was an alumna of McGill and a donor to the university. She said she had written to the principal, Dr. Bernard Shapiro, demanding that I be dismissed. When I contacted the principal, he reassured me, saying that the real reason that we still need tenure is to allow us to say what we believe we must without losing our jobs. And one of my students reported that he had been listening to Howard Stern—the "shock-jock" on American radio whose program had been taken off the air in several Canadian cities because his comments were thought to offend the norms of public decency—who was strongly endorsing me and the position I had taken on infant male circumcision. As my student remarked in something of an understatement, "It's not really the kind of endorsement you need at the moment."

As the debate was raging in the media (our contemporary public square), I was in Ottawa for a colloquium and hailed a cab to go to the airport. The driver asked if I worked for the Canadian government—he had just picked me up from the government conference centre where I had been co-chairing the xenotransplantation forum. When I said no, he asked where I did work.

"McGill University," I replied.

"Do you know that woman at McGill who is speaking against circumcision?" he asked and then added, "I'm a Muslim."

I gulped and said, "That's me."

He swung around with a look of astonishment, and the car veered to the side of the road. He then turned back and we engaged in a respectful conversation in which he explained the basis of his disagreement with my views. He said to me, "My father did it [circumcision] for me when I was eight years old and I would do it for my son, if I had one. I only have daughters."

As I got out of the cab at the airport, he also left the car. He held out his hand to shake mine, smiled and said, "By the way, my wife and her friends agree with you." This was not as surprising to me as it would have been a few weeks earlier. Several young Jewish women who felt they had faced a terrible choice in deciding whether to have their sons circumcised had contacted me after the circumcision debate erupted in the media, to say that they were grateful that the debate was occurring.

We need to analyze carefully and sensitively what is required by a respect for children—a respect for their physical and mental integrity, and for their right not to be harmed, in particular, not to have pain intentionally inflicted upon them without medical and therapeutic justification. We must also carefully delineate the boundaries of parents' claims and rights with respect to their children. Finally, we must articulate what is demanded by respect for religion and freedom of religion, for traditional and cultural norms, for the institutions of family, community and society, and for ethical and legal principles in relation to our attitudes, practices and beliefs about infant male circumcision.

This complex and difficult area that at first glance can seem so simple touches on many of our most profound values and beliefs. It is, indeed, a very important area of individual and societal ethics talk that crosses millennia of human existence. We have learned much about it and we need to continue to learn more.

9. Denying Health Care to Individuals

The Ethics of Access

Do we have any recourse against physicians who fail to provide us with health care because resources are limited? Or against those people or bodies who decide whether a health-care system will provide or pay for certain treatments? What are their ethical and legal obligations? Let us look first at one man's challenge to the systems-level decision-makers who denied him the treatment he desperately needed.

Barry Stein, a practising lawyer and father of young children, was forty-one years old in 1995 when he was diagnosed with colon cancer with metastases to his liver. In January 1996, he was operated on in Montreal to remove part of his colon. However, the cancer had spread to Mr. Stein's liver. These metastases could not be removed at that time because the hospital lacked a key piece of equipment, an intra-operative ultrasound machine. Mr. Stein's doctors told him that these metastases had to be removed no later than four to eight weeks after the original surgery. They also told him of a treatment that was available in New York—the insertion of an internal pump under the skin, the "Infusaid pump," which would continuously inject chemotherapy drugs directly into his liver in order to help to prevent further metastases—but it was not available in Canada.

Mr. Stein was placed on a waiting list for surgery at another Montreal hospital that had the piece of surgical equipment the original hospital lacked. But he was continuously bumped by other cases regarded as more urgent. In April 1996, well past the time limit recommended for the treatment of the metastases, Mr. Stein's Montreal doctors wrote to the Régie de l'assurance-maladie du Québec, the province's health insurance plan, requesting its permission, "on an urgent and compassionate basis" for the treatment to be carried out in New York. The doctors pointed out that the time factor was critical and that this treatment was "not classified as experimental, however, it is very specialized, [and] there is published evidence of an important benefit to patients of this kind." The Régie wrote back refusing to give permission for both the surgery to be carried out in New York and the Infusaid pump treatment.

The Régie refused to authorize the surgery in New York on the basis that it was available in Canada. They refused the Infusaid pump on the grounds that it was an experimental treatment, because there was a "lack of multi center, double blind, randomized studies [which meant that] proof has not been made that this therapy improves survival and, therefore, authorization cannot be granted." The physician from the Régie to whom Mr. Stein spoke when he telephoned to discuss these refusals "advised him to forget further surgery and live his remaining days in peace saying, 'You know, Mr. Stein, maybe you should just accept it, maybe you should just enjoy your life and not do anything'." How would we feel hearing a physician, who has the power to grant or refuse access to life-prolonging or even life-saving treatment, say this? Remember, if we were in Mr. Stein's situation, we would be hearing this gratuitous advice from a stranger who was not our physician and had not examined us, knowing that the cancer was probably spreading, that time was of the essence if we were to have the best chance of survival, and feeling powerless to make the system respond. The reaction of most of us if faced with this situation can best be summed up in one word, outrageous—we would find it outrageous.

Barry Stein decided not to heed the advice of the Régie's physician and instead to follow his treating doctors' recommendations. He went to New York for two operations, the first on April 16, 1996, the second in January 1997. He paid the bill himself. When Mr. Stein returned from New York, he applied again to the Régie, this time for reimbursement for the cost of these treatments. The Régie rejected his claim on the grounds that "part of the treatment was available elsewhere in Canada, and part was experimental." The Tribunal administratif du Québec (Administrative Appeals Tribunal), to which Mr. Stein appealed this refusal, upheld the Régie's decision. Mr. Stein then appealed to the Superior Court of Quebec for judicial review of the tribunal's decision. Madam Justice Carol Cohen overturned the tribunal's decision on the basis that it was manifestly unreasonable. In doing so, she noted that at the time of reviewing Mr. Stein's case, August 1999, he was "free of any recurrence of the liver lesions. Both he and his treating physicians credited this state of good health to the treatments received . . . in New York." The court sent the matter back to the Régie for reassessment and it reimbursed Mr. Stein. In a subsequent judgment, Madam Justice Cohen made a special award of $18,000 in legal costs to Mr. Stein on the grounds that in seeking judicial review of his case by the Superior Court, he had undertaken an important test case. The judgment of the Superior Court in the *Stein* case is interesting in relation to many issues relevant to the provision of health care and Canadians' access to it.

THE COURT HELD THAT the Administrative Appeals Tribunal, in reaching its conclusion to uphold the Régie's refusal to pay for the treatment Mr. Stein received in New York, "failed to respect the rules of natural justice" in relying upon "hearsay medical evidence," that is, the evidence of the Régie's physicians, who had not personally examined Mr. Stein. If this evidence was not acceptable to the court, should it have been used as the basis of the Régie's decision to refuse treatment to Mr. Stein? In other words, this finding by the court raises the issue of whether the Régie was under some obligation to have a medical examination carried out before it refused treatment that had been strongly recommended by the patient's own physicians, one of whom is an eminent cancer specialist. These doctors, of course, had examined Mr. Stein and were intimately familiar with all the medical facts of his case. They had explained these facts to the Régie and why the treatment in New York was necessary in pleading with the Régie to authorize that treatment.

Mr. Stein based his claim on section 10 of the Quebec Health Insurance Act. This section provides that people entitled to medical care under the act can be reimbursed for the cost of care received outside Quebec, but only if the care is medically required, not available in Canada, and not experimental. (There are similar laws in all provinces of Canada.) The court held that

> it was [not] reasonable to make Stein continue to wait for surgery in Montreal when the danger to his well-being increased daily. [To do so] is irrational, unreasonable and contrary to the purpose of the *Health Insurance Act* which is designed to make necessary medical treatment available to all Quebecers.

In other words, the court held that the absence of reasonably prompt access to treatment for which time is of the essence meant that the treatment was not available in Quebec, and, it would seem, in Canada. Consequently, the surgery Mr. Stein received in New York fulfilled the condition in the act for reimbursement of its cost, that it was unavailable in Canada.

The Appeals Tribunal had based its refusal to pay for the Infusaid pump on the grounds that the pump "must be experimental because it is not known in the Canadian medical community and because there is no Canadian standard for the procedure [of using it for a patient]." It recognized, however, that the pump was routinely used in certain large American centres. Madam Justice Cohen states, in relation to this evidence:

> On this basis *every* procedure which is not performed in Canada would be experimental as it would necessarily be "unknown" to the Canadian medical community. This is irrational as there can be no Canadian "standard" for a procedure which is not performed here. To conclude otherwise imposes a tautology that will prevent the coverage of all procedures performed regularly elsewhere, but not within the country.

Thus the court recognized that Canadians can sometimes expect reimbursement of their costs for new procedures not yet available in Canada but regarded as standard elsewhere, when, as Mr. Stein did, they seek them outside Canada. Obviously, such claims for reimbursement cannot be unlimited or open-ended. But what the limits might be are not explored by the court.

In technical legal terms, the ruling of a Superior Court judge does not set a legal precedent. Such rulings are, however, influential. The ruling in the *Stein* case, which has not been appealed, tips the scales towards Canadian patients gaining access to treatments that are currently available in Canada but not readily so in relation to the urgency of treating the patient's disease, or are not available in Canada but are regarded as standard treatment in the United States or, we can assume, comparable countries.

Mr. Stein's case is the tip of an iceberg of cases in which Canadians will seek access to new treatments for serious illnesses such as cancer and especially those treatments regarded as standard in the United States. We can see this just by reading the daily newspapers. For instance, in the late summer of 1999, Canadian patients' access to new treatments for cancer suddenly became a major news story. A front-page headline in the *Globe and Mail* read: "Breast cancer drug creates cost dilemma. Expensive new treatment can prolong life, but will governments pay?" Carolyn Abraham, the reporter, wrote:

> Health Canada has approved the first genetic therapy to fight breast cancer, a costly designer drug that can extend life for certain patients in advanced stages of the disease. But the drug's approval, which the federal government fast-tracked over the past nine months, leaves the provinces to find a way to pay for it and there is no guarantee that each of them will.

The drug, Trastuzumab, is expected to cost $3,000 a month or $36,000 a year for each patient. Clinical trials suggest that it can increase median survival time by five months, at best.

Yet another front-page *Globe and Mail* headline read: "Tenacious woman scores medical victory. Fiona Webster's fight opens access to genetic breast cancer tests." Women with a strong family history of breast cancer have needed to make decisions whether to have preventive, bilateral mastectomies and ovarectomies as a precaution against developing breast cancer, without knowing whether they carried the genetic mutation that leads to familial breast cancer. The new genetic test means that they can determine if they carry the gene and need not undergo the surgery if they do not, and, if they do, they can make the decision regarding surgery on an informed basis. The test was available in Ontario only within a research setting and results could take up to two years. Results were available within a few weeks in the United States. Ms. Webster's initial request to have the Ontario Health Insurance Plan pay for the test in Utah was rejected on the grounds that the test was experimental. With the help of a lawyer working *pro bono*, Ms. Webster appealed this decision and

The Ethical Canary

226   convinced the province to pay for the test for all women who need it. Cancer Care Ontario (an agency of the Government of Ontario for advising on and co-ordinating programs in cancer detection, care and research) has now asked the Ontario government for $4.5 million to provide this clinical testing service.

As well in the summer of 1999, a group of breast cancer survivors and their advocates, who were concerned about timely access to new treatments for breast cancer, carried out an enquiry across Canada to find out how decisions that determine whether new drugs for cancer are made available are taken. They wrote to government officials responsible for cancer care in each of the provinces, territories and federal government. They focused their enquiry on a treatment for adjuvant node positive breast cancer, adriomycin plus cyclophosphamide followed by Taxol*. This is standard treatment in the United States for women with adjuvant node positive breast cancer, but is unavailable in Canada outside a research protocol. The results of their enquiry show wide variation in the way these decisions are made and, in some cases, difficulty in determining who made them, the basis on which they were made, and who is responsible and accountable for them.

It is not an accident that issues of access to health care have emerged in the public forum at this particular time. Baby boomers, who as a group are used to having both their needs and their desires met, are aging and increasingly facing diseases such as cancer. They are appalled at the thought that they would be denied the best health care. The Internet is a major asset in helping them become a particularly medically well-informed group, and they are articulate and not intimidated at the prospect of using the legal system to advance their claims. The illusion that all Canadians receive the highest standard health care and all such care that could benefit them has been shattered. In the

*Disclosure: I acted as a consultant on this enquiry and was paid by Bristol Myers Squibb, the manufacturer of Taxol.

past, this illusion exerted a calming effect on Canadians and made it unlikely they would challenge any failure by the healthcare system to deliver. This is no longer true.

IN THE REST OF THIS chapter, I briefly survey the ethical and legal obligations, first, of the systems-level decision-makers who decide which treatments will be paid for by the provincial healthcare systems, and then of the physicians who treat individual patients, with respect to their decisions about Canadian patients' access to new or emerging tests or treatments. Together, these two groups will be pivotal in deciding how the competing issues of access and cost will be reconciled in relation to particular new treatments or particular patients' or groups of patients' access to them.

The macro-level question of whether we, as a society, can afford to pay for all the costly new tests and treatments that are becoming available almost daily is very difficult and also of the utmost importance. This question also arises in private health insurance schemes—it is just that the source of the funds and the tradeoffs are different. It is dealt with only indirectly in the following discussion.

To explore the ethics and law of Canadian patients' access to new medical treatments, we have to understand some of the current basic principles and ethical and legal rules that govern the provision of health care in Canada. (Although I use Canada as an example, the "ethical and legal scene" these rules establish is, in general, typical of that to be found in comparable countries.)

First, of course, physicians have a primary obligation of personal care to their patients. They must not place the interests of others ahead of those of the patient they are treating and must not be in a conflict of interest in making decisions regarding treatment for the patient. But physicians also need to be concerned not to waste healthcare resources, and in this respect, they have secondary obligations to other patients and to society. As a result of the restraints that those who pay for health care—whether governments or, in other countries, private insurers or Health Maintenance Organizations (HMOs)—seek to impose, physicians have increasingly been caught between these two obligations.

Second, as a condition of receiving federal transfer payments, the Canada Health Act requires that each of the provinces provide beneficiaries in its province with comprehensive medical services. These services are defined as "all medically required" or "medically necessary" treatment. One important issue, therefore, is the definition of such treatment. Experimental or research treatment falls outside the scope of medically required treatment. Consequently, one way a province can avoid paying for a certain treatment is to label it as experimental or research treatment. This same approach is used by some private healthcare insurance companies in the United States.

Third, again as a condition of receiving funds, each province must ensure that the provision of medically required services is publicly administered. This requirement means that the provinces do not allow a privately funded, for-profit system to provide these services and have implemented this prohibition by legislation. In preventing a private healthcare system from running parallel with the public one, Canada is unique among comparable countries.

Fourth, some provinces have set up statutory authorities to make decisions about the availability of treatments. For example, in all provinces except New Brunswick, Prince Edward Island and Quebec, central cancer agencies or boards undertake the decision-making about which new cancer treatments should be made available to patients and when. These agencies are directly associated with the particular provincial government to varying degrees. We can compare some of the functions of these bodies to those of the arm's-length appeal bodies that legislators in the United States have been proposing for several years as a way of resolving cases in which conflict arises because private insurers or HMOs have refused patients access to treatment. Patients can appeal to these bodies in an effort to have a refusal overturned.

Fifth, medically necessary treatment within the provincial healthcare systems does not include pharmaceuticals except those made available within a hospital context.

IF PATIENTS HAVE NO ethical or legal claims to experimental treatment but they do to standard treatment, it is important to differentiate between them. One of the few "official" documents that examines the borderlines between experimental and standard treatment is the *Belmont Report* of the United States' President's Commission. This report was written in 1978. At the time, the main concern was that people were being wrongfully subjected to new or experimental treatments. Today, on the other hand, many patients are concerned that they are not being given access to such treatments quickly enough, and that they are being unethically deprived of new advances in medicine. The *Belmont Report* speaks of three groups of treatments: research, practice and innovative medical procedures. It defines "practice" as procedures "designed solely to enhance the well-being of an individual patient" that have "a reasonable expectation of success." By contrast, the term "research" "designates an activity designed to test a hypothesis, permit conclusions to be drawn, and therefore to develop or contribute to generalisable knowledge expressed, for example, in theories, principles and statements of relationship." The definition of innovative practices is unclear, but, probably, some of them are research and some practice.

Applying these definitions is not a straightforward task, either in general or to a particular treatment intervention: If we equate standard medical treatment to "practice" and use the definition of practice to identify standard medical treatment, it is relatively easy to determine whether a medical intervention is intended and "designed to enhance the well-being of the patient." But how should we determine whether it fulfils the "reasonable expectation of success"? And which basic presumption should we use when we disagree about whether a treatment is standard or experimental: that the treatment is research or experimental until it is shown to be practice or standard, or the opposite, that it is standard until shown to be experimental?

A basic presumption that treatments are standard favours patients' access to treatment more than one that presumes they are experimental. This is true, because in cases of equal doubt as to whether the treatment—for instance, a new treatment for cancer—is experimental or standard, if we assume that it is standard, patients will be given access to it unless the person who claims that it is still experimental can prove that it is. The opposite is true if we assume that the treatment is experimental until it is shown to be standard. The latter presumption saves on the cost of new or emerging treatments. The former presumption favours patients being given access, as quickly as possible, to all potentially valuable new treatments. The circumstances in which this decision that characterizes the treatment as either standard or experimental must be made, and the decision-making process that gives rise to these two opposite outcomes, are identical. The outcome depends only on which basic presumption is used. We sometimes fail to recognize this and, therefore, overlook the importance of our choice of basic presumption.

Because the choice of a basic presumption is not neutral, this choice must also be governed by ethical principles. Both as societies and as individuals responsible for decision-making for society (healthcare administrators, government bureaucrats, politicians and taxpayers), we usually favour the cost-saving presumption. (This is even more true when health care is a for-profit enterprise.) However, as patients, we strongly favour the access presumption. The conflict between these two aims cannot, in reality, be avoided, and it is not necessarily bad. Rather, we must deal with this conflict (which can also be more neutrally described as creative tension) in a way that ensures that the decisions about making new treatments available are ethical in their process and outcome.

The basic presumption also determines who has the burden of proof: The person whom the basic presumption favours can simply rely on it being the case. In contrast, the person relying on the exception must prove that it should apply. For instance, if the basic presumption is that a certain cancer test, such as the one Fiona Webster wanted, is still experimental, she would have to prove that it had become standard in order to gain access to it (assuming for the moment that patients will be given access to standard treatments). But should patients need to prove that a new treatment has become standard in order to gain access to it, or should those making the decision that it is still experimental need to justify their decision? The approach of the courts to the allocation of the burden of proof, in general, could be instructive in this regard. Courts often look to fairness and equity in ease of access to proof, the parties' resources and their relative power in determining who should have the burden of proof. In other words, the stronger party, the one most easily able to prove his or her case, is most likely to have the burden of doing so. On the other hand, the usual legal rule for burden of proof is that "he or she who alleges or makes a claim must prove," that is, the person making the allegation or claim must prove the validity of that allegation or claim.

One possible way to gain access to new treatments is to claim a legal right to health care. Quebec is the only province in Canada with such a legislated right. This right is, however, carefully circumscribed and may not in practice offer any broader range of treatments than would be available in other provinces. But the statutory provision does establish that there is such a right and, arguably, means that the person denying treatment has the burden of proof to justify the denial. This situation could place Quebec patients at an advantage compared with those in other provinces. When there is a dispute as to whether a new treatment should be available and there is equal doubt as to whether it is still experimental or has become standard, the legislated right to health care could be interpreted to mean that the treatment should be provided.

When a treatment is still experimental, it is much more difficult to use the law to establish any claim to have access to it, at least outside a research protocol. Consequently, as a cost-saving measure, governments, institutions, insurance companies or HMOs that will be responsible for paying for treatments for beneficiaries for whom they must provide health care may seek to keep them classified as experimental in order not to have obligations to provide them. One hears stories about foot-dragging by provincial authorities who decide when a treatment has become standard. These same allegations can be heard in relation to private health insurance companies in the United States. There have been suggestions that the main reason for such delays is concern about the cost of many new treatments and a desire to save money through the delay. In this respect, it is interesting to note that, although in the *Stein* case the official reason given for refusing the Infusaid pump was that it was experimental, the Régie's doctor acknowledged that the Infusaid pump was "not available in Canada because of the cost of the pump."

One way to argue that a new treatment should be regarded as standard in Canada is to show that it is regarded as standard in countries whose healthcare norms are comparable to those in Canada, for example, the United States, England or Australia. A relevant example in this respect can be found in the final report of the Commission of Inquiry on the Blood System in Canada, chaired by Justice Horace Krever. Part of the evidence that the commission relied on to find that the delay by the Canadian Red Cross in implementing certain tests for HIV contamination of the blood system constituted wrongdoing was that these tests had been adopted in the United States well before their adoption in Canada. While the commission carefully avoided making findings as to legal liability, it ruled that the U.S. practice was evidence of a reasonably safe standard of care that should have been adopted in Canada much sooner than occurred. But just because a healthcare practice has been adopted in the United States does not necessarily mean that failure to adopt it in Canada is negligence. It depends on all the circumstances. The point is, rather, as the Krever Commission's approach shows, that U.S. standard practice is likely to be seen as relevant and taken into account in deciding what constitutes reasonable (that is, non-negligent) care in the Canadian context.

In this manner, treatments characterized as standard in countries similar to Canada are likely to influence what is regarded as a legally required reasonable standard of care in Canada. But must all these standard treatments be classified as "medically necessary" for those who need them and, therefore, be made available under Canadian medicare? Until very recently, most ethical and legal commentators would probably have agreed that all standard treatments should be regarded as medically necessary for patients who need them. The Nova Scotia Court of Appeal's ruling in the *Cameron* case, however, if it is allowed to stand and followed in other Canadian jurisdictions, puts the continuing accuracy of these commentators' views in doubt.

The plaintiffs, Alexander Cameron and Dr. Cheryl Smith, an infertile Halifax couple, argued that the province's Health Services and Insurance Act required it to pay for *in vitro* fertilization treatment on the grounds that it was medically necessary for them and that failure to pay for it breached both the province's obligations under the act and the plaintiffs' constitutional rights not to be discriminated against. The majority of the Court of Appeal (Justice Chipman with Justice Pugsley concurring) recognized infertility as a physical disability requiring medical treatment. With respect to the range of treatment for this disability to which the plaintiffs were entitled, they ruled, however, that

> of necessity, what is or is not medically required must be judged by those placed in charge of the administration of the [health funding] policy. The judgement call requires an appreciation not only of medical procedures, but the availability of funds to finance them.

This ruling represents a radical change in the definition of what constitutes medically required treatment. It means that medically required treatment is no longer assessed just in relation to the individual patient (or even a group of patients suffering from a certain condition), but also the provincial healthcare scheme's ability to meet the costs of the treatment. This requirement goes even further than a cost-benefit assessment, which asks: Is the treatment worth the cost and, if not, may it be regarded as not medically required?—which, itself, is open to ethical and legal challenge. It is not that cost or the provinces' ability to pay is irrelevant; on the contrary. The issue raised by the court's ruling is whether this ability should be factored into decision-making about provision of the treatment through the definition of medical necessity.

In holding that cost should be a factor, Justice Chipman cites the Canadian Bar Association's Task Force on Healthcare Reform, to the effect that "the scope of 'medically required services' and, indeed, all 'insured health services,' is a policy decision." He also refers to the trial judge's ruling that "neither 'medically indicated' nor 'standard medical procedure' equates to 'medically required.'" Justice Chipman acknowledges that *in vitro* fertilization is recognized as standard treatment for the type of infertility that afflicts the plaintiffs, but concludes as follows:

> In the scheme of things—in the order of priorities—these two [*in vitro* fertilization] procedures [which the plaintiffs seek to have covered by the province's health insurance scheme], having regard to costs, the limited success rate and the risks, do not, at this time, rank sufficiently high to warrant payment for them from public funding. From a review of the entire record, particularly the history of IVF before the [Royal] Commission [on New Reproductive Technologies], the history of the tariffs and the evidence . . . I am satisfied that this is the real explanation why these procedures were considered not medically necessary and did not find their way into the tariffs.

With no intention of disrespect to the court, I suggest that if cost is to play a direct role in deciding whether a standard treatment should be made available to patients, then cost should not be taken into account by making it part of the definition of medically required treatment. Thus, cost should not be factored in by taking an approach that if a treatment is too expensive (which itself is a value judgment) it is not "medically" required. Factoring cost into the definition of medically required treatment makes the definition of this so arbitrary and vague as to be useless. It also creates a strong possibility that decisions will be made that are ethically unacceptable and open to legal challenge. If cost is to be taken into account in this context, it should instead be as an ethical and a legal justification or excuse for not providing medically necessary treatment. In the *Cameron* case, for instance, rather than saying that the treatment for the Camerons' infertility is not medically required because it is too expensive, the government should be asked to show that even though this treatment is medically required, it is justified in not providing it because of its cost.

The problem for the provinces in adopting the latter approach proposed above is that their failure to provide medically necessary treatment to a person entitled to it can be challenged, as the plaintiffs did in the *Cameron* case, on the grounds that it is a breach of the comprehensiveness requirement of the Canada Health Act. The Nova Scotia Court of Appeal dealt with this difficulty in two ways. First, they held that "the hospital and medical care available under the policy of the [Nova Scotia Health Services and Insurance Act] . . . is comprehensive, but by no means all-inclusive." This raises the question: Which standard treatments can be excluded from coverage and yet still allow the province to say that the coverage it provides is comprehensive? If Mr. Cameron or Dr. Smith had, as Mr. Stein did, needed treatment for cancer rather than for infertility, and this treatment had been refused, would the court have ruled in the same way? And second, the Court of Appeal ruled that even if the Nova Scotia act, in failing to cover the costs of *in vitro* fertilization, failed to meet the standards or objectives of the Canada Health Act, it did not follow that the Camerons could base a legal claim on this failure. Such a failure, the court said, raised only "a political, not a justiciable issue." In other words, the Camerons could pursue a claim to the

236   infertility treatment that they needed only through political, not legal, action.

This decision of the Nova Scotia Court of Appeal also seems to shift the locus of decision-making about what is medically required treatment from individual physicians to a governmental level. The decision-making body could decide that the cost of a standard treatment was such that the treatment was not medically required even though reasonable physicians strongly believed that it was essential. Would making this shift breach the Canada Health Act? It is not possible to answer this question from the *Cameron* case, because the physician expert witnesses in that case agreed with the province's decision not to fund the *in vitro* fertilization treatment. Moreover, it remains to be seen whether the findings in the *Cameron* case will be restricted to the provision of new reproductive technologies or analogous treatments, or will be applied more generally. We are comfortable with not providing access to cosmetic surgery through the publicly funded healthcare system. We would be appalled if access to, at least, standard treatment for cancer were not provided. In which of these categories should infertility treatment be placed? Or should it be regarded as one of a third group of treatments to which we should have a new and different approach? The approach taken to infertility treatment in some provinces might reflect such a change. Some elements of the overall treatment needed by infertile people are covered under medicare and other elements must be paid for privately.

One important issue that the *Cameron* case demonstrated is the possibility that people who are unable to obtain access to medical treatment as a result of decisions by governmental bodies can challenge these decisions as a breach of constitutional rights protected by the Canadian Charter of Rights and Freedoms. Such decisions could be challenged as being unconstitutional, if, for instance, they interfered with people's rights to life, liberty or security of the person (Charter, section 7) or constituted wrongful discrimination (Charter, section 15). If, however, any breaches of these rights or protections by a government in not providing certain treatments are in accordance with the principles of "fundamental justice" (Charter, section 7), or are "reasonable limits prescribed by law as can be demonstrably justified in a free and democratic society" (Charter, section 1), then these breaches will not be unconstitutional. The use of a "Charter challenge" is a relatively new approach in arguing rights of access to certain treatments within the Canadian healthcare scheme. A few early approaches were made to the courts, but recently there appears to have been a marked increase in these approaches.

TO TURN FROM THE LAW to ethics, ethically what role should cost play, and what role must it not play, in a governmental body's decisions about making treatments, especially new ones, available? Whose values should be given priority in deciding the very sensitive and difficult issue of whether giving people an additional period of life merits the cost involved? What if the life of a young single mother with advanced breast cancer could be extended by five months by a very expensive treatment, and she says this extension is of the utmost value to her and her children? Should this desire on her part mean that cost should be irrelevant? Moreover, if cost plays a role in restricting treatment, are there obligations to disclose this policy?

Most of the decisions that seek to balance access to treatment against its cost involve complex value judgments, and values can conflict. Many of the values conflicts that arise in a healthcare situation are between physicians and patients or their families, as we saw in the *Krausz* case. In these cases, the shift in ethics and law, from physician-centred decision-making to patient-centred decision-making, would be relevant. This shift means that the patient's values should take priority over the physician's when the two conflict.

But whose values should take priority when the conflict is between a patient and a person, committee or other body with responsibility for the allocation of healthcare resources? In practice, up to the very late 1990s, the "committee" has prevailed. But, as we have seen, such decision-makers are now being challenged in the courts. Anyway, who, ethically, should prevail in any given case is a separate question from who legally can prevail. Moreover, in these cases the values conflict is between different levels of decision-making. In a physician-patient values conflict, the conflict is entirely at the individual level. In a patient-resource allocator values conflict, the conflict is at two and possibly three levels: individual, institutional and governmental. The aims that may ethically be given priority at an institutional level (for example, efficiency and cost-saving on the part of a hospital) may not be ethical at the individual level. In trying to resolve these conflicts, once again we enter a world of competing sorrows. In making the decisions about the provision of and access to health care that we cannot avoid making, we must never forget that either immediately or ultimately these are decisions about whether the suffering of real people is relieved or continues, about whether their quality of life is improved or restricted, and whether their life is prolonged or cut short. These are not, to say the least, trivial matters or hypothetical or academic ones.

WHAT ARE THE ETHICAL and legal obligations of individual physicians treating individual patients in relation to patients' access to new or emerging treatments?

First, in both ethics and law, the physician has a primary obligation of personal care to the patient. A subsidiary, emerging obligation, which flows from this obligation, is that of the physician to act as the patient's advocate in obtaining the treatment that the physician considers therapeutically most appropriate for the patient. Thus, the physician must take those steps that a reasonably careful and competent physician would take to try to obtain the treatment the patient needs.

The physician also has ethical and legal responsibilities with respect to obtaining the patient's informed consent to the treatment that the patient decides to undergo, and the patient's informed refusal

of those treatments the patient rejects. Failure to obtain informed consent is medical negligence.

As well, the physician must not be in a situation of conflict of interest with respect to the patient. If the physician stood to gain or lose personally, either financially or in other ways, by not offering a certain indicated treatment to the patient, the physician would be in a conflict of interest. In this respect, hospital administrators have certain obligations towards physicians. For instance, it would be unethical, and could be negligent, to establish a hospital system that punished physicians who used more than a certain amount of resources. Such deterrents would only be acceptable in relation to the unreasonable use of resources. The difficulty here, again, is to decide: Who is to draw the line between what is reasonable and unreasonable, on what basis, and using which process?

Moreover, in recent times, the Supreme Court of Canada has recognized that physicians have fiduciary obligations to their patients. These are duties of undivided loyalty on the part of the fiduciary—the physician—and require that the physician establish with the patient a relationship of the utmost trust, good faith and confidence. Such obligations underscore and provide additional legal weight to the long-standing obligations of physicians, outlined above.

The physician's duties regarding the range of treatments that should be offered to the patient and the duty to obtain informed consent are closely linked. The physician must non-negligently decide what this range of treatments should be and must disclose to the patient the existence of each of these treatments, and their benefits, potential benefits, risks and harms.

Deciding on the range of treatments that should be offered to the patient is currently an ethical and legal minefield for physicians. If the physician believes that a treatment not available under medicare or other healthcare insurance is better than those that are available but does not tell the patient, or, possibly, does not try to obtain it for the patient, the physician is in breach of the primary obligation of personal care to the patient and, from a legal point of view, may not have

240   taken reasonable care. In theory, cost should not determine the range of treatments that the physician offers to the patient, but in practice, it is an unavoidable reality. Those who pay for health care—whether governments or insurance companies—or healthcare institutions that must operate within restricted budgets—such as hospitals—place restrictions on physicians, both directly and indirectly. And the remedy is not nearly as easy as simply saying that everyone involved should just be open and honest about the role that cost plays in the choice of treatment. Most of us react with horror if people admit to not believing that prolonging our or others' lives or reducing our or their suffering is worth what it would cost and, therefore, they are not offering us or them certain treatments. But the reality is that cost does play a role. And when this is the case, it is better to be open and honest about it than to hide it.

Patients must be able to trust their physicians; they need to be able to enter into a therapeutic alliance with them. Patients need to be able to believe, with good reason, that the physician will not allow the interests of others to interfere with their best interests. Nowhere are such factors of greater importance than in the treatment of patients with life-threatening diseases. Discussions that involve physicians explaining to patients with such a disease that better treatments are available but will not be provided because of cost and the need to conserve resources for others threaten all of these elements of the physician-patient relationship.

The idea that the physician would place the interests of others before those of the individual patient is completely contrary to the traditional ethics and ethos of medicine, and to the legal obligations of physicians as they have evolved to this time. And the view that the physician could be justified in doing so, or even have obligations to others or to society to do so in certain circumstances, is a very recent concept, which so far has a very uncertain place in both ethics and law. Strong arguments can be made for maintaining the strength and integrity of physicians' traditional obligations to patients, but difficult, real-life situations challenge our capacity to do so.

There is debate as to which treatments the physician must include in the range of treatments and must disclose to the patient. A view is emerging in the ethics and law literature that physicians must include all treatments that might reasonably benefit their patients, even those not available under medicare, and must disclose all of these options to the patient. Other authors argue that there is an obligation to offer only those treatments that are reasonably available. They also argue that there is no ethical or legal obligation to disclose information about treatments that they have no ethical or legal obligation to offer. The case study sometimes used to support this view concerns the use of non-ionic, as compared with ionic, contrast medium for intravenous pyelogram (IVP) X-rays. The difference between the two dyes lies in their minor to moderate side effects; the non-ionic has fewer, but the fatality rate for both dyes and their efficacy in providing good X-rays of the kidneys are the same. Some hospitals have decided to restrict the use of the more expensive non-ionic contrast medium to patients who might be more likely to have an allergic reaction to the iodine in the less expensive medium. The argument is that there is no need to disclose the existence of the more expensive, non-ionic dye to those patients who are not at such increased risk. Even if we accept that non-disclosure of the more expensive diagnostic intervention is justified in this case, we need to question whether this line of reasoning could be applied if, unlike the two dyes, the fatality rate and efficacy of two other alternative treatments were not the same.

It is fully understandable that physicians would be reluctant to believe they had ethical and legal obligations to include among a range of reasonably indicated treatments those treatments that were not reasonably available or not available at all. Making disclosures to patients about such treatments will give rise to distress, anxiety, conflict and tension, which the physician will need to handle. Many physicians' response, which is a reasonable one, to the proposal that they should make such disclosures is to ask why they should be required to complicate their professional lives in this fashion. The reason is that they have ethical and legal obligations to the patient that require them to do so.

When considering the effect of economic restraints on physicians' obligations, one question that arises is whether these constraints could justify the physician's breach of an obligation to the patient that would otherwise be medical negligence. It was sometimes argued that there was a rule in the common law that in setting the reasonable standard of care, the courts would take into account the economic reality of any given situation in which negligence was alleged. The Supreme Court of Canada has, however, overruled this approach. The court held that if a business (in this case, selling ice cream from a small van that toured the streets) could not be undertaken reasonably safely and make a profit, then the answer was not to allow it to be undertaken unsafely without attracting legal liability, but rather not to allow it to be undertaken at all. The ice cream vendor would have made a loss if he had employed two people to staff the van in order to make the situation safer for children who had to cross roads to visit the van. But while we can manage to do without ice cream, the same is not true of health care. How would the courts deal with health care that fell below a reasonable standard of care if, because of cost constraints, the physician did not offer the patient the best or even reasonably adequate treatment? Would this attract negligence liability to the physician, as it did to the ice cream vendor, even though from an economic point of view, the physician had no other reasonable option? Is it preferable to have a healthcare system that operates below a reasonable standard of care than to have no healthcare system at all?

To the extent that a Canadian court has been faced with the issue of sacrificing the individual patient's interests for the greater good of cost-saving in the interests of others, one court at least has been clear and blunt. After Jason Law, a fifty-one-year-old man, died from a cerebral aneurysm, the diagnosis of which was delayed, his estate sued several physicians. One reason for the delay was a failure to order a CT scan until late in the patient's illness. Justice Spencer of the British

Columbia Supreme Court, in finding two of the four physicians sued liable in negligence, stated:

> I must observe that throughout this case there were a number of times when doctors testified that they feel constrained by the British Columbia Medical Association standards to restrict their requests for CT scans as diagnostic tools. No doubt such sophisticated equipment is limited and costly to use. No doubt there are budgetary restraints on them. But this is a case where, in my opinion, those constraints worked against the patient's interest by inhibiting the doctors in their judgement of what should be done for him. That is to be deplored. I understand that there are budgetary problems confronting the healthcare system. I raise it in passing only to point out that there were a number of references to the effect of financial restraint on the treatment of this patient. I respectfully say it is something to be carefully considered by those who are responsible for the provision of medical care and those who are responsible for financing it. I also say that if it comes to a choice between a physician's responsibility to his or her individual patient and his or her responsibility to the medicare system overall, the former must take precedence in a case such as this.

So the judge makes clear that the physician's primary legal obligation is to patients—which exactly parallels the ethical obligations—and points out that responsibility extends beyond physicians to healthcare institutions, systems and government. But, apart from calling on physicians to fulfil their obligations to patients, the judge, like the rest of us, does not have any precise proposals as to what physicians should do when this is not possible because of cost constraints.

HOSPITAL ADMINISTRATIONS have a major role to play in the decisions that determine the range of treatments physicians will have available to offer to patients. They must also act non-negligently in making these decisions and must ensure that they run a non-negligent hospital system. As discussed in the next chapter, hospitals are not just a business like any other business and must not be run as such. For example, efficiency and cost-saving, while always important aims and even ethically required, should not always be the main priorities for hospitals, especially when they would conflict with caring, in the broadest sense of this term, for patients.

A central question, in both a patient obtaining access to treatment and a physician obtaining the patient's informed consent, is the scope of disclosure of information about each of the indicated treatments that must be given to a patient in order to obtain the patient's informed consent to the treatment which is given and informed refusal of those which are rejected. Both are necessary.

The Supreme Court of Canada, in the case of *Hopp v. Lepp*, made it clear that even if certain information is not required to be disclosed under the usual test of what the reasonable patient would want to know, if the patient asks questions, the physician has an obligation to answer those questions honestly and fully. Consequently, even if there is no initial obligation to tell a patient about a certain treatment, if the person asks about that treatment, a full and honest disclosure about it is required. The same is true if the patient asks whether there are any other or better treatments that could be considered, or if the patient asks if any new or research treatments have been developed.

A wrongful or negligent failure to disclose the existence of a treatment about which the patient should be informed can negate the patient's informed consent to the treatment that is given. It is not enough that the patient understands the benefits, potential benefits, risks and harms of the treatment he or she receives. Rather, the patient has to understand this information in relation to all treatments that could be of benefit to him or her. Failure to obtain such an informed consent and informed refusals is negligence.

The doctrine of informed consent has many aims, but an early and still primary one is to allow patients to exercise their rights to autonomy and self-determination in deciding which risks they will run and which benefits they will forgo. This requires that patients be informed about all the alternatives open to them. Even if a governmental agency, committee or hospital decides that a treatment will not be made available (and, particularly, if the principal basis for this decision is the cost of the treatment, rather than its unproven status or doubtful effectiveness), the physician may still have an obligation to advise a patient of this treatment. If such a treatment falls within the range of treatments that the reasonable physician would disclose to a person in the same circumstances as the patient, or if it is a treatment that the reasonable patient would want to know about, almost certainly the physician has an ethical and legal obligation to disclose the existence of this treatment to the patient.

As we saw in the *Stein* case, as physicians fulfil their ethical and legal obligations of disclosure, conflict within the healthcare system will likely increase, as will resorting to the courts. No one welcomes this, but the alternative is worse. Patients must be able to have the utmost trust in their physicians, and medicine itself must maintain a general climate of "earned trust," as a crucial element of its overall ethical tone. Hiding information about possible treatments or failing to inform patients of them, especially those patients with serious illnesses, is antithetical to earning trust. And with the Internet, it is increasingly likely that patients will learn about the treatments that are available. An advertisement for the *New England Journal of Medicine*, aimed at physicians, underscores the likelihood of this happening. It reads: "Don't wait for the library or hospital copy of the *Journal* to be circulated to you. Take out your own subscription and read the latest articles before your patients do."

AS A CANADIAN SOCIETY, under our present publicly funded healthcare system, we will have to admit that we cannot afford to offer every new treatment to everyone who might benefit from it. Although we almost certainly have never been able to do this, we have lived with the illusion that it was otherwise. The difference now is that decisions not to provide certain treatments can no longer be taken indirectly, or behind closed doors, or be caused to appear as inevitable outcomes. Canadians are challenging the acceptability of both the process and the substance of some of the decisions that affect the availability and allocation of health care. This "coming out of the closet" of health policy decision-making has benefits, but also risks and harms. Can we accept, as individuals and as a society, that a choice has been made by someone, somewhere, that we or our loved ones will not receive all the medical care that is likely to be of benefit to us or them?

The one matter of which we can be certain, and on which we can all agree, is that there are no easy answers.

10. Structuring Healthcare Systems

The Ethics of Allocation

n the previous chapter, we examined how decisions that resulted in a denial of health care could be challenged on ethical or legal grounds. In this chapter, we look at the principles, concepts, approaches and ideas that might help us to act ethically when we face tough decisions as institutions or governments as to what health care will and will not be provided.

In exploring the ethics of limiting health care, as in many areas of ethics, we often focus on dramatic individual cases. Front-page stories involving the lack of access to health care are reported in the Canadian press every day. In one story, a forty-five-year-old man with end-stage cystic fibrosis was called into hospital for a lung transplant, but no intensive care unit (ICU) bed could be found for him. The surgeon could not proceed because the patient could not be cared for post-operatively. The lungs available for transplantation to this desperately ill man were wasted. He could well die before other matching organs become available. The reason the ICU bed was not available was that a large number of hospital beds had been closed. In some cases, beds have been closed because of a shortage of nurses.

In contrast, two stories that described prominent Canadians who were politically well connected, seventy-two-year-old Dalton Camp (an adviser to former prime minister Brian Mulroney) and seventy-nine-year-old Ray Nelson (a director of the government-owned Alberta Treasury Branches) who received heart transplants in 1993 and 1999, respectively, also raised our concerns, in these cases about the ethics of providing treatment to a certain person. Each man at the time of his surgery was the oldest person in Canada to have received a heart transplant. Questions were raised as to whether, in our purportedly totally egalitarian Canadian healthcare system, all patients are equal or some are more equal than others. Did these patients have access to heart transplantation mainly because they were prominent people and politically well connected or was it a coincidence that they shared these characteristics and, moreover, were both men? Let me be clear here. We have laws against discrimination on the basis of age, and access to health care is one of the most important contexts in which to apply these laws. But such laws must be used to protect everyone, not just selected people.

Of the many difficult issues discussed in this book, limiting medicine and doing so ethically are among the most complex for a wide variety of reasons. The decisions we would make about limiting medicine as a taxpayer in a socialized system or a person buying an insurance policy in a private system differ substantially from what we would want if we or our loved ones are ill and in need of health care. As well, we all personally identify with the need for health care and with people who require it, especially if it is denied to them. What's more, the decisions that must be made are diffuse, multiple, complex, interlinked, and frequently must be made concurrently at individual, institutional, governmental and societal levels. What we decide as a

politician might be very different from what we would want for ourselves in health care—a reality that itself raises ethical issues that are
discussed shortly.

It is easy, however, to focus on the rights and wrongs—the ethics—
of individual stories about lack of access to health care, or unfair
access. It is much more difficult to place them in a larger context and
to examine the ethics of the allocation of healthcare resources at the
institutional, governmental or societal level. For instance, at the
governmental level, what is the ethical responsibility to allocate
resources to health care? And at the institutional level, what is the
ethical responsibility for allocating resources within health care?

Trying to answer these questions is a daunting task. We have, however, no other option than to try to do so. The approach I propose has
two main features: to use the lens of ethics, and to attempt to structure a framework of questions that will function as a conceptual tool
we can use to help us make these decisions. In this chapter, I first outline some of the features of the approach I have in mind. Then I use
this approach to address selected aspects of the following questions:
Who decides? On what basis? Using which procedures? And for
which purposes?

THE FRAMEWORK OF QUESTIONS that I propose is complex, multi-
dimensional, transdisciplinary, nuanced, and fluid rather than fixed.
It must be structured to identify new questions that should be added
and old ones that need to be deleted, and be able to easily accommodate such changes. Most importantly, it must be a carefully integrated
whole. At present, the nature of decision-making in the healthcare
system often seems like a cubist painting that presents disconnected
pieces of a given reality. For instance, we might have the operating
rooms and surgeons available, but there is a permanent shortage of
anesthetists, which means that surgery cannot be performed. Or there
is an expensive pain-relief treatment that would enable a patient to
stay out of hospital and avoid the cost to the system that a hospital

admission involves, but the pharmacy budget has been exhausted and, therefore, the treatment is not available. The framework should help us to integrate our decision-making about health care as, indeed, we must do if we are to act ethically.

Such a framework of questions must be able to accommodate a wide range of ethical concerns, ranging from everyday ones—like access to basic treatment, the level of nursing care, or the length of waiting lists for elective treatment—to the most avant-garde, like access to expensive new diagnostic techniques or cancer treatments developed as a result of genetic research, or the issues raised by xeno-transplantation. As I have said before, many of these avant-garde issues can rightly be labelled "the costs of our success." This description carries an important message in the context of concern over the cost of health care. Much as we would like to avoid our current "scarce healthcare resources" dilemmas, we face them precisely because we have been so successful in developing new medical technology, not because we have failed. Failure would have been very inexpensive financially, but unbearably expensive in pain, suffering and harm to our quality and length of life.

The framework of questions must also be able to accommodate analysis, especially ethical analysis, at different levels. For instance, at the institutional level it could be ethically acceptable for a hospital to decide, as a cost-saving move, not to install an ICU. But at the individual level it would not be ethical for a physician to deny such treatment to a patient who needs it, because the physician wanted to save the ICU resources for other patients whom the physician regarded as having a better prognosis or quality of life.

Examining the ethics of the different levels necessarily opens up the question of whether we have obligations to provide some minimal level of health care to everyone in our world. Can we argue that there is a universal right to health care, and then accept that this right extends only to people living in affluent Western societies with socialized healthcare systems? Is "rights talk" the most appropriate language in which to explore our obligations to provide health care, especially to those who live outside our borders? Would "justice talk" or "ethics talk" be more appropriate?

As is so often true in doing ethics, the language we use in our dialogue about health care is not neutral. The ways in which allocation of resources are described in the community and societal-level debates can make a difference to the decisions we reach. In looking at obligations to those outside our borders, should we consider using a tripartite concept of human ethics, human rights and human responsibilities to articulate such obligations? Or would we achieve a more ethical, just and humane outcome if we placed more emphasis on practice than theory, and explored more fully and imaginatively practical ways of providing the most disadvantaged people in our world with basic health care? For instance, Dr. Solomon Benatar, a leading South African physician and ethicist, proposes that we should divert a small percentage of the money currently spent on military and militarism to provide some minimally adequate level of health care for people in the developing world.

The framework of questions must also be aimed at evolving a specific field of ethics to govern healthcare institutions and systems. This field is called, alternatively, healthcare organizational ethics or healthcare institutional ethics and has emerged only recently. Its focus is to create ethical communities and an ethical climate within healthcare organizations. Kevin Wildes, an ethicist at the Kennedy Institute of Ethics at Georgetown University, proposes that institutions can possess both integrity and conscience—which means they can also lack them. Organizational ethics should be aimed at helping to articulate and develop the moral culture that will promote them.

We can contrast healthcare organizational ethics with clinical ethics, which has developed over the past thirty years and focuses largely on the individual healthcare professional-patient relationship and what is required to maintain the ethical integrity of this relationship. Our initial approach to healthcare organizational ethics was to write on the large screen the principles and approaches we had developed in this individual clinical context—for instance, the principle that the interests of the individual patient must come first. When we recognized the shortcomings of this approach, we often tried to deal with the larger issues through the application of business ethics. The difficulty with doing this is that, while health care has aspects of being a business, it is not just a business like any other, because while hospitals are in the business of caring, they also have a public mission and trust in relation to caring (even if they are privately owned hospitals). Therefore, unlike other businesses, to always give priority to efficiency, for example, in running a hospital, would be unethical when this priority conflicts with what is needed to care properly, in the broad sense of this phrase, for patients.

In many ways, healthcare organizational ethics is a mixed system, which, as Jane Jacobs points out in her book *Systems of Survival,* is the most difficult system to govern ethically because the safeguards of one system do not work in the other and we can end up with no functioning checks and balances. We can see this, for instance, when we look at the nature of hospitals' obligations to patients. In acting as a healthcare provider to the patients, the hospital is governed by clinical ethics; in acting as a supplier to a customer, by business ethics. The problem is, as the American Joint Commission on Accreditation of Healthcare Organizations says, that the boundaries between these two roles of the hospital—between "clinical" ethics and "business" ethics and the different obligations to the patient they create—are not clear or are nonexistent. Moreover, the primary aims of the hospital in acting in one capacity or the other are not the same and can often conflict. When acting as a business, the hospital is concerned to guard against over-utilization or under-utilization of its resources. When the hospital is acting as a provider of health care in the clinical context, its primary aim must be the patient's well-being. We need institutional structures that can protect patients' welfare, but at the same time realize that goals such as efficiency and effectiveness are also ethically required. It will take deep thought (dare I say wisdom), integrity, courage, honesty and time to design and implement these structures. Many of us and

many of our societies might have a rough ride—including ethically—before this process is completed.

We also encounter difficulties with developing organizational ethics
because our basic presumptions are not neutral. Organizational ethics
could ask us, for instance, to regard hospitals and other institutional
healthcare providers—which could include governments that fund
health care—as co-fiduciaries (co-trustees) for populations of patients.
But what might be in the best interests of a population of patients can
often not be in the best interests of an individual patient, and this is
where the ethical conflict arises. Our current resolution of this conflict
is to have individual healthcare professionals, especially physicians, act
as fiduciaries for their patients. This role sometimes requires them to
challenge the system on a particular patient's behalf, creating severe
stress for both the physician and the system. One response to this
dilemma is to argue that we need medicine that is appropriately—that
is, ethically—economically disciplined: For instance, as discussed in
the previous chapter, it is suggested that physicians need not tell their
patients about more expensive treatments if the less expensive one is
adequate but not as good as the other. But as ethicist Lawrence McCul-
logh has pointed out, being an economically disciplined fiduciary is an
ethically unstable situation. The nature of being a fiduciary is to act in
the utmost good faith, trust and confidence towards the other person.
Physicians' not telling their patients about better treatments clearly
breaches these obligations. There is no point in creating a fiduciary
obligation and then voiding it of any content. In fact to do so is more
dangerous than not creating such an obligation.

We need institutional structures that ensure ethical behaviour, and
we must eliminate those that do the opposite. In implementing organizational ethics, we must make certain that our efforts do not detract
from a feeling of ethical responsibility on the part of individuals.
Organizational ethics must be in addition to, not in place of, individual
ethical responsibility. Indeed, individual ethical responsibility is
crucial to the practice of institutional ethics. Moreover, individuals
must understand that they can play an important role in developing

institutional ethics. An approach taken by the Quebec government is interesting in this regard. Instead of legislating a code of ethics for healthcare institutions, it legislated that each institution, after wide consultation with its staff, must draft and adopt its own code. This approach ensures that institutions take "ownership" of ethics within their milieu.

In establishing a framework of questions, we must also keep in mind that decisions about health care are never just about health care. In democratic Western societies, what we do and what we do not do in providing health care establishes important values and symbolism for society as a whole, particularly with respect to whether we espouse a fundamental value of caring for one another. Moreover, the ethical and legal tone of a society can best be judged by how it treats its weakest, neediest and most vulnerable members. In our Western societies, many of us experience such vulnerability only when we are among those who have, to use Susan Sontag's words in her book *Illness as Metaphor*, temporarily or permanently left the "kingdom of the well" to reside in the "kingdom of the sick." Health care—its presence or absence, its availability, and the conditions of its availability—can be regarded as one of the most important ethical canaries in the societal mineshaft. If the healthcare-system canary is sick, we need to be concerned about the viability of our society, or at least the ethical and moral "air" on which its well-being depends.

I HAVE SPOKEN ELSEWHERE in this book about the need to learn to live comfortably with a certain degree of uncertainty in doing ethics. Nowhere is this more true than with respect to our decisions regarding healthcare institutions and systems. Politicians will need courage in deciding both what must be done and what must not, and—perhaps most difficultly—what will not be done although it could be, even though not doing it harms some people.

Courage requires being open and honest about the fact that these decisions are being taken and the reasons for them. It also requires that the decision-makers be responsible and accountable, if trust is to be maintained in both the decision-makers and the system they establish. Ultimately, and I have found most controversially, it requires, in my view, that in publicly funded healthcare systems, the decision-makers at the political or governmental level and their loved ones should choose to be subject to the same healthcare system as the people they represent. If we look at the healthcare system as a lifeboat—and that is what it is—then the politicians and their constituents must travel together. It is too easy to deny others access to certain treatment when you are confident that if you or your loved ones needed that treatment you would never personally face the same denial.

Some important insights are emerging in relation to what is required in devising ethical limits on health care in the context of medicine without limits. I will mention just a few of these "ethical limiting devices" here.

First, though it may seem obvious that public policy must be ethical, we are only very recently starting to articulate this requirement. It was in facing the fear and sometimes hysteria and stigmatization that erupted at the beginning of the HIV epidemic, and trying to formulate ethical public policy to govern issues raised by HIV infection and AIDS, that we became most aware of the need for ethics to guide both the formulation and application of public policy. This development might have been late in coming because governmental discretion and Crown immunity have meant that governmental agencies —which in many countries are the main decision-making bodies for the healthcare system—have not been subject to legal liability for their decisions. Consequently, ethical accountability was assumed to be, likewise, excluded. It is interesting to note that it was after the Supreme Court of Canada handed down groundbreaking judgments holding statutory authorities legally liable for some of their negligent decisions that consideration of the ethical obligations of bodies formulating public policy, which includes healthcare policy, started in Canada. For instance, while a statutory authority would most probably not be held legally liable for failing to have safety standards to govern the public water supply, it might be liable for failing to ensure that those standards it did have were properly applied by its inspectors when this failure resulted in death or injury to people who used that water supply.

Second, there is an emerging recognition that in some, or even many, situations, we may not be able to "do ethics" directly. Rather, we can set up conceptual spaces in which it becomes more likely that the decisions taken will be ethical. For instance, if, in our main hospital, we have neither a pediatric intensive care unit nor a coronary intensive care unit and need, but cannot afford, both, using a conceptual space to make this decision might be the most ethical way to choose. We can imagine these spaces as metaphysical public squares in which all those who should be present are present and interacting with one another. It is from this interaction that decisions on healthcare policy should emerge. These spaces need to be inhabited by decision-makers who act morally, without conflict of interest, from a basis of earned trust and earned authority, and are accountable.

Third, increasingly, decision-making about health care involves different sectors. As well as the obvious players from the healthcare sector itself, government, business, industry and academia are all also now involved in healthcare decision-making. The ethical rules and bottom lines governing each of these sectors are not the same, a discrepancy that can lead to ethical conflict and ethical distress when we are prevented from doing what we believe is ethically required. The conflict can be between physicians and nurses or, as has become all too commonplace lately in the United States, between a physician who wants to provide a certain treatment for a patient and an insurance company that refuses to pay for it; or between researchers and a pharmaceutical company that challenges the researchers' results because they will be harmful to sales of its products.

In a complex and acrimonious case, physician-researcher Dr. Nancy Olivieri of the Hospital for Sick Children in Toronto became embroiled in a dispute with the pharmaceutical company Apotex Inc., which was funding her research on a drug, L1 (deferiprone), which, among other indications, is given to children with thalassemia major (an inherited disorder of the oxygen-carrying red blood cells). Dr. Olivieri had signed a confidentiality agreement with the company, but based on her research findings she said that she felt morally and ethically obliged to breach it. She believed that her research showed a loss of effectiveness of the drug and adverse side effects and she wanted to warn of those dangers. She felt a particular responsibility, because her earlier research on deferiprone had promoted its use. The pharmaceutical company disagreed with her findings and responded with a statement that data from their clinical trials supported the safety and efficacy of the drug and that they were proceeding to obtain the approvals necessary for marketing it. Apotex threatened to take legal action against Dr. Olivieri if she published her findings. They did not do so, but the fallout from this dispute received intense public attention in Canada for a considerable period of time. It elicited a broad societal discussion of the ethics that must guide medical research carried out as a cooperative venture between hospitals, universities and industry, an increasingly common partnership.

Healthcare professionals who believe they are ethically required to act in a certain way, but are prevented from doing so by some person or body with authority over them, suffer not only ethical distress, but often also professional and financial harm. For instance, HMOs may "de-select" a physician (that is, not renew a contract with a physician to provide services to people insured with the HMO) if the physician's billing is above the norm.

Fourth, as discussed in other chapters, there is increasing concern in Western democracies that we have lost a sense of the common good and that no one is acting to protect the well-being of the community as a whole. Our decisions concerning health policy are important and rarely neutral in these respects. If they do not offer such protection, they are likely to harm the sense and reality of the common good and social cohesion. In some ways, we are never more alone than when we are ill, especially seriously ill. And yet in this situation we also need and can experience the most intimate and profound support of others. Most of us want this support to include whatever care and treatment might benefit us—indeed, we often feel entitled to it. And yet this care might be provided at the expense of others who also need health care. Can these conflicts be accommodated?

As a tentative suggestion, if we moved from using individualism as only a basis for rights and, as well, partnered these rights with correlative individual responsibilities, people might recognize responsibilities to the community and even engage in activism to fulfil them. Thus, individualism could, paradoxically, fuel a living sense of community. My friend and colleague Dr. Norbert Gilmore has been musing for some time on what he identifies as a lack of gratitude on the part of many of us—perhaps, sadly, a culture of ingratitude. If to our feeling of individual entitlement to health care we added one of gratitude that it is available, could this cause us to use health care differently? Might we feel obligations to maintain, protect or contribute to the healthcare system that we would not otherwise recognize? Could gratitude for health care give us back a sense and reality of community? Might the loss of a sense of gratitude have contributed to a loss of a sense of community?

And fifth, we must accept that there is no magic solution, formula or bullet to solve the difficulties we face in the allocation of and access to health care. There are multiple considerations, concerns, players, issues, structures, decisions, values, norms, attitudes and beliefs—to name just some of the important elements that must be factored into any decision-making about health care. The answers to what is being called a crisis in health care in many industrialized Western countries with publicly funded healthcare systems are not just more money or a simple redesigning of the system. We must engage in real collective moral thinking and decision-making about the provision of health care. Beleaguered health ministers and other politicians are often tempted to turn just to statistics, including economic statistics, to "fix" the healthcare system. But this approach rarely allows for a careful, in-depth, broad exploration of the values that should govern health policy decision-making.

If, as is being said, we are moving from materialism—where economic values predominate—to post-materialism—where other values are at least as important as economic ones—this new climate will affect both the content and process of our decision-making about health care. It will certainly mean that economic statistics are not, alone, an ethical basis on which to decide on health policy and healthcare funding. And yet some of our publicly funded healthcare systems—and, of course, privately funded ones—seem to have moved instead to a sole dependence on economics. We must go back to the ethical drawing board in this regard.

I believe that, at present, decision-making about health care is in the "chaos" or second phase of the triad of phases (which are also discussed in the next chapter) that we pass through in evolving new knowledge. Until the late 1960s, we were in the "true simplicity" phase. At that time, decision-making was not difficult, mainly because the health care we had developed was limited compared with what we can offer now; because we were not as sensitive as we are today to the ethical obligation to provide everyone in our society with reasonable access to health care; and because the power of health care to do harm was as limited as its power to do good. Because all these factors and others changed, we have moved with increasing momentum into a chaos phase with respect to health policy decision-making, and we are still experiencing that phase. We know and can do much more; we recognize obligations to provide access to health care; and we are aware of the power of health care for good and, sometimes, harm. But we have not yet structured our knowledge in a way that allows us to feel reasonably certain we are "doing the right thing." When we have structured this chaos, we will move to "apparent simplicity." This last stage can look very like the first one, and the decisions we make may be the same as or very similar to those that we made at the true simplicity stage. This decision-making is different, however, because unlike decisions at the true simplicity stage, these decisions are based

260   on in-depth knowledge. We could also regard this progression in the sophistication of our decision-making as an example of our using reason at the third or apparent simplicity stage, to verify the intuitive responses we had at the first or true simplicity stage.

LET'S NOW EXAMINE the four questions, the responses to which are major determinants of the system we will find waiting for us when we need health care: Who decides? On what basis? Using which procedures? And for which purposes?

WHETHER YOU OR MEMBERS of your family receive certain types of health care depends mainly on your physician. The final allocation of nearly 80 percent of all healthcare resources is made by physicians. This allocation mechanism is sometimes described as "*de facto* gate-keeping" and physicians necessarily have to undertake it—it is an intrinsic element of the practice of medicine. As explained in the previous chapter, because the physician has a primary obligation of personal care to the patient, the physician must act without conflict of interest and in the patient's sole interests in undertaking *de facto* gate-keeping. The interests of others—other patients, family or society—are secondary. *De facto* gate-keeping by physicians can be compared to "*positive* gate-keeping"—in undertaking this action the physician benefits personally from allocating resources to patients—and "*negative* gate-keeping"—in which the physician benefits personally from restricting patients' access to resources. Some commentators believe that the latter two forms of gate-keeping are inherently unethical. Certainly, if they are allowed, great care needs to be taken to ensure that physicians engaging in them act ethically.

Unethical incentives for physicians can range from financial or other benefits for using certain companies' products, to being a part-owner of a diagnostic laboratory to which patients are referred, to health insurance companies paying physicians a bonus for denying patients' access to necessary medical treatment. Giving physicians financial rewards for refusing patients' access to treatment matters, especially when that treatment might be life-prolonging or even life-saving as could be true of some treatments for diseases such as cancer. Physicians employed by some HMOs in the United States have given evidence to hearings investigating the healthcare insurance industry that they received bonuses for rejecting other physicians' applications for approval of certain treatments for patients. Some of these decisions might have been unethical. For instance, a physician whose terms of employment included such a bonus scheme gave evidence that she deeply regretted rejecting a certain treatment for a woman who was suffering from breast cancer—in fact, she said the case haunted her—because she believed the woman should have been given it. Let's think about the ethics of this: It is one matter to reject a treatment because it is inappropriate—or even, perhaps, because it is just too expensive. It is quite another matter to reward a physician for issuing such a rejection.

Physicians can also be placed in conflict of interest by the policies governing the allocation of resources adopted by the healthcare institutions in which they work or by the healthcare system or insurance company that reimburses them for their services. To say the least, healthcare policy-makers and institutions such as hospitals must take care not to place physicians who must allocate resources in unethical situations and cause them to face unethical choices. In short, the systems that institutions establish must themselves be ethical. Ethical difficulties can arise at the interface where the physician's primary obligations of personal care to the patient—for instance, to obtain the patient's informed consent to treatment—meet the reality of healthcare policy. For example, physicians find themselves in difficult ethical situations when they know that the patient requires treatment as soon as possible, but the waiting lists will result in serious delay that threaten the patient's life or health. Or, as discussed already, physicians can face ethical difficulties when a hospital or healthcare system limits the range of treatments a physician can offer

262   to a patient, because these limitations can mean the physician is acting unethically.

For instance, if a cardiac surgeon is told that she may implant a
maximum of only ten intracardiac assist devices per year, when the
surgeon and the hospital know that, on average, at least fifty patients
will need and could benefit from this potentially life-saving treatment
(the device is a defibrillator that is automatically activated if the person suffers a cardiac arrest), the surgeon faces horrible choices in
using the ten devices that are available. Ethically, the only acceptable
way to allocate them is on the "first-come, first-served" basis for those
who need and could benefit from them. Some people propose that
there is another ethical alternative, a lottery. But most of us react with
shock to this proposition, a response that may reflect a moral intuition that there is something unacceptable about it. Imagine actually
pulling a number out of a hat in the presence of a person who needed
such a device. The person is probably at increased risk of cardiac
arrest on the spot. How we will allocate such devices is a current ethical dilemma in Canada. Some estimates are that if everyone in the
country who could benefit from such a device were given it, the cost
could be as high as 4 percent of the total Canadian healthcare
budget—and that is the cost for only one item of the new technology.

Decision-makers about health care must also "think outside the
box" in assessing how, ethically, to limit healthcare costs. For instance,
acting ethically by respecting people's autonomy and right to decide
for themselves which treatments they want or do not want can
reduce costs: Many people refuse expensive, invasive, minimally life-
prolonging treatments. Sometimes lateral thinking about cost-saving is
also productive. For instance, helping people to deal with their fear of
death and offering them palliative care can give patients a wider range
of choices about care and treatment at the end of their lives. Some of
their choices could also be cost-saving—but even if they are not or cost
more than other options, ethically we might still be obliged to offer
them. So saving healthcare resources and augmenting ethics are not
always or necessarily antithetical; rather, the contrary can be true.

In the same vein, those making decisions about health care must be careful not to assess its costs within too narrow a framework. Some of our healthcare cost accounting may be warped because we adopt a "silo mentality"—we artificially divide costs into different streams (hospital care, home care or pharmaceuticals) and fail to recognize that small or moderate extra spending in one stream can save major costs in another. This mentality gives skewed results, which can, in turn, lead to unethical decisions, especially with respect to the allocation of resources. For instance, better pain-relief treatment can mean that a patient does not need hospitalization and can thereby save hospital costs. But our reluctance to spend money on very expensive pain-relief treatment may blind us to the greater overall saving that it could produce, quite apart from the fact that we would be doing the right thing ethically by making such treatment available. To give healthcare decision-makers the benefit of the doubt, they might not be aware of the suffering they cause with some of their cost-saving strategies. The alternative explanation is that they are acting grossly unethically in making certain cost-saving decisions. For instance, leaving people on waiting lists for treatments does not ultimately save the cost of the treatments these people need—unless they die while waiting. Surely, this could not be an anticipated outcome? Indeed, such patients' needs for stop-gap measures often increase the overall cost.

We need to see the big picture. We must apply the calculus of how much reduction in suffering each healthcare dollar we spend achieves and how much suffering each healthcare dollar we refuse to make available inflicts. But at the same time we must take great care not to use this calculus unethically—for instance, by wrongfully using our perception that the amount of reduction in suffering delivered does not merit the cost of the treatment in question. These are difficult calculations and are values-based. Moreover, how do we balance the suffering of one individual with that of a large group? Should we give priority to relieving the great suffering of one person over relieving the lesser suffering of many? Old questions, but ones that must still be addressed in the context of contemporary health care. Suffering can also be very hard to assess. Often it is not open to being measured quantitatively; rather it requires qualitative assessment, and healthcare administrators and policy-makers can be suspicious of qualitative assessment. This suspicious attitude is a mistake and can lead to unethical decisions in relation to both the provision of health care and the formation of health policy in that these decisions fail to give proper weight to fulfilling ethical obligations to relieve suffering. Macro- and meso-level decision-making about health care and policy is, indeed, an area in which it can be easy to say what is required from an ethical stance, but very difficult to translate it into concrete terms.

The ethical need to involve the public in health policy decision-making in general has been brought to the fore by new technologies, such as xenotransplantation and human cloning, that pose risks to everyone, whether at the physical or metaphysical level. I believe direct public consultation is likely to become increasingly common. It will be necessary as a political reality—if not for any other better reason. Perhaps the most serious danger in such consultations is that it will be only a façade. The public is already cynical about how decisions affecting it are made, especially those related to new technologies, as recent controversy over genetically modified crops and food has shown. To undertake public consultation that was anything other than open, honest, genuine and substantive would do harm to public trust, not only in the immediate situation to which it was relevant, but also much more widely. Such harm is of the most serious concern because ultimately the survival of our kind of society and democracy itself depends on public trust. We must therefore be fully conscious, at all times, of our obligations to act in such ways that public trust is honoured and reinforced.

Acting ethically at the level of societal decision-making also requires that macro-level decision-makers be held accountable for the decisions they make. The greatest source of mistrust, fear and anger on the part of the public occurs when they encounter a faceless bureaucracy and politicians who deny responsibility. Our systems have not always functioned well in the past in relation to such accountability, as the tragedies surrounding the transmission of HIV and hepatitis C through the blood system have shown.

This same context also provided, however, a remarkable example of a Canadian politician standing up to be accountable. The Government of Canada set up a royal commission (the Commission of Inquiry on the Blood System in Canada, the Krever Commission) in 1993, to investigate how the Canadian blood-supply system became contaminated with HIV and hepatitis C. The Honourable Monique Bégin was Minister of Health for Canada during part of the time these tragic events occurred. A lawsuit was launched seeking an injunction to prevent the commission from specifically naming certain people in its report as potential wrongdoers. These were all people who had made decisions or given advice about the blood-supply system at relevant times, and Mme. Bégin was one of these people. The court granted all the political decision-makers, including Mme. Bégin, immunity from being named by the commission. Mme. Bégin waived her immunity—no other politician or bureaucrat who had likewise been granted immunity took such a stance publicly. She made this decision because she believed passionately that ethically she must take responsibility. But she was very unsure what might happen as a result of doing so. As she left my office having made her decision, her parting words were "Wish me *bon courage*." The public's response to her act was overwhelming. Hundreds of people telephoned, faxed or wrote letters, all more or less along the same lines: "Thank God, that at last a politician has said, 'I will be held accountable'." There is an important and powerful lesson here.

THE TOPIC OF WHAT should be the basis of our decision-making about health care is enormous. It is not possible, here, to do more than identify some of the considerations that must be addressed. What one considers to be ethical and unethical in decision-making about health policy and health care can vary. For instance, someone deciding on the allocation of healthcare resources on the basis of a virtues-ethics approach (that is, deciding on the basis of acting morally or virtuously in making the decision) might reach a different decision than someone who valued utility foremost. The former might give priority in access to health care to the least privileged and most vulnerable people—homeless people, for example. The latter could base their decision on achieving the greatest health benefits for the largest number of people, who might be more privileged young adults.

The interaction of law, ethics and guidelines also matters in decision-making about access to health care and healthcare policy. There is a difference between assessing the acceptability of a decision about health care on the basis of whether it is, first, legal and, second, ethical, as compared with the converse. It is especially important in this area for ethics to inform law and for law not to limit ethics. Working from ethics to law makes this preferred result much more likely than working from law to ethics. We can see this difference by asking, for example, whether people have a right to have access to adequate pain-relief treatment. Ethically, the answer is clear: They do. Some health-care institutions have been more concerned, however, to ensure that pain-relief drugs are not misused (because the institutions could be legally liable if the medications were misused) than to ensure that patients have access to all necessary pain-relief treatment. Consequently, they have set up systems that make it difficult to provide patients with adequate pain-relief treatment. This is a case of law informing ethics. We must bring the law into line with ethics in such situations, which is more likely to occur if we start our analysis of any given situation from ethics.

Internal hospital policies are also used as a basis for decision-making about health care. Guidelines that articulate an institutional policy that requires, for example, that "do not resuscitate" (DNR) orders are to be placed on all patients raise ethical problems. Patients have a right to individualized personal care. To treat them as a group to which a blanket decision may be applied—especially one concerning life-saving treatments—is unethical and could often, as well, result in legal liability. Sometimes, in the past, these types of decisions have been taken on the basis of age—for instance, no one over sixty-five years of age will be given haemodialysis for terminal kidney failure. These decisions are unethical and also breach the law against discrimination on the basis of age. Care must be taken that such decisions are not still being taken, but under a medical cloak—it is common to hear healthcare professionals explain that a person would not benefit from a certain treatment because he is too old. Sometimes this judgment is correct, but sometimes it is latent, age-based discrimination. Guidelines used as a code for a series of decisions that are not made explicit also raise ethical concerns. For example, in some institutions, a DNR order does not simply mean that the people to whom such an order applies will not be given cardiopulmonary resuscitation should they have a cardiac arrest. Rather, it is a code for the withdrawal of all life-support treatment, including antibiotics or other therapies.

As discussed in the previous chapter in relation to access to research treatments, the basic presumptions on which we base our healthcare decision-making can also have an effect on our decisions. In situations of equal doubt as to whether we should provide certain health care, the basic presumption will govern and, therefore, will determine the outcome. If the basic presumption is one of access, it will be provided in situations of equal doubt. If the presumption is against access, the opposite will be true.

There are four basic presumptions. When they are applied to access to health care, let us say to the intracardiac assist device we have already considered, these become no access—it is too expensive; no access except on certain conditions—you must first try all less expensive treatments, such as drug therapy, and have these fail before access is given; access but limited on certain conditions—the treatment will be given but not to people with (to use a hypothetical example because there is no research data on this yet) end-stage congestive cardiac failure, because it has been shown to be minimally life-prolonging or ineffective in such cases; and access freely given. In general, the presumption that should, I believe, apply is access to all medically necessary health care, but limited if certain carefully defined conditions are fulfilled. The people denying access to health care should have the burden of proof; they must show they are justified in withholding it.

One question being asked is whether health care is a special "public good" with priority over other public goods such as education, welfare or housing. One could argue that it is a special public good on the basis of justice; on the basis that respect for persons and their human dignity requires the provision of health care to them; and on the basis that a right to health care is essential to the enjoyment of all other rights because one cannot exercise them if one is sick. In practice, health care claims can take priority over other comparable claims, through the often innovative use of law. Relevant law, ranging from public international, human rights and humanitarian law, to constitutional and private law—such as tort and contract liability—can be used to establish and implement a right to health care. Although such cases usually directly involve only one individual, they can set precedents that affect everyone as the *Stein* and the *Cameron* cases, which we discussed in the previous chapter, show.

At a policy level, there are arguments both for and against establishing a right to health care. Those who support such a right worry about people not having adequate access to health care and seek to ensure that their healthcare needs—if not all their healthcare desires—are fulfilled. Those who oppose such a right worry about the costs of universal access. As is often the case, there needs to be a careful balance between these two arguments: We need adequate access and we need adequate, ethically acceptable, controls on access.

Another way to assess the amount of health care to which people should ethically be given access is to work from a "mutual responsibilities" concept. If we belong to a family, community or society, we have responsibilities to the others who also belong and they have responsibilities to us—we are inter-dependent. In some cases this approach will lead to the same conclusion as a "rights-based" analysis, but in other cases it might not do so. For instance, a state that has encouraged its citizens to rely on it to provide health care in return for their paying taxes to support this service may have obligations to citizens who have relied to their detriment on the state's undertaking in this respect. Let us imagine, for instance, that the state decides to privatize its healthcare system. People who have contributed to the state healthcare system throughout their lives through their taxes, and who are now old and ill and consequently unable to buy private insurance, would in my view have a strong ethical claim against the state for the provision of all necessary health care. Whether the state would have legal obligations to these people under a mutual-responsibilities approach is not clear. Such obligations would be more likely to exist under a rights-based approach to access to health care.

It also merits noting that our view of the nature and content of mutual responsibilities with respect to the provision of health care will differ markedly depending on how we view the nature of a profession and professionals' obligations to the community. If a profession is seen largely as a free-enterprise business venture, it will entail very different responsibilities than it will if it is seen as a trust given to healthcare professionals by the community to be used on behalf of the community for the good of each of its members. While some countries adopt one or other of these approaches, in Canada we have a mixed system that can be a basis for confusion and ethical difficulties. Sometimes when we expect healthcare professionals to act as the holders of our trust, they act on a "business" basis. This is seen most starkly when healthcare professionals take industrial action—especially strike—in order to improve their working conditions. We are shocked at their doing this because we experience their actions as a profound breach of one of our most important areas of trust. In contrast, the healthcare professionals who are prohibited from striking regard themselves as being penalized in comparison with other kinds of workers who can use such tactics to further their claims. Sometimes the situation is reversed. Healthcare professionals, in particular physicians, claim privileges of professional autonomy and self-regulation on the basis that they are a trusted profession, when the public, as is currently happening in Ontario, seeks to have greater input into the regulation of the profession and individual practitioners, and a greater say in their control.

Yet another way to approach decisions about health care, especially healthcare policy, is to look at the values that inform such decisions. Australian medical law professor Philip Bates and his colleagues have suggested that we can divide these values into a series of six clusters: paternalistic; maternalistic; liberty; social conscience/fairness/equity; social efficiency/managerialist/economic rationalist; and "rule of law"/democratic. Which of these clusters we adopt, and which we give priority to when there is conflict between them, will differ according to our own values, beliefs, professional background and experience. Our decisions concerning health care will vary depending upon which value cluster is given priority. Often, we can obtain insights into the acceptability of our decision-making about health care, especially its ethical acceptability, by identifying the cluster of values that is given priority in making any given decision. For instance, a decision that has a harmful outcome for some people may be ethically acceptable if this decision is taken on the basis of social conscience, fairness and equity. The same decision may be unethical, however, if taken on the basis of social efficiency and managerialist and economic rationalist aims. A decision to spend healthcare dollars on socio-economically disadvantaged pregnant women at high risk for giving birth to premature babies, which means that we cannot afford a state-of-the-art intensive care nursery, may be ethically acceptable. But a decision simply to cut funding for intensive care nurseries in order to reduce the government's budget deficit, no matter the need for such nurseries or the harm done, would not be ethical.

We react more powerfully to some failures to uphold values than to others, not because of a difference in the seriousness of some failures as compared with others, but because of differences in the way in which these occur or the features of the decision-making that gave rise to them. For instance, we are often more appalled by a lack of adequate medical facilities for a very sick newborn child than we are by the avoidable damage that is suffered by a premature newborn baby whose mother did not receive adequate care during her pregnancy. Overt, direct threats to important values that cause obvious harms are much less ethically tolerated than are latent, indirect threats caused by difficult-to-identify decision-makers to difficult-to-identify victims. This reality can be unethically manipulated in decision-making about health care, especially at the institutional or governmental level. We fund the intensive neonatal nursery and make a large public fuss about it, which overshadows the other less obvious decisions not to provide health care that people need. Diffusing the decision-making and the responsibility for it, making it difficult to find out who decided and who should have decided, and failing to keep adequate records or to monitor the harms that result from decisions about health care—these are all ways in which decision-making can be unethically manipulated.

THE PROCESS USED FOR healthcare decision-making can have a major effect on the decisions that are made. Ethics committees are a relatively recent but increasingly used mechanism for decision-making about health care at the individual, institutional and societal levels. One important task for ethics committees in the future will be to help to develop the area of organizational or institutional ethics. In doing so, they should have a strong emphasis on "preventive ethics"—that is, what is needed to establish ethically sensitive institutional structures and systems and to identify situations that present risks of unethical conduct, especially in formulating and implementing health policy that governs the allocation of resources and access to health care.

But ethics committees are not without dangers. One danger lies in the choice of members. Some people assume that doing ethics is nothing more than a matter of good personal conscience and, as a consequence, some ethics committees operate without any member who has training in ethical analysis or adequate access to professional consultation on the matter. I have had this fact brought home to me in reviewing research projects the funding for which has been refused on ethical grounds, or reviewing an ethics committee's approval of a certain project that raises serious ethical concerns. The projects were being carried out at major Canadian universities or teaching hospitals.

In one case the ethical approval had been given by a committee that had no member with ethical expertise. The principal researcher on the project recognized that the research raised serious ethical concerns and was nervous about relying on the approval given; as she phrased it, she "didn't want to be hung out to dry" if, when knowledge of the research became public, there were concerns about its ethical acceptability. The project was sent to me when she asked the funding agency to obtain a "second opinion" on its ethics. Twelve months later, we are still working on addressing the ethical issues that this important research raises, so that it can go forward.

In another case, a well-known ethicist was listed as a member of an ethics committee that had approved a research project involving children. This project needed, as well, the approval of the research ethics committee of the granting agency funding the research. I chaired this second committee. We believed the research raised serious ethical concerns and agreed I should contact the ethicist member of the first committee. When I did so, she said she was a member of that committee but had never seen this project. We had been sent a list of the members of the institution's ethics committee, not those members who had actually reviewed this research protocol.

In yet another case, the principal researcher had acted as a member of the ethics committee and as its expert adviser on the risks involved in his own research project on premature newborn babies. The committee had approved the research as ethical, but the funding agency rejected this finding simply on the basis that the research, as described in the proposal, was on its face unethical. The funding agency did not know about the conflict of interest problem. The researcher appealed the rejection, arguing that funding agencies had no right to second-guess an ethics committee as to what was and was not ethical. It was as part of the appeal process that this conflict came to light. The researcher's appeal was dismissed.

I do not want to leave the impression that ethics committees are not effective or act unethically. They are effective and none, in my experience, act in bad faith. But sometimes they can best be described as struggling to do a good job because they do not necessarily or always have the ethical knowledge or expertise that they need. In large part, it is because applied ethics is a new field in which Canadian students, like others around the world, are only now specializing.

There is also another danger in having safeguards, such as ethics committees, if they are not effective. If safeguards are present, most people are much less concerned about a situation than they would otherwise be. We are better off not having any safeguards than we are with ones that do not function effectively and provide a false sense of security. Care also needs to be taken that there is not an abnegation of personal responsibility on the part of the members of an ethics committee. We can feel safer in groups than when we are a lone decision-maker. Committees can sometimes reach decisions that no one member acting alone would ever take.

An ethical process for decision-making about health care should include mechanisms that allow patients or institutions to appeal decisions they see as harmful to themselves or others to whom they owe obligations. For example, if an insurance company refuses to pay for an experimental treatment for an insured patient, there should be a mechanism for appeal to an impartial body of decision-makers who can review and, where appropriate, reverse the decision. Similarly, people suffering from fatal illnesses for which no standard treatment is available need to have mechanisms in place for the compassionate release of treatments that are currently being tested in clinical research trials. For instance, under the Canadian Food and Drugs Act, experimental drugs can be made available on an individual *ad hoc* basis

274   when they are a person's only hope for treatment of a life-threatening condition, such as AIDS or cancer.

Some decision-making about health care ends up in the courts, whether as a result of claims to a right to health care or as medical malpractice litigation. These cases, some of which have been discussed in earlier chapters of this book, often have a powerful impact on the access of large numbers of people to health care or the standard of care they receive. In the future, advocacy groups will likely use the courts either to make governments deliver health care or to hold them liable for failing to have done so. As mentioned already, while the Supreme Court of Canada has recognized that statutory bodies have legal immunity for their discretionary decisions, it has held them legally liable for their negligent operational decisions. These cases arose outside the healthcare context, but similar actions will likely arise in the future in that context. For example, while the government's allocation of funds to health care is discretionary and, therefore, could not be legally attacked, the decisions that a board, which is responsible to provide certain services, makes about the use of the funds it receives are more likely to be operational and, therefore, open to challenge and potential liability if a decision is negligently made.

Healthcare advocacy groups are becoming an increasingly forceful voice in decision-making about health care. They have influenced the allocation of healthcare resources and, to a large extent, have improved the access to health care of people whose interests they represent. The efforts, starting in the early 1980s, of those advocating for medical research on HIV infection and AIDS and health care for people with AIDS provided a model that others have now followed. Advocates for women with breast cancer used the "AIDS advocates" as a model and went on to point out the large discrepancies between the amount of money spent on research on AIDS as compared to that on breast cancer, although breast cancer was also a potentially fatal illness that affected a greater proportion of the population (who were mainly women) than did AIDS. In doing this, they were not proposing that the funding for AIDS research should be reduced, but that resources for breast cancer research should be increased. They have been successful in raising awareness of breast cancer and increasing funding for research and treatment. Advocacy groups do much good, but we must remember that not all those people or diseases that have an ethical claim on healthcare resources have a group advocating for them and these people's claims and needs can be overlooked. While advocacy groups have an important role, competition between these special interest groups for a share of the necessarily limited healthcare pie may not be the most equitable way, overall, to distribute healthcare resources.

Macro-level decision-making about health care is undertaken as part of the bureaucratic and political process and is therefore likely to be driven by social efficiency, managerialist, economic rationalist values. Pursuant to these values, bureaucrats often want to implement quality-control mechanisms. But while there is a valid role for quality control, we must ensure that it is used ethically. One problem is that although quality is sometimes treated as an objective criterion, in fact it is often values-based, leading to questions of whose values should predominate when there is conflict. Moreover, some of the most important aspects of health care, such as healthcare professionals' empathy and compassion for patients, may not be readily amenable to a quality-control assessment. We must be careful in deciding what elements or characteristics of a healthcare system should be assessed for quality. As physician and ethicist Howard Brody says, sometimes the measurable drives out the important.

Mark Schacter, a journalist, points out in an article in the *National Post* titled "Health-care report cards" that health care improves our lives in ways that cannot be measured in dollars and cents, and that health care does not have clear simple goals that can be assessed. He asks what factors should be measured: the overall health of a country's residents? The geographic distribution of facilities and personnel? The time you wait to be treated in an emergency room to see a specialist or have surgery? The efficiency of hospital bed management? The availability of advanced equipment? The frequency of malpractice? Courteous treatment? He says:

> Each measure reflects an aspect of what we demand from the system. Some are about quality of care, some about fairness, some about efficiency and some about effectiveness. Danger lies in a measurement system that unduly emphasises one to the detriment of others. Imagine a system where hospitals are judged on the basis of rapid turnover of hospital beds. Likely outcome? Too many patients sent home too early. A mistaken view of efficiency tramples quality and effectiveness.

Rather, he says, we need "a good mix of efficiency, effectiveness, equity and quality." But even then the media and politicians could use reporting on health care to seek scapegoats. Therefore, we must develop a healthcare reporting system "wisely and use it responsibly."

As Schacter outlines, a wise healthcare reporting system will require that we make changes when needed and admit our mistakes; it will also require a broad involvement, especially of the public; a mixture of measures covering efficiency, effectiveness, equity and quality; assessment of some final outcomes (for example, healthier citizens), but acknowledgement that some outcomes are beyond government control; that we learn from failure rather than stigmatizing it; and that we stop looking for someone to blame except those who fail to learn from failure. This is, indeed, wise advice.

OUR PURPOSE IN ENGAGING in decision-making about health care can also affect the ethical acceptability of the decisions we make. For example, to subject a person to compulsory treatment for infectious disease in order to protect public health is ethically acceptable under certain conditions and if this is the only reasonable way to prevent the spread of a serious infectious disease. Compulsory immunization of children can be justified on the same basis. An analogous question is: To what extent are we ethically justified in rejecting some individuals' claims to health care in order to protect the viability of the healthcare system as a whole? Does this reason for rejecting these claims—that is, our purpose in doing so—mean that we are ethically justified in doing so, but if this purpose were absent, so would the ethical justification?

One of the most contentious decisions in health care at the macro level is to allocate resources with an obvious aim of gaining political advantage. All such decisions should be assessed for ethical acceptability, and some will be found to be unethical. We cannot, however, lay all of the blame for these unethical decisions at the feet of the politicians involved. We, as the public, must also act ethically by not re-electing politicians whose actions are unethical, especially in relation to their decisions concerning health care. We should ask who is responsible for unethical responses on the part of the politicians, and we should recognize that sometimes, in part, we the public are.

IT HAS BEEN SAID THAT psychoanalysis is an impossible profession and sometimes it is more difficult than others. Likewise, formulating and applying health policy and designing and running a healthcare system—especially ethically—is an impossible task and sometimes it is more difficult than others.

In his book *How to Do the Impossible*, Andy Nulman, a Montreal entrepreneur, lists his rules: Have dreams and visions about what you want to do; believe that it is possible to achieve them; live in tomorrow, but not for tomorrow; and regard your failures as learning experiences, not defeats. This is probably good advice to apply in our efforts to maintain our healthcare systems.

I have merely touched on the vast and complex range of ethical issues that our healthcare systems are confronting in trying to balance fulfilling individual needs and maintaining community confidence and protecting the common good. You may feel, rightly, that I have presented only problems, not answers. In my view, however, asking as many as possible of the right questions about our health policy and healthcare system is likely to be more important than the finding of any one answer—or even many answers. Questioning necessarily involves uncertainty, and to return to a theme I have mentioned before, living with uncertainty—certainly consciously choosing to do so—requires courage. Because science and technology continue to advance at astonishing speed, we will all—whether as patients, families, healthcare professionals, healthcare administrators, government bureaucrats or politicians—need courage and compassion and wisdom in full measure in ethically limiting medicine without limits.

11. Creating an Ethics Toolbox

What Does "Doing Ethics" Require?

I n this final chapter I want to briefly explain what we mean when we say we are "doing ethics" and to introduce some concepts and methodologies that are tools with which we do ethics. Many of these tools have been used throughout this book, but explicitly identifying them can help us to understand the way in which a certain ethical position or conclusion is reached. This, in turn, helps us to see more precisely how we might agree or disagree with a stance regarding a certain matter taken on the basis of ethics. But first I want to introduce an idea I have been evolving over the past year. I call it "ethics time."

We need time in which to do ethics. The speed of the new discoveries leads to ethical exhaustion. New science is travelling much faster than either ethics, law or social and public policy in their efforts to keep up with it. In the early 1970s, an eminent Australian judge remarked that law and medicine were marching together, but law was in the rear and limping a little. The advances in genetics over the last two years of the twentieth century and the beginning of this one have caused me to question whether ethics and law are still in the same race with science. There is, of course, a grave danger if they are not. But there is an even bigger danger if we believe that our ethics and law are keeping pace with science, when, in fact, they are not. There is no more dangerous situation than believing we have safeguards that are operating adequately, when in reality this is not the case. We are lulled into a false sense of security and are much less likely to identify the harms and risks that are present than if we had no safeguards at all.

"Ethics time" is not on the same scale as "science time," "medical time," "business time" or "political time." This difference can be a source of great difficulty in doing ethics with respect to the new science. As we have seen, extraordinary scientific developments are announced almost daily, especially in the fields of genetics and molecular biology, and scientists, understandably, have an enormous drive and enthusiasm for discovery. They want to get on with what they are doing as fast as they can. The same is true, as it should be, for physicians faced with a seriously ill patient for whom some new development offers the only hope. But what if the discovery—as could be true, for instance, of xenotransplantation—poses a risk to the public? Likewise, business wants to proceed as quickly as possible with "doing business." Political time is more complex. In politics, there needs to be at least an appearance of considered and wise decision-making. But, at the same time, politicians are subject to the "do something" pressure of the electorate, especially in relation to threats to health or life, such as the shortage of organs for transplantation. Moreover, political viability can often depend on short-term answers, not approaches that would, over the long term, be the most appropriate ones. New technologies such as xenotransplantation might, therefore, be attractive to politicians not least because they could also help to

establish their country as a world leader in medical uses of biotechnology, which, in turn, would stimulate the economy. This currently
appears to be happening in Canada. In contrast to all these time-lines,
we might not be able to compress the time needed to do ethics in relation to the new science. An irreducible minimum time is needed both
to obtain the necessary facts on which to base good ethics and for a
sedimentation-of-values process that is essential to doing ethics.

Let us consider xenotransplantation. Certain risks of this technology—for instance, the emergence or identification of new infective
agents (such as we have seen with the human immunodeficiency
virus [HIV] which causes AIDS, or the prions that cause mad cow disease)—might take a considerable period of time to become manifest.
Should we, therefore, require carefully isolated, long-term studies on
xenotransplantation between different species of non-human animals
before involving humans? And when we involve humans, should we
limit this technology to a very small number of cases until we can be
reasonably certain whether the risks crystallize? To do so could take
ten, twenty or even thirty years. What are our ethical obligations to the
individuals who at present could be helped by participation in clinical
trials of xenotransplantation? What is the ethically appropriate balance
between science time, medical time and ethics time in developing
xenotechnology?

A minimum amount of time is also needed for the public to
become familiar with the benefits, potential benefits, risks and harms
of a new scientific development, not only at the physical level, but
also at the level of its potential impact on values, norms, traditions,
customs, culture, beliefs and attitudes. There is, as well, a difference
between simply delivering information on ethics to the public and
engaging the public in ethics talk about a new technology. The latter
takes time. One of the basic principles of applied ethics is that doing
ethics requires shared decision-making among all the people who
ought to be involved. The public must be one of the participants in
the decision-making, especially when, as is true in xenotransplantation, they are subject to the risks of medical research. It is difficult,

282   however, to define what constitutes sufficient public involvement in decision-making concerning new technologies and their risks, and it is unclear how we can adequately and effectively engage the public in ethics talk. At present there is, I believe, often only a façade of public consultation and involvement in decision-making. This is both less ethically acceptable and much more dangerous than a complete absence of any public involvement.

Because the scope and power of the new science is unprecedented with regard to what we could do to ourselves and our world in using it, we must be much more concerned that we might have been in the past about the discordance between science time and ethics time. As well, our communications technology and modern travel make this new science and technology instantly global in its use and impact, in a way that new scientific and technological developments never were before. In the past, limited experiments on the benefits, risks and harms of new developments were undertaken in only one location and only slowly picked up elsewhere. This geographical limitation gave many communities a delayed time-line for establishing their ethical stance on new scientific developments and, before adopting them, the advantage of having a reasonably accurate assessment of their risks and benefits.

The current instant worldwide access to new scientific developments, in itself, also raises ethical issues. Countries without the research infrastructure needed to develop, for instance, human cloning technology can use it when it has been developed elsewhere. And even if we do not regard the use of a technology as inherently wrong—as many do not with respect to xenotransplantation—in some countries the new technologies might not be used safely for either the research subject-patients involved or the public, and they may not be used ethically.

A related ethical issue is that some scientists who are prohibited from carrying out certain research in their own countries, because of its unacceptably high levels of moral or physical risks, threaten to or do take their research to countries where there are no restrictions. But while ethical restrictions are geographically limited, the risks—both physical and metaphysical—that they are meant to protect against are not. Thus, many new scientific techniques, such as xenotransplantation and human cloning, need trans-national ethical regulation.

And then there is "nature time." We can now choose to make changes in nanoseconds that would have been matters of chance and taken millions of years in natural evolution. We must carefully consider what ethics requires of us with regard to respect for nature and its time-lines. Again, we should adopt a precautionary ethical principle: Doing so would mean we would have the burden of showing that it is reasonably safe to interfere with nature time and our interference is likely to be of benefit to society before we are justified in doing so. In this way, ethics requires that we consider what the old (but currently unfashionable) virtue of prudence or restraint might require of us in pursuing the new science. In suggesting this, one risks being characterized as a neo-Luddite or as "someone who does not live on this planet"—both descriptions that the media reported have been applied to me recently, in response to my views on ethics time.

We must not assume, however, that scientific progress at any cost is worth the price, and we must also make moral progress. One way to view the new science, which some might find surprising, is as opening up ways—perhaps even unprecedented opportunities—to make moral progress. But this will require wise restraint of two kinds. First, we must take the time necessary to keep scientific progress and moral progress moving forward together. Second, we must decide what we must *not* do with the new science, no matter what benefits are promised, because to do it would be inherently wrong. We need an extremely wise balance of progress and restraint to inform our collective decisions about what we both will and will not do with the new science and technologies. In other words, we must do science in ethics time and not vice versa.

We have profound responsibilities to consider not only our own well-being, but also that of future generations in developing new science and using new technologies. We need adequate time to undertake this decision-making. Science and ethics must march forward together. Therefore, when ethics is in the rear and limping a little, science will need to wait and help ethics catch up. We should, as it is said some aboriginal people do when faced with difficult communal decisions, look back seven generations and forward seven generations to inform ourselves how to decide. This is a truly profound appreciation and implementation of ethics time and we would be wise to learn from such wisdom.

I TURN NOW TO LOOKING in more detail at what doing ethics means and the conceptual tools we need. This is necessarily a broad-sweep overview, which means that in the rest of this chapter we shift, sometimes abruptly, between the different concepts, ideas, methodologies or metaphors that are used in doing ethics.

Many people believe that the beginning and end of doing ethics is to act in good personal conscience. They are right that this is the beginning, but wrong that it is the end. We all need to do ethics and, therefore, to learn how to do it. But doing ethics is not always a simple task: It is a process, not an event, and, in many ways, a life-long learning experience.

Good ethical judgment can be elusive. Often certain kinds of knowledge related to ethics can be sought only by setting up a conceptual space—made up of images, analogies and other intangible tools of the mind—within which we hope to encounter this knowledge. And some ethical insights can be difficult to communicate, at least verbally: It might be that we can only comprehend them through experience or moral intuition. Consequently, we have to construct the conceptual space we need for doing ethics in such a way that it can accommodate and foster both theoretical and experiential knowledge and allow us to use this knowledge to generate the full range of insights necessary to doing ethics.

Much of the ethics talk about scientific developments, especially at the societal level, purports to be based only on reason. However, other human ways of knowing are also essential to this discussion. A **285** major challenge in doing ethics is to accommodate these other ways of knowing in a structure that fully integrates them with both reason and each other. Ways of knowing other than reason include "examined emotions" such as empathy and compassion; intuition, especially moral intuition; human memory (to use John Ralston Saul's term for history); common sense; and imagination and creativity.

We can compare doing ethics to the situation of a five-year-old boy who wants to bake a cake. His mother gives him the ingredients— butter, milk, flour, eggs, sugar, flavouring, raisins—and he simply throws them into a bowl and stirs them with a wooden spoon. The result will be a lumpy mess, not a cake and probably not even a pan-cake. The boy's mother knows how these ingredients must be com-bined in order to achieve the necessary blending. Moreover, she knows that, depending on how she treats these ingredients—both before they are put into the mixture and the way in which they are introduced—she will obtain a very different kind of cake. If she sepa-rates the egg whites from the yolks and beats the egg whites and lightly folds them in at the last moment, she will have a light sponge cake; if she uses the eggs whole, a dense tea cake. In both cases, she ends up with a cake, but they are of very different natures.

In much the same way, depending on how we treat and "mix" the "ingredients" that we use in doing ethics, analogous variations may occur. Transdisciplinarity is based on a belief that the learning or methodologies of any one discipline are too confining to enable us to deal with the complexity of many of the most important and urgent societal issues, in particular, to do ethics properly in relation to these issues. Transdisciplinarity recognizes the major impact that our choice of methodology can have on the decisions we make, espe-cially concerning ethics. This approach, which is still in the process of development, has an aim of embedding various streams of knowl-edge in one another and seeks to re-create integrated knowledge through doing this. A transdisciplinary approach can be contrasted with parallel disciplinary activity (which is what most people mean by interdisciplinary work) and seeing ethics as an "add-on" after the "real" work—for instance, the science—is completed.

Transdisciplinarity will compel us to find a common vocabulary between the disciplines. But we also need integrated and integrating language that goes beyond the disciplines, especially in the form of metaphor, narrative or even poetry (in the broad sense of this word). These literary forms can help us to identify ethically important emotions and intuitions, to integrate what we know with what we feel, and then to critically examine, from the perspective of ethics, the knowledge that results. This may seem a loose and uncertain approach and it can be difficult for some people to accept that they cannot be in direct control of doing ethics, but must simply enter the process with honesty, integrity and "good faith" and see what results. To do this requires, as I have said often in this book, that we learn to live at least reasonably comfortably with necessary and justified uncertainty.

Our language problems in doing ethics do not end here. One of the great difficulties we face is that our secular societies lack a secular vocabulary that can adequately capture the metaphysical reality essential to our human well-being, both as individuals and as a society, regardless of whether we are religious. Traditionally, we have used the language of religion to capture the dimension made up of the human spirit, and we often still do so, but this can cause serious difficulties for those who reject religion. One of the challenges of multiculturalism, pluralism and, indeed, globalization is to find a language and vocabulary that will cross the boundaries of religion, ethnic and national origin, and culture, and capture the profound shared realities of the human spirit that can give meaning to our lives. Finding this language is fundamental to doing ethics, and, from some perspectives—for example, an environmental one—it might also be critical to our survival as a species and planet. It is telling that we frequently speak of our planet as a spaceship or a lifeboat. What this tells us is that we are all travelling together. But even today we seem not to have a sufficient awareness that our fate—to a greater rather than a lesser extent—will be a common one.

WE NOW LOOK AT FIVE features of doing ethics: the levels at which we do this; the basic presumptions we can use; the integration of "old" values with new ones; the stages of the evolution of ethics; and the relationship of law and ethics.

We do ethics at different levels—mega or global, macro or societal, meso or institutional, and micro or individual—and the level at which we address a problem can make a difference ethically. What is ethical at one level might not be at another. For example, it can be unethical not to consider maximizing efficiency and cost-saving in designing and operating a healthcare system, but doing so can make it difficult, and sometimes impossible, for physicians to fulfil their obligations of "personal care" to the individual patients who use the system. Similarly, the protection and promotion of some elements of a healthcare system, such as caring, might not be seen as ethically required or relevant above the micro or individual level—a view that is often in error.

Many people do not recognize that the basic presumption on which an ethical analysis is based in a given situation can have a major impact on the decision as to what is or is not ethical. For instance, we can compare a basic presumption that genetically altered food may be marketed until there is evidence that it is unsafe (this is a "yes, but . . . " presumption—yes, it may be marketed, but not if it is shown to be unsafe), with a presumption that genetically altered food must not be marketed unless it is shown to be reasonably safe (a "no, unless . . . " presumption). People wanting to market such food are favoured by the former presumption, those opposing it by the latter one. In situations of equal doubt as to safety, the stance of the person favoured by the basic presumption will prevail. The person relying on an exception must prove that, in all the circumstances, the exception should apply. This may not be easy to do, especially in relation to the rapidly appearing and unprecedented breakthroughs we are witnessing in science today. Unlike the "yes, but . . . " and "no, unless . . . " basic presumptions, the two other possible basic presumptions are unconditional: These are "no" (it is inherently wrong) and "yes" (there are no restrictions—a fully libertarian approach).

288   Lately, we have often heard calls for a return to "old" moral values or statements that previous generations were more ethical than the present one, and that we should emulate them. This view implies that changes in ethics swing as a pendulum, moving towards new approaches and then reversing to re-adopt old values when difficulties arise. This image is not correct. A preferable image is that of a spiral—like the DNA double helix—that goes upwards. If we view doing ethics as a process of developing a complex of values intertwined in a three-dimensional structure, we can imagine ourselves as moving from "old ethics" to new insights. In this way we can "re-spect" (look back on) the old values that we need and bring them forward into the present. Our task, then, is to accommodate the old in the new, giving rise to a very different version and vision of ethical reality than would simply returning to the old. Whereas the pendulum model limited our approach to two dimensions, the three-dimensional helix approach is likely to produce a much wider variety of ethical insights that are more finely nuanced.

In doing ethics in relation to new scientific developments, we pass through three stages: true simplicity, chaos and apparent simplicity. In the *true simplicity* phase, often we do not know enough to be confused about what is ethically right and ethically wrong. Interestingly, though, our responses at this stage are often ethically correct, typically because of a reliance on moral intuition. When we know more, we enter the *chaos* phase. Structuring this chaos usually results in our being able to identify clear ethical approaches that can frequently be very similar to those we adopted at the true simplicity phase. The difference is, however, that at the *apparent simplicity* phase, unlike the true simplicity one, our decisions are based on a deep understanding of the ethical issues involved.

Sometimes ethics and law can conflict, and it can make a difference to the outcome of our ethical decision-making in these situations whether we start from law or ethics. If we enquire, first, what is the ethics, and then ask what is the law and whether this conforms with the ethics, we might come to a different conclusion than if we start with an enquiry as to the law. A good example in this regard is how we view the ethics and law of withdrawing life-support treatment. In the past, some physicians were frightened to withdraw such treatment even though the patient wanted it done, because the physicians believed the law prohibited it. But if we start from ethics, it is clear that for a physician to impose treatment on a competent adult patient who refuses it is a breach of ethics—it fails to show respect for the patient and the patient's rights to autonomy and self-determination. Consequently, the law has been interpreted to allow (indeed require) physcians to respect the informed refusals of this treatment. This approach can be summed up as having ethics informing law rather than law informing ethics when there is conflict between the two and the conflict must be resolved.

I WANT NOW TO OUTLINE three concepts that are fundamental to doing ethics: values, trust and risk. They are related; for example, shared values help us to trust others and we tolerate higher degrees of risk being imposed by the decisions of those people we trust than those we do not.

Ethics deals with values. For one thing, doing ethics requires us to identify our values. Moreover, we must justify the choice of the values on which we base our ethical decisions. These different justifications correspond to different ways of doing ethics, which can be loosely separated into groups that are sometimes called "schools of ethics." Among the diverse schools are principle-based or deontological ethics; situational ethics; utilitarian ethics; consequentialist ethics; casuist or case-based ethics (an approach similar to the legal doctrine of precedent); narrative ethics; feminist ethics; hermeneutical ethics (an approach based on interpretation of a context or text); and virtues or character ethics (virtuous or moral people decide what is ethical).

When each of the different schools of ethics gives the same response with respect to how we should act regarding a given ethical issue, there is no ethical dilemma. Although our reasons for acting in a particular way may differ, we all agree on what should be done in this case. Often, however, we disagree. Moreover, even if we use the same school of ethics as the basis of our ethical analysis, there can still be disagreement: When values conflict—that is, when they cannot all be simultaneously honoured—we may not agree on the relative weight and priority that we should give to the different values.

One way to envision what is involved in doing ethics is to imagine the situation that raises the ethical issues as the centre of a circle and the people who should be included in the decision-making about how to deal with this situation forming a ring along the circumference. Each person has a light that they shine on the centre to make visible the perspective of that person's discipline or school of ethics or some other relevant perspective on the situation. Each of these lights shows up different features or "truths" about the situation, some of which can be seen only with a particular light. When we are fortunate, the combination of these different coloured lights gives rise to a white light of ethical insight. When the various lights cannot be integrated, we must identify the values each "lit-up area" represents and put these values in order of priority. When this happens, we experience values conflicts and ethical distress; that is, some of us have to live with a situation in which values that are important to us are being breached.

In doing ethics, we must also be cognizant of the fact that we react more powerfully to some failures to uphold values than to others. This results not from a difference in the seriousness of the failures, but because of differences in the way they occur. The more overt a threat to values, the more important the societal values, such as respect for people's life and health, that are threatened; the more obvious the harm caused by the breach, the more serious the harm and the higher its probability; the more clearly identified the potential victim before the breach occurs, the more clearly identified the decision-maker and the decision-making process; and the more directly the decision-maker can be seen to have inflicted harm, then, the more likely it is that this decision-maker will be held both ethically and legally liable for the harm his or her decision causes. The corollaries to this are equally true. Thus decision-making can be manipulated to make it seem less ethically concerning. For instance, if we cannot identify who decided it was too expensive to implement a new test for HIV in the blood system or refused to reclassify a new cancer treatment as standard treatment and not research and thereby make it readily available, we might not see those actions as ethically wrong. This is partly because we are less aware that such a decision was made; the absence of the test or treatment seems to occur through chance, not human choice. Sometimes people in authority intentionally use decision-making structures that make it difficult to identify a clear decision-maker or that inflict harm only indirectly or threaten values only latently. They may do so for reasons ranging from cost-saving to avoiding responsibility or liability. Some decisions that can at first glance appear to be ethical might not be in substance, when we review them with these factors in mind.

Trust is an increasingly talked about and, if we believe the thrust of this talk, a rapidly decreasing feature of our relationships with one another and our societal institutions. But this might be an unwarrantedly pessimistic view. Just one example can show that we have greater degrees of trust now than in the past. A hundred years ago, how many people did we need to trust to feel that the food we ate for breakfast was safe? How many do we need to trust today? A century ago, we grew our own vegetables, exchanged food with neighbours and personally knew the butcher and baker. Today our grapefruit might have come from one continent, the grain for our cereal from another and the bacon from yet another. Thousands of people had access to these products, but we trust that they are safe for us to eat. Nevertheless, we can have problems in feeling that we can trust others, especially those people or institutions with the power to affect our lives, which today include scientists and science as major players. Because of its unprecedented new discoveries and powers, science is now one of the areas where many of us are concerned to ensure trust and trustworthiness.

What do people expect of scientists with regard to trust? And what do scientists expect from the rest of us with regard to our trusting them? At the World Conference on Science in Budapest in 1999, which was attended by over three thousand of the world's leading scientists, I frequently heard scientists repeating the old mantra: "Science is value free." They were arguing that no restrictions should be placed on the discovery of knowledge, and that only when knowledge is applied should ethics come into the picture. This split reminds me of the one we used to make between the mind and the body, but have abandoned as a result of stunning advances in psychoneuroscience. Perhaps, just as science showed us the great error of that dichotomy, ethics might show the same in relation to pure and applied science. These scientists believed that all that ethics required of them as scientists was that they should act in good personal conscience. While this is necessary, it is not enough.

Like medicine, science has traditionally been governed by "blind trust," largely because of the huge gulf in understanding between those "who knew"—the scientists—and the general public. Today this gap is greatly diminished. Indeed, ethics requires that scientists explain their science to the public along with the issues, including the ethical ones, that their research raises. Scientists must now earn the public's trust, that is, show the public that it should place its trust in them and continuously demonstrate this. Earned trust, unlike blind trust, is a process, not an event; it must be earned throughout a relationship and, of course, it can be lost at any time.

Earned trust requires that those whom we trust be responsible and accountable when something goes wrong that harms us. It requires, as well, that before we place people at risk, we obtain these people's consent to actually being put at risk. If physicians have ethical and legal obligations to obtain their patients' informed consent to the risks involved in accepting or refusing medical treatment, do scientists have an obligation to inform the public of the risks of their research or those of its potential applications and uses? Should we regard the public as a research subject and, therefore, obtain its consent to these risks? Such consent is mandatory under all codes of ethics governing research involving human subjects. Are some agreements between scientists and corporate sponsors unethical— for example, those under which scientists agree to bans on discussing their research in public while it is in progress, or to delay publishing their results, or not to publish them at all unless the sponsors agree? Might the purposes for which the research results could be used indicate that undertaking the research is, in itself, unethical? Or are the scientists correct who believe that knowledge—and the science that reveals it—is value free? Do scientists' ethical obligations vary according to whether they are funded by society or privately? Should we regard scientists as having fiduciary obligations to the public and to future generations and, if so, what would this mean?

Risk is yet another ethical issue. "Applied ethics"—ethics in practice—flows back and forth between facts, including scientific facts, ethics and law. This is not accidental: Good ethics depends on good facts, and good law depends on good ethics. Risk is often among the most important of the ethically relevant facts.

Assessment of risk and communication of information about risk, including that involved in scientific research and development, are complex tasks and our reactions to this information are a complex phenomenon. Even when we turn just to physical risks, there can be uncertainty, because the scientists cannot agree on the magnitude and prevalence of a given risk. This means that we cannot insist on certainty. What we can insist on is honesty, good faith (especially an absence of conflict of interest) and non-negligence in risk assessment. We must also recognize that almost all our decisions about risk involve value judgments. Thus we should identify the values that inform these decisions and, from an ethical perspective, be able to justify our choice of the values we use to inform our decisions about risk.

The levels of risk we will perceive and accept ultimately relate to trust. If we trust the person or institution who estimates, evaluates or imposes the risk (which is more likely if that person or institution is

294   seen to be ethical), we will tolerate a higher level of risk than if these
factors are not present. People's perceptions of the seriousness and
probability of risks are magnified if there is an approach of secrecy,
arrogance or incompetence, or if the person or institution making the
decision seems to be independent of any regulatory or policy-making
process. People perceive the risks imposed on them in these circumstances as being outside of any trusted control. This increases the
unacceptability of the risk's dread factor and, therefore, of the risk.

There are also risks in risk assessment, especially in relation to the
new science and technology. One is that we tend to focus only on physical risks and not on those equally important intangible or metaphysical risks like deterioration of shared values. Humans are visually
oriented and activated and we react much more readily to risks when
we can see their effects. Even in pluralistic, democratic societies, we
can agree that certain physical risks are bad and that we do not, in any
circumstances, want to be exposed to them. Such a consensus is
rarely possible with respect to metaphysical risks. And yet we ignore
these at the peril of our society. In my more optimistic moments, I
view the resurgence of interest in ethics as a strong and hopeful sign
that we have recognized this danger and are acting to avert it.

It matters, as well, whether a risk is likely to be reversible should
it occur. We have the most serious obligations not to engender irreversible harms. I have referred, previously, to Bill Joy's article, "Why
the Future Doesn't Need Us," published in *Wired* magazine. Joy
warns that the new technologies—genetic technology, nanotechnology
and robotics—could cause "something like the extinction" of
humankind within the next two generations. He spoke of being
deeply concerned about the power to create new forms of life that
could reproduce, that could unleash self-replicating, mutating,
mechanical or biological plagues. These organisms could not be
recalled and could create "a replication attack in the physical world"
comparable to the viruses and "worms" that have caused serious
damage to major commercial Web sites in the virtual world. He
believes that these new technologies are a much greater threat to

humanity than nuclear weapons, because unlike the latter, they are not hard to come by and they do not require a state to unleash them; they could be unleashed by a single individual. We would do well to generalize Joy's warning to all our new technologies. To advocate doing so is not intended to be fear-mongering with regard to new science and technologies or to promote an anti-science reaction. Rather, it is meant to reflect the profound sense of respect and responsibility that we should feel for the immense powers the new science and technologies have placed in our hands.

FINALLY, VIRTUES AND VICES—in particular, the concept of evil— could provide insights in doing ethics.

The virtues have been around for a long time in human moral history. Indeed, to some they seem distinctly out of date. Could they, however, function as signposts to guide us and our reason and moral intuition in seeking ethical insights? Can we use them in new and imaginative ways that would give us access to ethical knowledge that would otherwise be unavailable?

Imagine a pile of bricks, with each brick representing a virtue. Humans have used bricks for many thousands of years, but how we arrange and combine them today is different from what we have done in the past and can radically change the structures we create. The same is true of the virtues when they are used as building materials for a contemporary ethics structure. Imagine, now, how the virtues might provide guidance in doing ethics in relation to the new science. *Honesty* speaks for itself. *Courage* is the courage to act with integrity, to say yes when it is ethically appropriate and the courage to say no when, likewise, that is ethically required. In our society the latter is often more difficult than the former. We use *restraint* when we ask what we ought not do, when we take the time, ethics time, to try to make wise, ethical decisions. *Fidelity* is expressed in a commitment to trying to do the right thing; for instance, when politicians make the laws and guidelines that will govern the new science, they implement fidelity when they act on the basis of promise-keeping and a commitment to the public good. The deepest expression of fidelity, one that underlies all other commitments, is commitment to respect for life and to the human spirit. The virtue of *generosity* can be honoured in relation to the new science, for instance, by acting justly in providing access to the benefits of scientific research, especially towards those who are most deprived and vulnerable. What would applying this virtue indicate as ethical or unethical approaches in relation to the patenting of human DNA or inserting terminator genes in crop seeds (the crops from these seeds are prevented from producing fertile seed)? We need *tolerance*—for instance, in dealing with our values conflicts—and *forgiveness*—perhaps of ourselves, for our inevitable mistakes in dealing with our extraordinary new scientific discoveries, as much as the errors of others. As is so often true in doing ethics, we must balance the application of each virtue with that of the others. For instance, tolerance that is not balanced by courage, restraint or fidelity could be just as ethically damaging as the failure to practise tolerance at all.

In recent times, the concept of evil has been equally as unfashionable as the idea of the virtues. Perhaps instinctively, we usually recoil from evil. We might even have an intuition that it could be "infectious." Sometimes we deal with evil by making it disappear through redefinition, often as sickness. Frequently this is justified, but sometimes we need to face the fact of evil. To recognize evil might also be to recognize that some things are inherently wrong, and this is not a popular stance in societies such as ours in which situational ethics is the predominant mode of values analysis. The concept of evil has, as well, strong religious associations. For these and other reasons, evil is a difficult topic to discuss.

In 1996, I was asked to speak at a conference at the Holocaust Museum in Washington, D.C. The conference was being held on the fiftieth anniversary of the Doctors' Trial before the Nuremberg War Crimes Tribunal. George Annas and Michael Grodin, in their book *The Nazi Doctors and the Nuremberg Code,* had written that among the most profound questions in medical ethics is "How could physician-healers have turned into murderers?" I decided to examine this question and to explore whether there were any ethical insights that could be gained by today's medical researchers and physicians, through considering, horrible as it is to do so, the Nazi doctors' involvement in euthanasia and human experimentation.

Some researchers and physicians whom I told that I was writing on this topic reacted with great anger. I hastened to explain I was not suggesting that today's researchers and physicians were evil or could be compared to the Nazi doctors, but they refused to be appeased. They rightly understood that to recognize there could be such lessons is to recognize the possibility that contemporary researchers and physicians, or science and medicine themselves, could be connected with evil, and this is, truly, a horrible thought.

While it is easy to understand why any scientist or physician would want intensely to disidentify from the Nazi doctors, it might not be the wisest course to take. We might, for instance, learn valuable lessons from asking whether there are any factors in our society, and its science and medicine, to which we should respond with concern and care because they are similar in some ways to factors that were present in German society, and its science and medicine, at the time of the Nazis.

Take for example the search for perfection. Perfecting ourselves—or at least our children—is one of the loudly trumpeted benefits of the new science, as we saw in discussing new reproductive and genetic technologies and possibilities such as cloning. Fascist ideology incorporated the notion of perfection, whether of people or the self-perfecting state. It is therefore not surprising that one feature of German medicine, just prior to the Holocaust, was that it saw itself as having a valid and important role to play in the search for what the Nazi state saw as perfection in people, institutions (including medicine) and the state, through an exclusively scientific, rationalist approach.

I have mentioned already our loss of awe and discomfort with mystery and our tendency to deal with this loss and discomfort by turning a mystery into a problem and then seeking a solution to that problem. This is to use a conversion technique—we convert one issue to another in order to be able to deal with it in a certain manner. In Nazi Germany, broad social problems (such as caring for mentally ill or physically disabled children or adults) were converted to scientific or medical problems in order to see them as open to rational solutions (in this case, eugenics programs involving sterilization or euthanasia). This may give the impression of solving the problem in question through a quick, technical fix. Moreover, when mentally or physically disabled people are characterized as a "problem," and this "problem" is seen as an obstacle to fulfilling a political agenda, dealing with it through medicine or science—placing a medical or scientific cloak on it—makes the ethical concerns less obvious. This becomes even more likely when the benefits and potential benefits of dealing with the "problem" through scientific or medical research are emphasized to the exclusion of other considerations—for example, the harm that carrying out the research aimed at remedying the "problem" or applying its results could cause to fundamental values, human rights, human ethics and our common human spirit and spirit of humanity.

Science is based on rationality and is an important institutional manifestation of this attribute. When rationality is our most esteemed human attribute and value, this connection of rationality and science means that science can be used in ways that are inappropriate or even unethical. For instance, most people, even those people who approve of the genetic manipulation of human embryos, do not, on the whole, believe that parents should be compelled to correct serious defects in their future children or be penalized for not doing so. But, occasionally, one hears a proposal to this effect. In particular, science can become a justification in relation to matters of vital human interest that are not essentially scientific matters and where, therefore, it is inappropriate and unethical for it to function in this manner. In other words, science can be used to replace morality or ethics as a justification of certain actions. I believe that this occurred in Nazi medicine and it would be easy for this same mechanism to operate today—which is in no way meant to imply that evil would likewise result. But until we recognized the need for ethical review of medical research involving human subjects, for example, we were using a scientific aim as the main justification for such research. And, indeed, those contemporary scientists who believe that ethics is irrelevant to "pure" science research and applies only at the level of its application are adopting a view that a scientific aim alone justifies their research.

One danger to which the Nazi horrors could alert us, which might pass unnoticed, is that we tend to place technology between us and those who are harmed by its use, in such a way that we see the technology, and not us, as causing the harm. This is a central message of Michael Ignatieff's book *Virtual War*, which points out the immense danger of such an anesthetization of our perceptions and emotions. In seeing technology and not ourselves as doing the harm, we often fail to recognize—as Raphael Sassower points out in his article "Responsible Technoscience: The Haunting Reality of Auschwitz and Hiroshima"—that in dealing with technoscience we are dealing with humans and their creations and that all those involved with the creation or use of technoscience must have a sense of personal responsibility. There is a price paid for pure objectivity and value neutrality with respect to science, he says. "If rationality is separated from the emotions, and if instrumental rationality is separated from morality as such, then it makes perfect sense to speak of the separation between science and ethics."

But personal detachment and disinterestedness are essential components of scientific integrity and some aspects of scientific morality. We must seek ways, therefore, to reconcile these values with ethical responsibility and ask what achieving this requires on the part of researchers. Sassower suggests a provisional "code" that may serve as a guide for increased personal responsibility of individual technoscientists (especially academic scientists and industrial engineers). In particular, he argues that scientists must not be value neutral about the evil uses to which their discoveries might be put, and that concerns about the ethics of the use of technologies that certain

300   research makes possible can indicate it is unethical to undertake that research.

An editorial in *The Lancet* provides a relevant example in this respect. It warns that as a result of decoding the human genome, new weapons targeted against specific individuals or populations could be developed: "Concern has slowly surfaced about biological weapons with selective ethnic targets." There is military interest in the ability to design biological warfare agents that would "evade natural immunity and existing vaccines." As a result of research programs such as the Genome Diversity Project, they might be designed "to attack known receptor sites for which differences exist at cell membrane level"—that is, to maim or kill people in certain ethnic or racial groups, but not others. *The Lancet* concludes that what we are talking about here is "an abuse of scientific knowledge . . . a hideous conception." Appallingly, and profoundly sadly, words that can be used to describe the horrors perpetrated by Nazi scientists in the name of science are still a relevant warning about some potential uses of science today.

Professor Upendra Baxi's concept of the functionalization of evil, which has been mentioned already, also warns of a serious danger in the approach taken to evil within our contemporary societies. This should alert us to the fact that we can lose our sense of the evil that is involved in certain conduct through looking for and focusing only on the good that did or could come out of the conduct. This is a concept that we should have in mind as we ponder and decide what we should and should not do with the new science and technology.

Constructing an ethics toolbox is an ongoing process, not an event. We must continue to construct a toolbox that will help us to hold safely in the palm of our collective human hand—for both ourselves and future generations—the extraordinary powers that the new science and technology are giving us.

Epilogue

As a child my father was an altar boy in a Roman Catholic church in a very small town in the vast Outback of Australia. When I knew him, he was first an atheist, later, an agnostic. And even later still, I am not sure what his beliefs were.

When he was dying, I asked him if he would like to see a priest. He answered wryly, "No, keep those black crows away from me," and asked why I thought he would want to do this. I replied he was one of the most religious—although *spiritual* would have been a better word—people I had ever met. He laughed and said that was not correct. I explained to him that I found his profound connection with nature, his way of seeing the world, his love of ideas and the "things of the human spirit" an expression of intense spirituality. He smiled and said, "Margo, that is not religion, that's living with the universe."

302   A priest friend to whom I told this story remarked that this was perhaps one of the best definitions of religion he had ever encountered.
As I have mentioned before, the word *religion*, after all, comes from
"re ligere"—to bind together—and the universe is the grandest scale
on which we can do this.

Several years after my father died, I gave a speech that I called
"Gazing at Stars and Patting Cats." Its basic theme was that in order to
live with equanimity and hope, to experience awe, wonder and joy,
and to deal with our tragedies, despairs and sorrows, we humans
need to have one hand patting an animal or in the earth at the same
time as we reach out with our other hand to the stars—to the universe. In a way, we humans are the medium through which the Earth
and the Universe meet—the window through which they can see each
other—because we can perceive them both. New science and technology have had a major impact on both poles of the spectrum of our
perceptions and knowledge and, in doing so, have lengthened the
spectrum dramatically. This spectrum now extends into the deep
inner space of ourselves through genetics and the vast cosmic outer
space and time of the universe through astrophysics. We have not yet
sufficiently expanded the scope of the ethics that must accompany the
expansion of knowledge the new science and technology bring. It will
take substantial thought, feeling, intuition, work and time to do this
and to integrate ethics with the new science and technology so that
we have a science-ethics window, not just a science one, a science-
spirit world-view that encompasses the Earth, the Universe and ourselves as part of both.

Sources

Note of explanation:
I have included many of my own articles in the following lists. These articles contain extensive references to the publications of other authors and are cited in order to give readers access to these other sources. Materials of special importance to a particular chapter in *The Ethical Canary* or those not referenced in one of my articles are listed individually.

PROLOGUE

Eckersley, R. "Universal Truths." *The Sydney Morning Herald*, 8 January 2000, p. 4s.

Books and Articles

Armstrong, Karen. *The Battle for God*. New York: Alfred Knopf, 2000.

Fukuyama, Francis. *The Great Disruption: Human Nature and the Reconstitution of Social Order*. London: Free Press, 1999.

Hein, G. "Interest Group Litigation and Canadian Democracy." *Choices IRPP* (Institute for Research in Public Policy), vol. 6, no. 2 (2000): 3–30.

Katz, Jay. *The Silent World of Doctor and Patient*. New York: Free Press, 1984.

Saul, John Ralston. *The Unconscious Civilization*. Concord, Ont.: Anansi, 1995.

Singer, Peter. *Animal Liberation*, rev. ed. New York: Avon Books, 1990.

Somerville, M.A. "Law as an 'Art Form' Reflecting AIDS: A Challenge to the Province and Function of Law," in *Fluid Exchanges: Artists and Critics in the AIDS Crisis*, ed. James Miller, 287–304. Toronto: University of Toronto Press, 1992.

————. "Messages from Three Contemporary Images of Medicine: Failed Medicine, Miracle Medicine and Science Fiction Medicine," in *From the Twilight of Probability: Ethics and Politics*, eds. W.R. Shea and A. Spadafora, 91–105. Cambridge, Mass.: Science History Publications, 1992.

————. "Planet as Patient." *Journal of Ecosystem Health*, vol. 1 (1995): 61–71.

Wright, Robert. *The Moral Animal: Evolutionary Psychology and Everyday Life*. New York: Pantheon Books, 1994.

Yankelovich, Daniel. "Trends in American Cultural Values." *Criterion* (August 1996): 2–9.

CHAPTER 2

Books and Articles

Atwood, Margaret. *The Handmaid's Tale*. Toronto: Seal Books, 1986.

"Dealing with Abortion" (editorial). *The Montreal Gazette,"* March 2000, p. B6.

Jones, D.J. "Artificial Procreation, Societal Reconceptions: Legal Insight from France." *The American Journal of Comparative Law*, vol. 36 (1988): 525–45.

Joy, Bill. "Why the Future Doesn't Need Us." *Wired* magazine, vol. 8, no. 4 (2000).

Kerenyi, T.D., and U. Chitkara. "Selective Birth in Twin Pregnancy with Discordancy for Down's Syndrome." *New England Journal of Medicine*, vol. 304 (1981): 1525–27.

Somerville, M.A. "Birth and Life: Establishing a Framework of Concepts." *University of Connecticut Law Review*, vol. 23, no. 3 (1989): 667–83.

————. "The Human Race—An Exclusive Club: What Are the Conditions for **305** Membership?, a review of *Defining Human Life: Medical, Legal, and Ethical Implications*, eds. Margery W. Shaw and A. Edward Doudera," *University of Detroit Law Review*, vol. 63 (1986): 347–59.

————. "Reflections on Canadian Abortion Law: Evacuation and Destruction, Two Separate Issues." *University of Toronto Law Journal*, vol. 31, no. 1 (1981): 1–26.

————. "Selective Birth in Twin Pregnancy" (correspondence). *New England Journal of Medicine*, vol. 305, no. 20 (1981): 1218–19.

————. "Weaving 'Birth' Technology into the 'Value and Policy Web' of Medicine, Ethics and Law: Should Policies on 'Conception' Be Consistent?" *Nova Law Review*, vol. 13, no. 2 (1989): 515–608.

Reports

Royal Commission on New Reproductive Technologies. *Proceed with Care*. Ottawa: Minister of Government Services Canada, 1993.

Legislation

Bill C-47, Human Reproductive and Genetic Technologies Act, 2d. Sess., 35th Parliament, 1996.

Civil Code of Quebec.

Criminal Code, R.S.C. 1985, c. C-46 (as amended).

Human Fertilisation and Embryology (Disclosure of Information) Act (U.K.), 1992, C.54.

Infertility (Medical Procedures) Act, 1984 (Vic.).

Cases

R. v. Morgentaler, [1988] 1 S.C.R. 301 (Supreme Court of Canada).

Winnipeg Child and Family Services (Northwest Area) v. D.F.G., [1997] 3 S.C.R. 925 (Supreme Court of Canada).

CHAPTER 3

Books and Articles

Annas, G.J. "The Shadowlands—Secrets, Lies and Assisted Reproduction." *New England Journal of Medicine*, vol. 339 (1998): 935–39.

————. "Why We Should Ban Human Cloning." *New England Journal of Medicine*, vol. 339 (1998): 122–25.

Blum, Len. "Going to the Movies, Eyes Wide Shut." *The National Post*, 30 July 1999, p. B1.

Callahan, D. "Cloning: The Work Not Done." *Hastings Center Report*, vol. 27, no. 5 (1997): 18.

306 Durkheim, Emile. *Suicide: A Study in Sociobiology*. Translated by J.A. Spaulding and G. Simpson. Glencoe, Ill.: Free Press, 1951.

Gearhart, J. "New Potential for Human Embryonic Stem Cells." *Science*, vol. 282, no. 5391 (1998): 1061.

"Human Cloning and Substantive Due Process" (note). *Harvard Law Review*, vol. III (1998): 2348.

Jonas, Hans. *Philosophical Essays: From Ancient Creed to Technological Man*. Englewood Cliffs, N.J.: Prentice Hall, 1974.

Katz, K.D. "The Clonal Child: Procreative Liberty and Asexual Reproduction." *Albany Law Journal of Science and Technology*, vol. 8 (1997): 1.

Kaye, H.L. "Anxiety and Genetic Manipulation: A Sociological View." *Perspectives in Biology and Medicine*, vol. 41, no. 4 (1998): 483–90.

Lewontin, R.C. "The Confusion over Cloning." *New York Review of Books*, vol. 44 (1997): 18.

McCabe, A. "Landry Riles D'Aquino at World Economic Forum." *The Montreal Gazette*, 1 February 1997, p. D5.

McGee, G., and A. Caplan. "The Ethics and Politics of Small Sacrifices in Stem Cell Research." *Kennedy Institute of Ethics Journal*, vol. 9, no. 2 (1999): 151–58.

Murray, Thomas H. *The Worth of a Child*. Berkeley, Calif.: University of California Press, 1996.

Nelkin, Dorothy, and M. Susan Lindee. *The DNA Mystique: The Genes as a Cultural Icon*. New York: Freeman, 1995.

Ricoeur, Paul. *Oneself as Another*. Translated by K. Blamey. Chicago: University of Chicago Press, 1992.

Robertson, J.A. "Embryos, Families and Procreative Liberty: The Legal Structure of the New Reproduction." *Southern California Law Review*, vol. 59 (1986): 939.

Shanner, L. "The Right to Procreate: When Rights Claims Have Gone Wrong." *McGill Law Journal*, vol. 40 (1995): 823.

Silver, Lee M. *Remaking Eden: How Genetic Engineering and Cloning Will Transform the American Family*. New York: Avon Books, 1998.

Wilmut, I., et al., "Viable Offspring Derived from Fetal and Adult Mammalian Cells." *Nature*, vol. 385 (1997): 810.

Reports

National Bioethics Advisory Commission (U.S.). *Cloning Human Beings: Report and Recommendations of the National Bioethics Advisory Commission*. Rockville, Md.: The Commission, June 1997.

National Bioethics Advisory Commission (U.S.). *The Ethical Use of Human Stem Cells in Research*. Rockville, Md.: The Commission, September 1999.

Books and Articles

Abraham, C. "Donor-organ Pigs Not Inspected by Health Canada." *The Globe and Mail*, 13 February 1999, p. A2.

Abraham, C. "Transplant Team Developing Animal Organs for Human Use." *The Globe and Mail*, 6 January 1999, p. A1.

Bach, F.H., J.A. Fishman, N. Daniels, J. Proimos, B. Anderson, C.B. Carpenter, L. Forrow, S.C. Robson and H.V. Fineberg. "Uncertainty in Xenotransplantation: Individual Benefit versus Collective Risk." *Nature Medicine,* vol. 4, no. 2 (1998): 141–44.

Binder, S., A.M. Levitt, J.L. Sacks and J.M. Huges. "Emerging Infectious Diseases: Public Health Issues for the 21st Century." *Science*, vol. 284 (1999): 1311–13.

Cartwright, W. "The Pig, the Transplant Surgeon and the Nuffield Council." *Medical Law Review*, vol. 4, no. 3 (1996): 250–69.

"The Frankenpig That Wasn't" (editorial). *The Globe and Mail*, 16 February 1999, p. A14.

Leake, Jonathan. "First CJD Baby Feared as Surge in Cases Is Forecast." *Sunday Times* (London), 27 February 2000, p. A1.

Malamet, E. "Um, Like How Does This Affect Me? Teenage Ethics." *National Post*, 21 June 1999, pp. D1–2.

Somerville, M.A. "Access to Organs for Transplantation: Overcoming 'Rejection.'" *Canadian Medical Association Journal*, vol. 132, no. 2 (1985): 113–17.

———. "Medical Interventions and the Criminal Law: Lawful or Excusable Wounding?" *McGill Law Journal*, vol. 26, no. 1 (1980): 82–96.

———. "'Procurement' vs. 'Donation'—Access to Tissues and Organs for Transplantation: Should 'Contracting Out' Legislation Be Adopted?" *Transplantation Proceedings*, vol. 17 (6 suppl. 4) (1985): 53–68.

Reports

American Medical Association, Council on Ethical and Judicial Affairs. "The Use of Anencephalic Neonates as Organ Donors." *Journal of the American Medical Association,* vol. 273 (1995): 1614–18.

American Medical Association, Council on Ethical and Judicial Affairs. *The Use of Anencephalic Neonates as Organ Donors—Reconsideration.* Council on Ethical and Judicial Affairs Report 1-I-95.

Law Reform Commission of Canada. *Criteria for the Determination of Death.* Working Paper 23, Protection of Life Series. Ottawa: Minister of Supply and Services Canada, 1979.

Nuffield Council on Bioethics. *Animal-to-Human Transplants: The Ethics of Xenotransplantation.* London: Nuffield Council, 1996.

308 *Proposed Canadian Standard for Xenotransplantation*. Ottawa: Therapeutic Products Programme, Health Protection Branch, Health Canada (Draft 14, prepared July 1999).

Recommendations for the Disposition of the Health Canada Primate Colony. Expert Panel Report prepared at the request of the Royal Society of Canada for Health Canada. Ottawa: 1997.

Report on National Forum on Xenotransplantation: Clinical, Ethical and Regulatory Issues November 1997. Ottawa: Health Canada, December 1998.

Legislation
Awarding of the Organ Donation Medal Act. The House of Commons of Canada, Private Member's Bill, April 1998.

CHAPTER 5

Books and Articles
Annas, G.J. "Death by Prescription: The Oregon Initiative." *New England Journal of Medicine*, vol. 331 (1994): 1240–43.

Becker, Ernest. *The Denial of Death*. New York: Free Press, 1973.

Berlin, Isaiah. *Four Essays on Liberty*. London: Oxford University Press, 1969.

Billings, J. Andrew, and Susan D. Block. "Slow Euthanasia." *Journal of Palliative Care*, vol. 12 (1996): 21–30.

Brodie, H. "Commentary on Billings and Block's 'Slow Euthanasia.'" *Journal of Palliative Care*, vol. 12 (1996): 38–41.

Callahan, Daniel. *The Troubled Dream of Life: Living with Mortality*. New York: Simon & Schuster, 1993.

Cassell, E. "The Nature of Suffering and the Goals of Medicine." *New England Journal of Medicine*, vol. 306 (1982): 639–44.

"Death on Request." Ikon Television Network, 1994.

"Death on Request" (excerpts). *Prime Time Live*, 8 December 1994.

Dickens, B. "Commentary on 'Slow Euthanasia.'" *Journal of Palliative Care*, vol. 12 (1996): 42–43.

"Doctors and Death Row" (editorial). *The Lancet*, vol. 341 (1993): 209–10.

"Dutch Doctors Revise Policy on Mercy Killing: New Guidelines Urge Terminally Ill to Take Matters into Their Own Hands." *The Globe & Mail*, 26 August 1995, p. A2.

Dyer, G. "Learning to Kill." *The Montreal Gazette*, 15 December 1995, p. B3.

"The Final Autonomy" (editorial). *The Lancet*, vol. 346 (1995): 259.

Foot, Richard. "Assisted Death Not Painless: A Dutch Study of Euthanasia Cases Found Drugs Did Not Always Work. Canadian Ethicists Say It Shows Doctors Require Specialized Training." *The National Post*, 25 February 2000, p. A3.

Ganzini, L., W.S. Johnston, B.H. McFarland, S.W. Tolle and M.A. Lee. "Attitudes of   **309**
    Patients with Amyotrophic Lateral Sclerosis and Their Care Givers Towards
    Assisted Suicide." *New England Journal of Medicine*, vol. 339, no. 14 (1998):
    967–73.

Gaylin, W., L. Kass, E.D. Pellegrino and M. Siegler. "Doctors Must Not Kill." *Jour-
    nal of the American Medical Association*, vol. 259: (1988): 2139–40.

Hendin, H., C. Rutenfrans and Z. Zylicz. "Physician-Assisted Suicide and Euthana-
    sia in the Netherlands." *Journal of the American Medical Association*, vol. 227,
    no. 21 (1997):1720–22.

James, P.D. *The Children of Men*. New York: A.A. Knopf, 1993.

Katz, Jay. *The Silent World of Doctor and Patient*. New York: Free Press, 1984.

Keown, J. "Restoring Moral and Intellectual Shape to the Law after Bland." *Law
    Quarterly Review*, vol. 113 (1997): 481–503.

Kolata, G. "Nurses Report Hastening Patients' Deaths." *The Montreal Gazette*, 23
    May 1996, pp. Al, A2, reprinted from *New York Times*.

Lewis, C.S. *A Grief Observed*. London and Boston: Faber & Faber, 1961.

Mount, B. "Morphine Drips, Terminal Sedation, and Slow Euthanasia: Definitions
    and Facts, Not Anecdotes." *Journal of Palliative Care*, vol. 12 (1996): 31–37.

Parrs, P. "Suicide Program Makes Me Uneasy." *The Montreal Gazette*, 25 May 1996,
    p. E21.

"Patient Death Probed. Doctor Obeyed Dying Wishes." *The Globe and Mail*, 20
    June 1992, p. A4.

Portenoy, R. "Morphine Infusions at the End of Life: The Pitfalls in Reasoning from
    Anecdote." *Journal of Palliative Care*, vol. 12 (1996): 44–46.

Sade, R.M., and M.F. Marshall. "Legistrothanatry: A New Specialty for Assisting in
    Death." *Perspectives in Biology and Medicine*, vol. 39, no. 4 (1996): 547–49.

Scarry, Elaine. *The Body in Pain: The Making and Unmaking of the World*. New York:
    Oxford University Press, 1985.

Seguin, Marilynne. *A Gentle Death*. Toronto: Key Porter, 1994.

Shepherd, H. "Unity Council Sets New Direction." *The Montreal Gazette*, 21 June
    1997, p. J-7.

Sneiderman, B., and M. Verhoef. "Patient Autonomy and the Defence of Medical
    Necessity: Five Dutch Euthanasia Cases." *Alberta Law Review*, vol. 34, no. 2
    (1996): 374–415.

Somerville, M.A. "Death of Pain: Pain Suffering and Ethics," in *Progress in Pain
    Research and Management*, vol. 2, eds. G.F. Gebhart, D.L. Hammond and T.S.
    Jensen, 41–58. Proceedings of the 7th World Congress on Pain, International
    Association for the Study of Pain. Seattle, Wash.: IASP Press, 1994.

————. "Death Talk in Canada: The Rodriguez Case." *McGill Law Journal*, vol. 39
    (1994): 602–17.

310   ———. *"Death Talk": The Case Against Euthanasia and Physician-Assisted Suicide.*
Montreal: McGill-Queen's Press, Fall 2000.

———. "Euthanasia by Confusion." *University of New South Wales Law Journal*,
vol. 20, no. 3 (1997): 550–75.

———. "Human Rights and Medicine: The Relief of Suffering," in *International
Human Rights Law: Theory and Practice*, eds. Irwin Cotler and P. Pearl Eliadis,
505–522. Montreal: The Canadian Human Rights Foundation, 1992.

———. "Inadequate Treatment of Pain in Hospitalized Patients" (correspondence). *New England Journal of Medicine,* vol. 307, no. 1 (1982): 55.

———. "Legalizing Euthanasia: Why Now?" *Australian Quarterly*, vol. 68, no. 3
(1996): 1–14.

———. "The Nature of Suffering and the Goals of Medicine" (correspondence).
New England Journal of Medicine, vol. 307, no. 12 (1982): 758–59.

———. "Pain and Suffering at the Interfaces of Medicine and Law." *University of
Toronto Law Journal*, vol. XXXVI (1986): 286–317.

———. "The Song of Death: The Lyrics of Euthanasia." *Journal of Contemporary
Health Law & Policy*, vol. 9 (1993): 1–76.

———. "Unpacking the Concept of Human Dignity in Human(e) Death:
Comments on 'Human Dignity and Disease, Disability and Suffering' by Sylvia
D. Stolberg." *Humane Medicine*, vol. 11 (1995): 148–51.

Truog, R.D., and T.A. Brennan. "Participation of Physicians in Capital Punishment." *New England Journal of Medicine*, vol. 329 (1993): 1346–49.

van der Maas, P.J., G. van der Wal, I. Haverkate et al. "Physician-Assisted Suicide
and Other Medical Practices Involving the End of Life in the Netherlands,
1990–1995." *New England Journal of Medicine*, vol. 335 (1996): 1609–1705.

van der Wal, G., P.J. van der Maas, J.M. Bosma et al. "Evaluation of the Notification
Procedure for Physician-Assisted Death in the Netherlands." *New England Journal of Medicine*, vol. 335 (1996): 1706–11.

Wolinsky, H. "U.S. Physicians Debate Capital Punishment." *The Lancet*, vol. 346
(1995): 43.

Young, Katherine K. "A Cross-Cultural Historical Case against Planned Self-Willed
Death and Assisted Suicide." *McGill Law Journal* 39 (1994): 657–707.

Reports

House of Lords. *Report of the Select Committee on Medical Ethics*. London: HMSO,
1994.

Law Reform Commission of Canada. *Euthanasia, Aiding Suicide and Cessation of
Treatment*. Working Paper 28, Protection of Life Series. Ottawa: Minister of
Supply and Services, 1982.

*Medical Practice with Regard to Euthanasia and Related Medical Decisions in the
Netherlands*. Ministerie van Justitie, 1991.

New York State Task Force on Life and the Law. *When Death Is Sought: Assisted Suicide and Euthanasia in the Medical Context*. Albany, N.Y.: New York State Task Force on Life and the Law, 1994.

Parliament of Canada. *Report of the Special Senate Committee on Euthanasia and Assisted Suicide: Of Life and Death*. Ottawa: Minister of Supply and Services Canada, 1995.

Parliament of the Commonwealth of Australia, Senate Legal and Constitutional Legislation Committee. *Consideration of Legislation Referred to the Committee: Euthanasia Laws Bill 1996*. Parliament House, Canberra: Senate Printing Unit, Department of the Senate, 1997.

President's Commission for the Study of Ethical Problems in Medicine and Biomedical and Behavioral Research. *Deciding to Forego Life Sustaining Treatment*. Washington: U.S. Government Printing Office, 1983.

Report of the Institute of Medical Ethics Working Party on the Ethics of Prolonging Life and Assisting Death. "Assisted Death." *The Lancet*, vol. 336, no. 8715 (1990): 610–13.

State Committee on Euthanasia. *Report on Euthanasia*. The Hague: Government Printing Office, 1985.

van der Wal, G., and P.J. van der Maas. *Euthanasia en Andere Medische Beslissingen rond het Levenseinde*. The Hague: Staatsuitgeverij, 1996.

Legislation

The Euthanasia Laws Act. 1997. Commonwealth of Australia.

Oregon Death with Dignity Act. 1994. Oregon State Legislature.

Rights of the Terminally Ill Act. 1995. Legislative Assembly of the Northern Territory of Australia.

Cases

Airedale NHS Trust v. Bland, [1993] 1 ALL E.R. 821; [1993]1 H.L.J. 7 (House of Lords).

Compassion in Dying v. Washington, 79 F 3rd 790 (9th Cir. 1996).

Compassion in Dying v. Washington, 122 F. 3d 1262 (9th Cir. 1997). Remanded to the district court of further proceedings consistent with the Supreme Court's opinion in *Washington v. Glucksberg*, S.Ct. 2258 (1997).

Lee v. Oregon, 107 F 3d 1382 (9th Cir. 1997).

Quill v. Vacco, 80 F 3rd 716 (2nd Cir. 1996).

Vacco v. Quill, 521 U.S. 793 (1997) (United States Supreme Court).

Washington v. Glucksberg, 521 U.S. 702 (1997) (United States Supreme Court).

Books and Articles

McGregor, Maurice. "Technology and the Allocation of Resources." *New England Journal of Medicine,* vol. 320, no. 2 (1989): 118–20.

Pellegrino, E. "Medical Ethics." *Journal of the American Medical Association,* vol. 256, no. 15 (1986): 2122–24.

Roberts, D. "Wife Battles Winnipeg Hospital to Keep Husband Alive." *The Globe and Mail,* 10 November 1998, p. A3.

Somerville, M.A. *Consent to Medical Care.* Ottawa: Law Reform Commission of Canada, 1979.

————. "Legal and Ethical Aspects of Decision-Making by and for Aged Persons in the Context of Psychiatric Care," in *Ethics in Mental Health Practice,* eds. D.K. Kentsmith, S.A. Salladay and P.A. Miya, 59–81. Fla.: Grune & Stratton, 1986.

————. "Legal Issues in Surgical Care of Elderly Persons." *Canadian Journal on Aging,* vol. 8, no. 2 (1989): 128–45; also published in *International Perspectives on Aging: Current Issues in International and Comparative Law,* vol. 3, ed. George J. Alexander, 185–208. Dordrecht/Boston/London: Martinus Nijhoff Publishers, 1992.

————. "'Should the Grandparents Die?': Allocation of Medical Resources with an Aging Population." *Law, Medicine and Health Care,* vol. 14, nos. 3–4 (1986): 158–63.

————. "Structuring the Issues in Informed Consent." *McGill Law Journal,* vol. 26 (1981): 740–808.

Reports

David, Coroner A-M. *Report on the Inquest into the Death of Herman Krausz.* File No. 97345, Opinion No. A-125446. 18 November 1999.

The Ethics Committee of the Society of Critical Care Medicine. *Consensus Statement of the Society of Critical Care Medicine's Ethics Committee Regarding Futile and Other Possibly Inadvisable Treatments.* Published in *Critical Care Medicine,* vol. 25, no. 5 (1997): 887–91.

Cases

Arndt v. Smith, [1997] 2 S.C.R. 539 (per McLachlin J.) (Supreme Court of Canada).

McInerney v. MacDonald, [1992] 2 S.C.R. 138 (per LaForest J.) (Supreme Court of Canada).

Nancy B. v. Hôtel-Dieu de Québec, [1992] R.J.Q. 361; 86 D.L.R. (4th) 385 (Quebec Superior Court) (translation from French).

Norberg v. Weinrib, [1992] 2 S.C.R. 226 (per McLachlin and L'Heureux-Dubé J.J.)   **313**
    (Supreme Court of Canada).
Rodriguez v. Canada (AG), [1993] 3 S.C.R. 519; 107 D.L.R. (4th) 342 (Supreme
    Court of Canada).

CHAPTER 7

Books and Articles
Anand, K.J., and P.R. Hickey. "Pain and Its Effects in the Human Neonate and
    Fetus." *New England Journal of Medicine,* vol. 317 (1987): 1321–29.
Somerville, M.A. *Consent to Medical Care.* Ottawa: Law Reform Commission of
    Canada, 1979.
———. "Governing Professional Intervention in the Family: Achieving and
    Maintaining a Delicate Balance." *Revue du Barreau du Québec,* vol. 44 (1984):
    691–718.
———. "Labels versus Contents: Variance between Philosophy, Psychiatry and
    Law in Concepts Governing Decision-Making." *McGill Law Journal,* vol. 39
    (1994): 179–99.
———. "Refusal of Medical Treatment in 'Captive' Circumstances." *Canadian Bar
    Review,* vol. 63 (1985): 59–90.
———. "Structuring the Issues in Informed Consent." *McGill Law Journal,* vol. 26,
    no. 4 (1981): 740–808.
Wolfe, J., H.E. Grier, N. Kilar, S.B. Levin, J.M. Ellenbogen, S. Salem-Schatz, E.J.
    Emanuel and J.C. Weeks. "Symptoms and Suffering at the End of Life in Chil-
    dren with Cancer." *New England Journal of Medicine,* vol. 342. no. 5 (2000):
    326–33.

Legislation
Civil Code of Quebec.
Public Health Protection Act, R.S.Q. c. P-35.

Cases
B.(R.) v. Children's Aid Society of Metropolitan Toronto, [1995] 1 S.C.R. 315
    (Supreme Court of Canada).
Re Dueck, [1999] 171 D.L.R. (4th) 761 (Sask.Queen's Bench).
Winnipeg Child and Family Services (Northwest Area) v. D.F.G., [1997] 3 S.C.R. 925
    (Supreme Court of Canada).

Books and Articles

Anand, K.J., and P.R. Hickey. "Pain and Its Effects in the Human Neonate and Fetus." *New England Journal of Medicine*, vol. 317 (1987): 1321-29.

Colvin, Eric. *Principles of Criminal Law*, 2nd ed. Toronto: Carswell, 1991.

Elchalal, U., B. Ben-Ami and A. Brzezinski. "Female Circumcision: The Peril Remains." *BJU International*, vol. 83 (suppl. 1) (1999): 103–8.

Fitzgerald, Maria. "The Birth of Pain." *MRC News* (London) (1998): 20–23.

Ganiats, T.G., J.B.C. Humphrey, H.L. Taras and R.M. Kaplan. "Routine Neonatal Circumcision: A Cost-Utility Analysis." *Medical Decision Making*, vol. 11 (1991): 282–93.

Goldman, Ronald. *Questioning Circumcision: A Jewish Perspective*. Boston: Vanguard Publications, 1997.

Howard, C.R., F.M. Howard and M.L. Weitzman. "Acetaminophen Analgesia in Neonatal Circumcision: The Effects on Pain," *Pediatrics*, vol. 93 (1994): 641–46.

Kaplan, G.W. "Complications of Circumcision." *Urologic Clinics of North America*, vol. 10 (1983): 543–49.

Kirkey, S. "Circumcising Baby Boys 'Criminal Assault.' Ethicist Says Society Must Consider Ban." *The Ottawa Citizen*, 17 October 1997, p. A1.

Kugler, I. "On the Possibility of a Criminal Law Defence for Conscientious Objection." *Canadian Journal of Law and Jurisprudence*, vol X (1997): 387–439.

Lawler, F.H., R.S. Bisonni and D.R. Holtgrave. "Circumcision: A Decision Analysis of Its Medical Value." *Family Medicine*, vol. 23 (1991): 587–93.

MacDonald, V. "Newborns Feel Pain Differently than Adults: Research." *The Montreal Gazette*, 3 August 1998, p. A9 (reprinted from *Sunday Telegraph* [London]).

Quinn, T.C., M.J. Wawer, N. Swenemkambo et al. "Viral Load and Heterosexual Transmission of Human Immunodeficiency Virus Type 1." *New England Journal of Medicine*, vol. 342, no. 13 (2000): 921–29.

Rogers, M.C. "Do the Right Thing. Pain Relief in Infants and Children." *New England Journal of Medicine*, vol. 326 (1992): 55–56.

Singer, F., ed. *The Jewish Encyclopedia: A Descriptive Record of the History, Religion, Literature and Customs of the Jewish People from the Earliest Times*, 93 vol. IV. New York: Ktav Publishing House, Inc., 1964 (Entry: Circumcision subheading: "In Apocryphal and Rabbinical Literature").

Somerville, M.A. "Death of Pain: Pain, Suffering, and Ethics," in *Progress in Pain Research and Management*, vol. 2, eds. Gerald F. Gebhart, Donna L. Hammond and Troels S. Jensen, 41–58. Proceedings of the 7th World Congress on Pain, International Association for the Study of Pain. Seattle, Wash.: IASP Press, 1994.

———. "Medical Interventions and the Criminal Law: Lawful or Excusable Wounding?" *McGill Law Journal*, vol. 26, no. 1 (1980): 82–96.

———. "Pain and Suffering at Interfaces of Medicine and Law." *University of Toronto Law Journal*, vol. XXXVI (1986): 286–317.

———. "Structuring the Issues in Informed Consent." *McGill Law Journal*, vol. 26, no. 4 (1981): 740–808.

Somerville, M.A., and D. Alwin. "Lidocaine-Prilocaine Cream for Pain During Circumcision" (correspondence). *New England Journal of Medicine*, vol. 337, no. 8 (1997): 568–70.

Stuart, Don. *Canadian Criminal Law*, 2nd ed. Toronto: Carswell, 1987.

Szabo R., and R.V. Short. "How Does Male Circumcision Protect Against HIV Infection?" *British Medical Journal*, vol. 320 (2000): 1592–94. (Correspondence re. Szabo and Short article. *British Medical Journal*, http://www.bmj.com/cgi/eletters/320/7249/1592, 2000.)

Taddio, A., G. Koren et al. "Effect of Neonatal Circumcision on Pain Response During Subsequent Routine Vaccination." *The Lancet*, vol. 349 (1997): 599–603.

———. "Effect of Neonatal Circumcision on Pain Responses at Vaccination in Boys." *The Lancet*, vol. 345 (1995): 291–92.

Taddio, A., B. Stevens, K. Craig, P. Rastogi, S. Ben-David, M. Shennan, P. Mulligan and G. Koren. "Efficacy and Safety of Lidocaine-Prilocaine Cream for Pain During Circumcision." *New England Journal of Medicine*, vol. 336 (1997): 1197–1201.

Taylor, J.R., A.P. Lockwood and A.J. Taylor. "The Prepuce: Specialized Mucosa of the Penis and Its Loss to Circumcision." *British Journal of Urology*, vol. 77 (1996): 291–95.

Toubia, N. "Female Genital Mutilation and the Responsibility of Reproductive Health Professionals." *International Journal of Gynecology and Obstetrics*, vol. 46 (1994): 127–35.

Van Howe, R.S. "Circumcision and HIV Infection: Review of the Literature and Meta-analysis." *International Journal of STD & AIDS*, vol. 10, no. 1 (1999): 8–16.

Williams, N., and L. Kapila. "Complications of Circumcision." *British Journal of Surgery*, vol. 80 (1993): 1231–36.

Yankelovich, Daniel. "Trends in American Cultural Values." *Criterion* (August 1996): 2–9.

Reports

American Academy of Pediatrics, Task Force on Circumcision. *Circumcision Policy Statement*. Published in *Pediatrics*, vol. 103 (1999): 686–93.

Fetus and Newborn Committee, Canadian Paediatric Society. *Neonatal Circumcision Revisited*. Published in *Canadian Medical Association Journal*, vol. 154 (1996): 776.

316 *Legislation*

An Act to Amend the Criminal Code (child prostitution, child sex tourism, criminal harassment and female genital mutilation), Stat. Inst. 97-66, c. 16 S.C. 1997.

Canadian Charter of Rights and Freedoms, 46 (as amended) Part I of the Constitution Act, 1982, being Schedule B of the Canada Act 1982 (U.K.) 1982, c.11.

Civil Code of Quebec.

Criminal Code, R.S.C. 1985, c. C-46 (as amended).

Cases

B.(R.) v. *Children's Aid Society of Metropolitan Toronto,* [1995] 1 S.C.R. 315 (Supreme Court of Canada).

CHAPTER 9

Books and Articles

Abraham, C. "Breast Cancer Drug Creates Cost Dilemma. Expensive New Treatment Can Prolong Life, but Will Governments Pay?" *The Globe and Mail,* 17 August 1999, p. A1.

————. "Tenacious Woman Scores Medical Victory. Fiona Webster's Fight Opens Access to Genetic Breast Cancer Tests." *The Globe and Mail,* 27 August 1999, p. A1.

Calabresi, Guido, and Philip Bobbitt. *Tragic Choices.* New York: Norton and Company, 1978.

Heinrich, J. "Medicare Challenged." *The Montreal Gazette,* 8 September 1999, p. A1.

Irvine, J.C. *Case Comment:* Law Estate v Simice, *Canadian Cases on the Law of Torts,* vol. 221 (1994): 259.

Katz, Jay. *The Silent World of Doctor and Patient.* New York: The Free Press, 1984.

Roy, D., B. Dickens and M. McGregor. "The Choice of Contrast Media: Medical, Ethical and Legal Considerations." *Canadian Medical Association Journal,* vol. 147 (1992): 1321–24.

Somerville, M.A. "Clarifying the Concepts of Research Ethics: A Second Filtration." *Clinical Research,* vol. 29 (1981): 101–5.

————. "Structuring the Issues in Informed Consent." *McGill Law Journal,* vol. 26 (1981): 740–808.

Reports

Canadian Bar Association Task Force on Health Care Reform. *What's Law Got to Do with It?: Health Care Reform in Canada.* Ottawa: The Canadian Bar Association, 1994.

Commission of Inquiry on the Blood System in Canada. *The Final Report.* Ottawa: Minister of Public Works and Government Services Canada, 1997 (Krever Commission).

The National Commission for the Protection of Subjects of Bio-medical and Behavioural Research. *The Belmont Report: Ethical Principles and Guidelines for the Protection of Human Subjects of Research.* DHEW publication number (WOS) 78-0012, Washington, 1978.

Legislation

Canada Health Act, R.S.C. 1985, c. C-6 (as amended).

Canadian Charter of Rights and Freedoms, Part 1 of the Constitution Act, 1982, being Schedule B of the Canada Act 1982 (U.K.) 1982, c.11.

Health and Social Services Act, R.S.Q., c. S-4.2.

Health Insurance Act, R.S.Q., c. A-29.

Health Services and Insurance Act, R.S.N.S. 1989, c. 20 and Regulations.

Cases

Arnold et al. v. Teno et al.; J.B. Jackson v. Teno, [1978] S.C.R. 287 (per Spence J., referring to and distinguishing *Bressington v. Commissioner of Railways* (1947), 75 C.L.R. 339 (Supreme Court of Canada).

Barratt v. District of North Vancouver, [1980] 2 S.C.R. 418; 114 D.L.R. (3d) 577 (Supreme Court of Canada).

Brown v. British Columbia (Minister of Health) (1990), 42 B.C.L.R. (2d) 294 (B.C. Supreme Court).

Cameron v. Nova Scotia (Attorney General) (1999), 177 D.L.R. (4th) 611 (N.S. C.A.) (On appeal to the Supreme Court of Canada).

City of Kamloops v. Nielsen, Hughes and Hughes, [1984] 2 S.C.R. 2 (Supreme Court of Canada).

Hopp v. Lepp, [1980] 2 S.C.R. 192 (Supreme Court of Canada).

Just v. B.C., [1989] 2 S.C. R. 1228 (Supreme Court of Canada).

Law Estate v. Simice (1994), 2 C.C.L.T. (2d) 228 (B.C. Supreme Court); [1996] 4 W.W.R. 672 (B.C. Court of Appeal).

McInerney v. MacDonald, [1992] 2 S.C.R. 138 (Supreme Court of Canada).

Norberg v. Weinrib, [1992] 2 S.C.R. 226 (Supreme Court of Canada).

R. v. Morgentaler, [1988] 1 S.C.R. 301 (Supreme Court of Canada).

Reibl v. Hughes, [1980] 2 S.C.R. 880; 114 D.L.R. (3d) 1 (Supreme Court of Canada).

Stein v. Québec (Régie de l'assurance maladie), [1999] R.J. Q. 2416 (Cour Supérieure du Québec).

Weiss v. Solomon, [1990] R.J.Q 731 (Cour Supérieure du Québec).

Wilson et al. v. Medical Services Commission of British Columbia et al. (1988), 30 B.C.L.R. 1. (B.C. Supreme Court).

Books and Articles

Bates, P.W., J. Cooper and C. Abela. "Public Health Legislation and Social Values," in *Public Health and Private Risk, 2nd Annual Conference, Australian Institute of Health Law and Ethics, Conference Proceedings, October 30–November 1, 1997.* Canberra: Australian Institute of Health Law and Ethics, 1997.

Benatar, Solomon R. "Global Disparities in Health and Human Rights: A Critical Commentary," *American Journal of Public Health*, vol. 88., no. 2 (1998): 295–300.

Bishop, L.J., M.N. Cherry and M. Darragh. "Organizational Ethics and Health Care: Expanding Bioethics to the Institutional Arena." *Kennedy Institute of Ethics Journal*, vol. 9, no. 2 (1999): 189–208.

Bodenheimer, T. "The HMO Backlash: Righteous or Reactionary?" *New England Journal of Medicine*, vol. 335 (1996): 1601–3.

Cruess, R.L., S.R. Cruess and S.E. Johnston. "Renewing Professionalism: An Opportunity for Medicine." *Academic Medicine*, vol. 74 (1999): 878–84.

Jacobs, Jane. *Systems of Survival: A Dialogue on the Moral Foundations of Commerce and Politics.* New York: Random House, 1992.

McCullough, Lawrence B. "Preventive Ethics, Managed Practice, and the Hospital Ethics Committee as a Resource for Physician Executives." *HEC Forum*, vol. 10, no. 2 (1998): 136–51.

Nulman, Andy. *How to Do the Impossible.* Toronto: Uphill Publishers, 1998.

Schacter, Mark. "Health Care Report Cards." *The National Post*, 14 January 1999, p. A18.

Somerville, M.A. "Ethical Issues and Challenges in Implementing a New Blood System." *Transfusion Medicine Reviews*, vol. 12, no. 3 (1998): 162–74. Also published in *Ethical Issues in Transfusion Medicine*, Colin R. Macpherson, Ronald E. Domen and Terry Perlin, 17–38. Bethesda, Md.: AABB Press, 2000.

———. "Justice Across the Generations." *Social Science and Medicine*, vol. 29, no. 3 (1989): 385–94.

———. "Making Health, Not War—Musings on Global Disparities in Health and Human Rights: A Critical Commentary by Solomon R. Benatar." *American Journal of Public Health*, vol. 88, no. 2 (1998): 301–3.

———. "'Should the Grandparents Die?': Allocation of Medical Resources with an Aging Population." *Law, Medicine and Health Care*, vol. 14, nos. 3–4 (1986): 158–163.

Sontag, Susan. *Illness as Metaphor.* New York: Doubleday, 1978.

"US Doctors Fight Gag Clauses in Contracts." *The Lancet*, vol. 347 (1996): 113.

"U.S. 'Gag Clauses' Under Renewed Attack." *The Lancet*, vol. 348 (1996): 1728.

"US HMO Cancels 'Gag Clauses.'" *The Lancet*, vol. 347 (1996): 463.

Wildes, Kevin W. "Institutional Identity, Integrity, and Conscience." *Kennedy Institute of Ethics Journal*, vol. 7, no. 4 (1997): 413–19.

Yiu, S. *The Corporate Take-over of Academic Research: The Nancy Olivieri Story.* www.utmj.org/76.1/news3contents.htm (1998).

Reports

Commission of Inquiry on the Blood System in Canada, The Hon. Mr. Justice Horace Krever. *The Final Report*. Ottawa: Minister of Public Works and Government Services Canada, 1997.

[American] Joint Commission on Accreditation of Healthcare Organizations. *Ethical Issues and Patient Rights Across the Continuum of Care*. Oakbrook Terrace, Ill.: The Commission, 1998.

Cases

Brewer Brothers v. Canada (AG.), [1998] 2 W.W.R. 48 (Man. Court of Appeal).

Just v. British Columbia, [1989] 2 S.C.R 1228 (Supreme Court of Canada).

Kamloops (City) v. Nielsen, [1984] 2 S.C.R. 2 (Supreme Court of Canada).

Kwong v. Alberta, [1979] 2 W.W.R.1 (Alta. Supreme Court [Appeal Division]).

Kwong Estate v. Alberta, [1979] 2 S.C.R. 1010 (Supreme Court of Canada).

Oosthoek v. Thunder Bay (City) (1996), 139 D.L.R. (4th) 611 (Ont. Court of Appeal).

Teno v. Arnold, [1978] 2 S.C.R. 287 (Supreme Court of Canada).

Weiss v. Solomon, [1990] R.J.Q. 731 (Cour Supérieure du Québec).

CHAPTER 11

Books and Articles

Annas, George J., and Michael A. Grodin, eds. *The Nazi Doctors and the Nuremberg Code*, 3–11. New York and Oxford: Oxford University Press, 1992.

Calabresi, Guido, and Philip Bobbitt. *Tragic Choices*. New York: Norton, 1978.

Dowrick, Stephanie. *Forgiveness and Other Acts of Love: Finding True Value in Your Life*. Ringwood, Victoria, Australia: Penguin Books, 1997.

"Gene Warfare—Unless We Keep Our Guard Up" (editorial. *The Lancet*, vol. 348 (1996): 1183.

Ignatieff, Michael. *Virtual War: Kosovo and Beyond*. Middlesex, England: Viking Penguin Group, 2000.

Joy, Bill. "Why the Future Doesn't Need Us." *Wired Magazine*, vol. 8, no. 4 (2000).

Katz, Jay. *The Silent World of Doctor and Patient*. New York: Free Press, 1984.

Proctor, R.N. "Nazi Doctors, Racial Medicine, and Human Experimentation," in *The Nazi Doctors and the Nuremberg Code,* eds. G.J. Annas and M.A. Grodin, 17–31. New York and Oxford: Oxford University Press, 1992.

320   Sassower, Ralph. "Responsible Technoscience: The Haunting Reality of Auschwitz and Hiroshima." *Science and Engineering Ethics,* 277–300, vol. 2 (1996).

Somerville, M.A. "The Right to Health: A Human Rights Perspective," in *SIDA, santé, droits de l'homme / AIDS, Health and Human Rights,* eds. J. Mann and C. Dupuy, 75–90. Lyon: Fondation Marcel Mérieux, 1993.

————. "La transdisciplinarité, vague de l'avenir: comment préparer nos rivages à l'accueillir," in *Entre Savoirs, L'interdisciplinarité en acte: enjeux, obstacles, perspectives,* 117–36. Colloque international sur l'interdisciplinarité organisé par l'UNESCO. Paris: UNESCO, 1991.

————. "Transdisciplinarity: A Response to 'Enticement by Methods' by Hanspeter Kriesi," in *The Responsible Scholar, Ethical Considerations in the Humanities and Social Sciences,* Gerald Berthoud and Beat Sitter-Liver, 241–54. Canton, Mass.: Watson Publishing International, 1996.

Somerville, Margaret, and David J. Rapport, eds. *Transdisciplinarity: reCreating Integrated Knowledge.* Oxford: EOLSS Publishers, 2000.

Thomasma, D.C. "Promisekeeping: An Institutional Ethos for Health-care Today." *Frontiers of Health Services Management,* vol. 13, no. 2 (1996): 5–34.

Turner, G., and B. Wynne. "Risk Communication: A Literature Review and Some Implications for Biotechnology," in *Biotechnology in Public: A Review of Recent Research,* ed. J. Durant, 122–23. London: Science Museum for the European Federation of Biotechnology, 1992.

Reports

Schrecker, T., B. Hoffmaster, M.A. Somerville et al. "Biotechnology, Ethics and Government," in *Renewal of the Canadian Biotechnology Strategy, Resource Document 3.4.1,* Background Research Papers, Ethics. Ottawa: Industry Canada, March 1998, 135–261.

Cases

Mount Isa Mines Ltd. v. Pusey (1970), 125 C.L.R. 383 (High Court of Australia).

EPILOGUE

Somerville, M.A. "Gazing at Stars and Patting Cats. Creativity, Emotions and Efficiency: The Male and Female Differences." *Canadian Speeches,* vol. 10, no. 5 (1996): 55–59.

Acknowledgements

This book, for better or worse, has its origins in my childhood. My first debt of gratitude is, therefore, owed to my parents, the late Gertrude Honora Ganley and George Patrick Ganley, who both grew up in the Australian Outback. Because of the place and era in which she was born, my mother did not have an opportunity for higher education. This was her greatest regret, and one of her passions in life was to ensure that my brother and I had the access she was denied. Throughout her life, my mother epitomized traditional feminine elegance and charm, and in her old age described herself as a feminist. She showed me that we are never too old to accept new ways of seeing the world and that we do not have to accept a "package" of ideas and ideals, but can choose those we hold dear from many diverse sources. My father regarded himself and me as being honoured by the

322   title of "perpetual student." I have only recently, especially in writing this book, realized the extent to which my philosophy of life is based on what he taught me.

My aunt, Veronica Rowe, as a nurse and later matron of a hospital, was my primary model of a professional woman. Her laughter, commonsense and love have sustained me in good and bad times, and I return her love with deepest thanks. Likewise, my deepest affection and thanks to the other members of my "Aussie" family, my brother, Bob—a truly ethical man—my sister-in-law, Carol, and my niece, Kate, and nephew, Benjamin.

I thank Anne McDonnell, who has been my soulmate through many years, for her caring, insight and wisdom, and for the summer verandah of "Rosemary," her cottage at Pearl Beach where many of the ideas in this book saw first light. No matter how many times I hear the kookaburras and currawongs, my heart still leaps at the beauty of their ancient welcome to the new day.

My deep gratitude is owed to the nuns who taught a generation of young Australian women, including me, that it was possible for us to make a difference in the world. Special thanks go to Sister Mary Ethelreda of the Sisters of Saint Joseph, my teacher in Grade 3, and my high school teachers Sister Mavis McBride and Sister Deirdre Jordan, of the Sisters of Mercy.

Across the Pacific to my other home in Canada, there are many people to whom I owe thanks in relation to this book.

First, my heartfelt thanks to my friends and colleagues—my surrogate Canadian family—Professor Norbert Gilmore, Doctor Irene Simons and Professor Katherine Young for personal and professional contributions to my life and work over many years and for help with this book. It is not possible to thank them adequately for all that they have done for me.

The establishment of the McGill Centre for Medicine, Ethics and Law was a very important event in my professional development. For their vision in making that possible and for friendship and understanding, I thank the Centre's three founding deans, Dean Richard

Cruess of the Faculty of Medicine, Dean Roderick Macdonald of the Faculty of Law and Dean Donna Runnals of the Faculty of Religious Studies. And for his persistence in persuading me against my will to undertake doctoral studies in medicine, ethics and law, I will always be grateful to Emeritus Professor Paul-André Crepeau of the Faculty of Law at McGill University.

Friends who provided professional expertise on certain issues in this book or other support in writing it to whom I express my thanks include John Antonopoulos; Professor Fritz Bach, Lewis Thomas Professor of Surgery at Harvard University; Dr. Donald Boudreau, asso-ciate dean of Medicine at McGill University; Germaine Gibara; and Edith Low Beer, CM.

Two other people, Doctor Peter Somerville, my former husband, and Knut Hammarskjöld, changed and enhanced my personal and professional worlds in many ways. I express my gratitude to each of them for the time we spent together.

One cannot create in a vacuum, and for me to be surrounded with the creativity of others is a major source of inspiration. I am especially grateful to two artists, Jacques Deshaies and Guido Molinari, for pro-viding such inspiration.

Illness has played a role in my life and work. For their care and empathy I thank Doctor Chaim Shustik, Doctor Joel Paris and Doctor Ken Flegel. And for being the Dragon Master of the fitness world, I thank Michael Murphy.

Without Jackie Kaiser of Penguin Canada, this book would never have existed. Despite my huge misgivings she diplomatically, mil-limetre by millimetre, created a situation in which I seemed to have already said yes and could no longer say no to writing it. Her sup-port while I was doing so has made the load much lighter and the task certainly a great deal more fun. Jennifer Glossop played a cru-cial role in helping me to structure this text and was outstanding as an editor. And Wendy Thomas, who copyedited it, made substantial improvements by constantly challenging me to clarify and explain. I am most grateful to each of them. I also thank all the other "Penguin

324   people"—in particular Cynthia Good, Debby de Groot and Sandra Tooze—for their efforts on my behalf.

The person without whom this book could not have been written is my assistant, Eileen Parle. Her sense of humour, balance, patience and wisdom, quite apart from the enormous amount of work that she has put into this book in helping me in so many of its aspects—from perceptive questions that have caused me to rethink certain positions, to suggestions for style change and editing—has gone far beyond even what such a demanding person as I am would ever expect. My thanks a thousand times go to her. And my sincere thanks to my long-term research assistants Ramona Rothschild and Hoi Kong, who unfailingly and cheerfully provided help to both Eileen and me.

And finally, to recognize that not only humans, but also the animals in our lives, are owed gratitude, I acknowledge Melba, Phoebe and Ozone who, with appropriate feline dignity, played the role of ethicist cats. I am grateful to them for strategic tail placements across manuscript pages in the tradition of their esteemed ninth-century Irish ancestor Pangur Bán.

Index

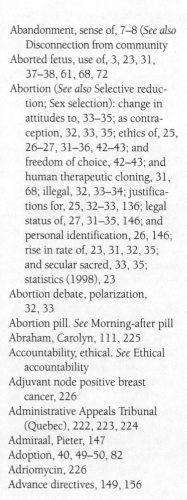